13 Ways to Not Suck at Being a Christian

A Survival Manual for Christians Who Mean Well but Kinda Suck at Discipline

13 WAYS TO NOT SUCK AT BEING A CHRISTIAN

Copyright © 2025 by Jean Benoit
All rights reserved.

No part of this publication may be reproduced, distributed, or transmitted in any form or by any means without prior written permission, except in the case of brief quotations embodied in critical reviews and certain other noncommercial uses permitted by copyright law. For permission requests, write to the publisher at the address below, or just pray really hard and see what happens.

ISBN: 978-1-0693787-5-0 (print)
ISBN: 978-0-0000-0000-0 (ebook)

First Edition

Published by Faith & Sass Publishing
1234 Narrow Road
Sanctification City, GA 30000
www.13waysbook.com

LEGAL STUFF: If you plagiarize this book, three things will happen: 1) Jesus will know, 2) Your grandmother will find out somehow, and 3) Ron Swanson will locate you and silently judge you while whittling something more useful than your stolen manuscript.

Despite heroic efforts, this book contains at least one typo. When you find it (and you will because Christians love pointing out errors), resist the urge to email us about it. Consider it a test of your spiritual maturity.

Scripture quotations are from the ESV® Bible (The Holy Bible, English Standard Version®), copyright © 2001 by Crossway, a publishing ministry of Good News Publishers. Used by permission. All rights reserved. Any paraphrases or overly casual references to biblical events are the author's attempt to keep you awake.

If this book made you uncomfortable, good. That was the point. Comfort is overrated and rarely leads to growth. The disciples didn't get comfortable until after Pentecost, and even then, most of them got martyred. So maybe "comfortable" isn't the goal here.

Printed in the United States of America on paper made from trees that died for your spiritual growth.

Let's Be Honest About This Jesus Thing.................................28
Chapter 1: A Grateful Heart – Learn to Say Thank You........33
    Why God Cares About Your Gratitude............................ 35
    The Problem of Ingratitude.. 36
    The Gratitude Muscle...38
        1. The Gratitude Journal (But Not the Fluffy Kind).39
        2. The Gratitude Alarm..40
        3. The Gratitude Visit.. 40
        4. Thankful Prayer First... 41
        5. The Gratitude Fast... 42
    The Hard Truth About Gratitude..43
    Gratitude When Life Actually Sucks.................................. 45
    The Gratitude Challenge..47
    The Gratitude Effect.. 48
    The Choice Is Yours.. 50
    The Kick in the Pants..51
Chapter 2:..54
Confession – Owning Your Crap..54
    The Confession-Avoidance Olympics.................................56
        The Blame Shift.. 56
        The Comparison Game..57
        The Technicality Defense..57
        The Justification Complex.. 58
        The Minimize and Dismiss...58
        The Spiritual Bypass...59
        The Self-Flagellation Show...59
    Why We Run from Confession... 60
        1. We're afraid of rejection... 60
        2. We're afraid of consequences................................ 61

    3. We're afraid of losing our image............................ 61

    4. We're afraid of feeling the full weight of our sin. 62

The Biblical Case for Confession... 63

What Confession Is (And Isn't).. 65

    What Confession Isn't:... 65

    What Confession Is:...66

The Practice of Confession: Getting Started....................... 67

    1. Establish a Daily Examination............................... 68

    2. Confess Specifically to God..................................... 69

    3. Develop Trusted Confession Relationships...........70

    4. Practice Immediate Confession............................. 70

    5. Embrace Regular Corporate Confession............... 71

Common Roadblocks to Confession.................................... 72

    Roadblock #1: "I don't feel bad enough about my sin.".. 72

    Roadblock #2: "I've confessed this sin before, but I keep doing it.".. 73

    Roadblock #3: "I'm afraid of what others will think if I confess."... 74

    Roadblock #4: "I can't forgive myself, even if God forgives me."..75

    Roadblock #5: "God seems distant despite my confession."..75

Beyond Confession: The Full Picture...................................76

    Repentance...76

    Receiving Forgiveness..77

    Walking in the Spirit..78

    Community Support.. 78

Confession and Mental Health... 79

The Transformative Power of Confession...........................80

    Freedom from Shame..80

- Deeper Intimacy with God...80
- More Authentic Relationships..81
- Greater Compassion for Others..81
- Accelerated Spiritual Growth...82
- A 30-Day Confession Challenge...82
  - Days 1-10: Daily Examination and Private Confession...83
  - Days 11-20: Scripture-Guided Confession...............83
  - Days 21-30: Communal Confession..........................84
- The Kick in the Pants: Stop Hiding, Start Healing..........84

Chapter 3:...88
Celebration – Finding Joy in the Mundane.............................88
- Why Celebration Matters...90
  - 1. Celebration is an act of spiritual warfare............. 91
  - 2. Celebration trains your attention......................... 92
  - 3. Celebration honors God..92
  - 4. Celebration sustains community............................93
  - 5. Celebration reminds us of our future.................... 94
- Why Celebration Is So Damn Hard....................................94
  - 1. We're chronically exhausted................................. 95
  - 2. We're distracted by comparison............................ 95
  - 3. We're addicted to outrage......................................96
  - 4. We're waiting for permission................................. 96
  - 5. We misunderstand what celebration is................. 97
- Celebration as a Discipline (Not Just a Feeling).............. 98
- Practical Ways to Celebrate the Ordinary........................ 99
  - 1. The Daily Joy List.. 99
  - 2. Sacred Interruptions..100
  - 3. Meal as Celebration... 100
  - 4. Sabbath Celebration.. 101

  5. Celebration Triggers..102
  6. The Celebration Circle... 103
  7. Declaring Good News..103
  8. Celebration Through Creativity........................ 104
  9. Celebration Memorials...105
  10. Celebrating Through Others...................... 105
Celebrating in Hard Seasons...106
  1. Celebrate smaller.. 107
  2. Celebrate honestly.. 107
  3. Celebrate in community.. 107
  4. Celebrate the unseen.. 108
  5. Celebrate past faithfulness..................................... 108
The Celebration Challenge.. 109
  Week 1: Notice...109
  Week 2: Express..110
  Week 3: Disrupt..110
  Week 4: Deepen.. 111
Overcoming Celebration Blockers....................................112
  The Perfectionist... 112
  The Productivity Addict.. 112
  The Expected Celebrator... 113
  The Anxious Anticipator... 113
  The Cynical Observer..114
Signs You're Growing in Celebration..............................114
The Relationship Between Celebration and Other Disciplines..116
The Kick in the Pants: Stop Waiting for the Big Stuff... 117

Chapter 4:.. 121
Submission – Letting Go of Control..121
What Submission Actually Is (And Isn't)...................... 123

- What Submission IS NOT: 123
- What Submission IS: 124
- The Control Addiction 126
  - The Overthinking Trap 127
  - The Worry Cycle 127
  - The Perfectionism Pattern 128
  - The Manipulation Game 128
  - The Planning Obsession 129
- The Biblical Case for Submission 129
  - Jesus Modeled Submission 130
  - Submission Shows Up Throughout Scripture 131
  - Creation Itself Reflects This Design 131
  - The Alternative Is Pride—And It Doesn't End Well.... 132
- The Freedom of Letting Go 133
- Practical Submission: How to Actually Let Go 135
  - 1. The Open-Handed Prayer Practice 135
  - 2. The "Not My Job" Discernment 136
  - 3. The Obedience Experiment 137
  - 4. The Reality Acceptance Practice 137
  - 5. The Control Inventory 138
  - 6. The "Fast from Control" Challenge 139
  - 7. The Sabbath Submission 140
- Submission in Key Relationships 140
  - Authority Structures 141
  - Marriage Relationships 142
  - Friendship and Community 143
- Common Roadblocks to Submission 144
  - Fear 144
  - Past Wounds 145

  Misunderstanding God's Character..........145
  Cultural Conditioning..................146
 Discerning Healthy vs. Unhealthy Submission..........147
  Healthy Submission:....................147
  Unhealthy Submission:..................148
 The Submission Paradox....................149
 The 7-Day Submission Challenge..............150
  Day 1: Acknowledge Reality.............151
  Day 2: Morning Surrender...............151
  Day 3: Schedule Interruption...........151
  Day 4: Authority Check.................152
  Day 5: Relationship Submission.........152
  Day 6: Outcome Release.................153
  Day 7: Sabbath Submission..............153
 The Kick in the Pants: Control Is Killing You........154

Chapter 5:..........157
Service – Doing the Dirty Work..........157

 What Real Service Looks Like...............159
  What Service Is NOT:...................159
  What Service IS:.......................160
 Why Service Is Non-Negotiable..............161
  1. Jesus Modeled It Himself............162
  2. Service Transforms Us...............163
  3. Service Demonstrates the Gospel.....163
  4. Service Is How the Church Functions.164
  5. Service Is an Antidote to Cultural Toxicity....165
 The Different Types of Service.............166
  Planned vs. Spontaneous Service........166
  Public vs. Hidden Service..............167
  Comfortable vs. Stretching Service.....168

Individual vs. Collective Service 169
The Heart of Service: Love, Not Duty 169
The Real-World Cost of Service 171
  Time You Don't Have 171
  Energy You'd Rather Conserve 172
  Comfort You'd Like to Keep 173
  Status You'd Prefer to Maintain 174
Practical Ways to Serve (That Actually Help) 174
  In Your Home 175
  In Your Church 175
  In Your Workplace 176
  In Your Community 177
Common Barriers to Serving (And How to Overcome Them) 178
  "I Don't Have Time" 178
  "I'm Too Tired/Stressed/Overwhelmed" 179
  "I Don't Know What to Do" 180
  "I'm Afraid I'll Do It Wrong" 180
  "I've Been Hurt in Past Service Situations" 181
The Savior Complex: When Service Goes Wrong 182
  Signs of a Savior Complex 182
  The Antidote to a Savior Complex 183
Service as a Lifestyle, Not Just an Activity 184
  1. Start Where You Already Are 185
  2. Make Service a Reflex, Not a Decision 185
  3. Examine Your Use of Power and Privilege 186
  4. Integrate Service Into Your Identity 187
The 30-Day Service Challenge 187
  Days 1-10: Home and Inner Circle 188
  Days 11-20: Community and Church 189

    Days 21-30: Stretch Zone... 190
    Service That Transforms You... 191
        Your Ego Shrinks to a Healthy Size......................... 191
        Your Compassion Grows..192
        Your Self-Sufficiency Diminishes............................ 192
        Your Joy Deepens..193
    The Kick in the Pants: Get Over Yourself and Grab a Towel.. 194

Chapter 6:.. 197
Worship – More Than Sunday Mornings..........................197
    What Worship Really Is (And Isn't)............................... 198
        What Worship IS NOT:...199
        What Worship IS:..200
    The Biblical Foundation for Whole-Life Worship..........201
    The Idolatry of Sunday-Only Worship............................204
    The Trinity of False Worship..205
        1. Comfort and Pleasure.. 206
        2. Success and Achievement......................................206
        3. Approval and Acceptance..................................... 207
    Practical Ways to Worship Beyond Sunday....................209
        1. The Morning Consecration....................................209
        2. Work as Worship... 210
        3. Gratitude Triggers... 211
        4. Sacred Listening..212
        5. Relational Worship...212
        6. Creation Appreciation.. 213
        7. Physical Worship... 214
        8. Financial Worship..215
    Transforming Sunday Worship Too................................. 215
        1. Prepare Your Heart...216

- 2. Participate, Don't Consume..................................217
- 3. Focus on God, Not Just Experience......................218
- 4. Connect Sunday to Monday................................219

When Worship Feels Impossible.. 219
- 1. Start with Honesty...220
- 2. Worship from Memory, Not Just Feeling........... 220
- 3. Borrow Faith When Necessary............................. 221
- 4. Offer Minimal Worship.. 222
- 5. Remember That Lament Is Worship....................222

The Worship Experiment: 7 Days of Intentional Worship 223
- Day 1: Work Worship... 223
- Day 2: Body Worship... 224
- Day 3: Relationship Worship.................................... 224
- Day 4: Creation Worship... 225
- Day 5: Resource Worship.. 225
- Day 6: Challenge Worship...226
- Day 7: Sabbath Worship.. 227

Signs of Growth in Worship...228

Common Worship Blockers (And How to Overcome Them)..229
- 1. Distraction..230
- 2. Hurry...230
- 3. Unconfessed Sin...231
- 4. Comparison and Competition............................. 232
- 5. Worship Consumerism...233

The Kick in the Pants: Worship or Worthless Ship?..... 234

Chapter 7:.. 238

Guidance – Seeking Wisdom Without the BS........................ 238

Why We Suck at Seeking Guidance................................... 240

1. Pride: "I Got This" 240
2. Impatience: "I Need Answers NOW" 241
3. Fear: "What If I Don't Like the Answer?" 242
4. Confusion: "How Do I Even Know It's God?" 243
5. Compartmentalization: "God for Sundays, Me for Mondays" 243

The Foundations of True Guidance 244
1. Scripture: The Authoritative Foundation 244
2. The Holy Spirit: The Internal Guide 246
3. Community: The External Confirmation 247
4. Circumstances: The Providential Alignment 248

Practical Steps for Seeking Guidance 250
1. Build the Daily Habit of Listening 250
2. Bring Everything to God, Not Just the "Big Stuff" ... 251
3. Learn to Recognize God's Voice 252
4. Develop a Personal Board of Directors 253
5. Make Peace Your Referee 254

How to Navigate Big Decisions 256
Step 1: Clarify the Real Question 256
Step 2: Consult Scripture First 257
Step 3: Pray Specifically and Persistently 258
Step 4: Gather Wise Counsel Strategically 258
Step 5: Evaluate Circumstances with Discernment 259
Step 6: Make a Faith-Based Decision 260
Step 7: Remain Flexible and Attentive 261

Common Guidance Myths and Mistakes 261
Myth #1: "If It's God's Will, It Will Be Easy" 262
Myth #2: "God Only Speaks Through Supernatural Signs" 262

    Myth #3: "God Has One Perfect Plan, and One Wrong Move Ruins Everything"..............263
    Myth #4: "God's Will Is Primarily About My Happiness and Success"..............264
    Myth #5: "I Don't Need to Seek Guidance Until I Face a Crisis"..............265
    Mistake #1: Seeking Confirmation Bias, Not Truth.....266
    Mistake #2: Confusing Feelings with Leading........266
    Mistake #3: Abdicating Personal Responsibility....267
    Special Guidance Challenges..............268
        When God Seems Silent..............268
        When Options All Seem Equally Good (or Bad)....269
        When Guidance Leads Where You Don't Want to Go 271
    The Lifelong Guidance Journey..............272
        Cultivate a Guidance History..............273
        Develop Guidance Community..............273
        Embrace Course Corrections..............274
        Deepen Your Knowledge of God..............275
    The 30-Day Guidance Challenge..............276
        Days 1-5: Foundation Building..............276
        Days 6-15: Daily Guidance Practice..............278
        Days 16-25: Guidance in Specific Life Areas..........281
        Days 26-30: Integrating Guidance into Life............284
    The Kick in the Pants: Stop Making Excuses and Start Listening..............286

Chapter 8:..............290
Simplicity – Cutting Through the Clutter..............290
    The Problem: We're All Drowning in More..............292
        Physical Clutter..............292

14

- Digital Overload 293
- Schedule Saturation 294
- Mental Clutter 294
- Relational Complexity 295
- Spiritual Accumulation 295

The Countercultural Nature of Simplicity 296
- The Fear of Missing Out 296
- The Allure of Identity Through Accumulation 297
- The Addiction to Stimulation 297
- The Status Quo of Complexity 298

Biblical Foundations of Simplicity 299
- 1. God is our provider, not our possessions 299
- 2. The kingdom of God is our primary pursuit 299
- 3. Contentment is a learned state of sufficiency 300
- 4. Generosity flows from simplicity 300
- 5. Material wealth brings spiritual danger 301
- 6. Jesus modeled a life of focused simplicity 301

Simplicity in Four Dimensions 302
- 1. Material Simplicity: Owning Less, Wanting Less 302
- 2. Calendar Simplicity: Doing Less, Being More 304
- 3. Digital Simplicity: Connecting Deeper, Scrolling Less 305
- 4. Mental Simplicity: Thinking Clearly, Worrying Less 306

The Unexpected Benefits of Simplicity 308
- 1. Increased capacity to hear God 308
- 2. Greater clarity about purpose 308
- 3. Deeper, more authentic relationships 309
- 4. Increased generosity 309
- 5. Freedom from comparison and status anxiety ... 310

6. Increased resilience during difficult times..........310
Practical Steps Toward a Simpler Life............................ 311
    Step 1: Identify Your Current Complexity Costs... 311
    Step 2: Clarify Your Core Priorities.........................312
    Step 3: Start with Quick Wins..................................... 313
    Step 4: Tackle One Life Area at a Time...................314
    Step 5: Build Accountability and Support.............. 316
Common Obstacles to Simplicity (And How to Overcome Them)..317
    Obstacle 1: Scarcity Thinking.....................................317
    Obstacle 2: Identity Attachment............................... 318
    Obstacle 3: Social Pressure.. 318
    Obstacle 4: The Complexity Creep...........................319
    Obstacle 5: All-or-Nothing Thinking....................... 320
Simplicity in Different Life Seasons................................ 320
    Young Adults / Single Season................................... 320
    Marriage / Partnership Season..................................321
    Parenting Season..322
    Mid-Life / Career-Focused Season........................... 322
    Later Life / Retirement Season..................................323
The 30-Day Simplicity Challenge..................................... 324
    Week 1: Physical Simplicity..324
    Week 2: Calendar Simplicity...................................... 325
    Week 3: Digital Simplicity.. 326
    Week 4: Mental Simplicity..327
    Week 5: Integration..328
How Simplicity Transforms Your Relationship with God 328
    1. From distracted to present..................................... 329
    2. From performance to trust..................................... 329

    3. From acquisition to gratitude.............................. 330
    4. From scattered to focused......................................331
    5. From drivenness to receptivity.............................332
  The Kick in the Pants: Your Soul Wasn't Built for This Much Noise..332

Chapter 9:..336
Silence – The Power of Shut Up...336

  Why We're Terrified of Silence...338
    1. Silence forces us to face ourselves.......................338
    2. Silence feels unproductive.....................................339
    3. Silence exposes our addictions............................ 340
    4. Silence feels socially awkward..............................341
    5. Silence opens us to hearing God........................... 341
  The Biblical Case for Shutting Up..................................... 343
    Elijah and the Sound of Low Whisper.....................343
    Jesus and His Rhythm of Withdrawal...................... 344
    The Psalmists and the Practice of Waiting Silently 346
    Ecclesiastes and the Discipline of Fewer Words.... 347
  The Transformative Power of Shut Up.............................348
    1. Silence reveals what's really going on inside us 348
    2. Silence trains our spiritual attention span.......... 349
    3. Silence creates space for discernment.................350
    4. Silence helps process grief and pain..................... 351
    5. Silence deepens our awareness of God's presence.. 352
    6. Silence transforms how we speak........................ 352
  Silence in a World That Never Shuts Up: Practical Steps.. 353
    Beginner Level: Getting Comfortable with Basic Silence...354
    Intermediate Level: Deepening into Reflective

Silence..........356
   Advanced Level: Extended and Communal Silence... 359
When Silence Gets Real: Navigating the Challenges....361
   Challenge 1: The Restless Mind..........361
   Challenge 2: Uncomfortable Emotions..........362
   Challenge 3: The Resistance of Others..........364
   Challenge 4: Spiritual Dryness.......... 365
Silence in Different Life Contexts.......... 366
   For Parents of Young Children.......... 366
   For Those in High-Pressure Careers..........367
   For Those in Communal Living Situations..........368
   For Those in Caregiver Roles..........369
The 30-Day Silence Challenge..........370
   Week 1: Establishing the Foundation.......... 370
   Week 2: Deepening the Practice..........371
   Week 3: Building Endurance..........372
   Week 4: Integrating Silence into Life.......... 373
Why Most People Won't Do This.......... 375
   1. Silence reveals what we're avoiding..........376
   2. Silence feels like a luxury we can't afford..........376
   3. Silence requires swimming upstream.......... 377
   4. Silence demands patience in an instant world...378
Signs of Growth in the Silence Journey.......... 379
   1. Increased awareness of internal states..........379
   2. More comfortable gaps in conversation..........380
   3. Reduced reactivity to triggers..........380
   4. Greater discernment of inner voices..........381
   5. Increased capacity to be present..........381
The Kick in the Pants: You Won't Hear God if You Never Shut Up..........382

Chapter 10: 386
Evangelism – Sharing Your Truth Without Being a Jerk 386
   The Evangelism Problem: Where We Went Wrong 388
      The Sales Pitch Approach 388
      The Information Dump Approach 389
      The Fear-Based Approach 390
      The Argument-Winning Approach 391
      The Cultural Warrior Approach 391
   A Better Way: Biblical Foundations for Effective Evangelism 392
      1. It Starts with Relationship 392
      2. It Requires Authentic Living 393
      3. It Involves Actually Opening Your Mouth 394
      4. It's Empowered by the Holy Spirit 395
      5. It Requires Listening, Not Just Speaking 395
      6. It's About Making Disciples, Not Just Converts .. 396
      7. It Respects Human Dignity and Freedom 397
   Practical Steps: How to Share Your Faith Without Being a Jerk 397
      1. Start with Your Own Story 397
      2. Ask Good Questions and Actually Listen 398
      3. Find Common Ground 399
      4. Address Actual Questions, Not Assumed Ones .. 400
      5. Speak Their Language, Not Church-ese 401
      6. Prioritize Relationships Over Results 402
      7. Live a Compelling Life 403
      8. Embrace the Process 404
   Navigating Difficult Evangelism Scenarios 405
      When They're Hostile to Christianity 405
      When They Ask Tough Questions You Can't Answer 406

19

- When the Conversation Gets Derailed.................... 407
- When They Seem Completely Uninterested........... 408
- When You Fear Damaging the Relationship.......... 408

Digital Evangelism: Sharing Faith Online Without Being That Person... 409
- 1. Be a Real Person, Not a Christian Bot................. 409
- 2. Ask Questions Rather Than Make Pronouncements.. 410
- 3. Share Stories More Than Arguments................... 411
- 4. Engage Privately with Public Disagreement...... 411
- 5. Share Content from Diverse Christian Voices.... 411
- 6. Be Quick to Listen, Slow to Post........................... 412
- 7. Remember Real People Are Reading................... 412

Evangelism Styles: Finding Your Authentic Approach 413
- The Relational Connector.. 413
- The Intellectual Engager.. 414
- The Direct Communicator....................................... 415
- The Service-Based Witness...................................... 416
- The Story-Telling Illustrator.................................... 417
- The Invitational Host.. 418

The Long Game: Evangelism as a Lifestyle.................... 419
- 1. Pray Consistently for Non-Believing Friends..... 419
- 2. Build Genuine Friendships with Non-Christians.... 420
- 3. Create a Hospitable Life.. 420
- 4. Develop Your Story.. 421
- 5. Learn to Recognize Spiritual Openness.............. 421
- 6. Respond to Current Events with Gospel Perspective... 422
- 7. Live with Gospel Intentionality........................... 423

The 7-Day Evangelism Challenge.................................... 424

    Day 1: Prayer Foundation..424
    Day 2: Testimony Development............................. 425
    Day 3: Question Cultivation....................................425
    Day 4: Hospitality Action... 426
    Day 5: Gospel Clarity.. 427
    Day 6: Digital Witness Review................................ 427
    Day 7: Courageous Conversation............................428
  The Kick in the Pants: You've Got Good News—Stop Keeping It to Yourself...428

Chapter 11:.. 433
Stewardship – Managing Your Sh*t....................................433
  The Owner vs. Manager Mindset.......................................435
    The Owner Mentality.. 435
    The Manager Mentality... 436
  The Four Big Domains of Stewardship.............................437
    1. Time: The Non-Renewable Resource...................437
      The Time Stewardship Problem........................ 437
      Biblical Time Management................................ 438
      Practical Time Stewardship Steps..................... 440
    2. Money: The Visible Value System........................ 443
      The Money Stewardship Problem.....................443
      Biblical Money Management............................. 444
      Practical Money Stewardship Steps.................446
    3. Body: The Physical Temple.................................. 448
      The Body Stewardship Problem........................449
      Biblical Body Care.. 449
      Practical Body Stewardship Steps....................451
    4. Talents: The Gifted Investment............................454
      The Talent Stewardship Problem...................... 454
      Biblical Gift Stewardship....................................455

Practical Talent Stewardship Steps.................... 457
Common Stewardship Pitfalls.. 460
    1. The Compartmentalization Trap......................... 461
    2. The Tomorrow Fallacy... 461
    3. The Comparison Disease.. 462
    4. The Activity vs. Productivity Confusion............ 463
    5. The Ownership Reversion...................................... 464
The Stewardship Development Path.............................. 464
    Stage 1: Awakening to Ownership............................ 465
    Stage 2: Establishing Basic Management................ 465
    Stage 3: Developing Strategic Stewardship............ 466
    Stage 4: Multiplying Stewardship Impact................ 467
The 30-Day Stewardship Challenge................................ 468
    Week 1: Time Stewardship.. 468
    Week 2: Money Stewardship..................................... 469
    Week 3: Body Stewardship... 471
    Week 4: Talent Stewardship....................................... 472
    Integration Days.. 473
The Kick in the Pants: Stop Making Excuses and Start Managing Your Sh*t.. 474

Chapter 12:.. 477
Humility – Getting Over Yourself.. 477
The Many Disguises of Pride.. 479
    1. Perfectionism: "I can't fail or show weakness"... 480
    2. Chronic Comparison: "I need to be better than others"... 480
    3. Attention-Seeking: "Notice me!"........................... 481
    4. Victimhood: "Everything happens TO me"........ 482
    5. Excessive Independence: "I don't need anyone" 483
    6. Defensive Pride: "I'm never wrong"..................... 484

7. False Humility: "I'm just terrible at everything" 484
The Biblical Vision of Humility 485
   1. Humility Begins with God-Centered Reality 486
   2. Humility Acknowledges Both Dignity and Dependence 487
   3. Humility Expresses Itself in Christlike Service .. 488
   4. Humility Creates Space for Others to Flourish .. 489
   5. Humility Receives Grace Without Entitlement .. 490
The Surprising Benefits of Humility 491
   1. Humility Accelerates Growth 491
   2. Humility Creates Authentic Connection 492
   3. Humility Produces Inner Peace 493
   4. Humility Enables Resilience 494
   5. Humility Enhances Leadership 495
Practical Steps Toward Humility 496
   1. Start with a Reality Check 497
   2. Practice Strategic Self-Forgetfulness 498
   3. Volunteer for Invisible Service 499
   4. Cultivate Purposeful Gratitude 500
   5. Learn the Art of the Genuine Apology 501
   6. Seek and Implement Feedback 502
   7. Practice the Ministry of Celebration 503
The Humility Journey: Stages of Development 504
   Stage 1: Awakening to Pride 505
   Stage 2: Intentional Counter-Practice 506
   Stage 3: Growing Authenticity 507
   Stage 4: Habitual Humility 508
Humility in Different Life Contexts 510
   For Leaders and People with Influence 510
   For Those in Learning or Subordinate Positions 511

For the Highly Successful..512
　　　For Those Facing Limitation or Setback..................512
　　　For the Naturally Gifted... 513
　　　For Those Building Platforms or Public Personas..514
　　The 30-Day Humility Challenge..515
　　　Week 1: Awareness Building......................................515
　　　Week 2: Basic Pride Interruption..............................517
　　　Week 3: Deeper Humility Development.................. 519
　　　Week 4: Humility Integration................................... 522
　　The Kick in the Pants: Your Life Is Not The You Show 526
Chapter 13:.. 531
Perseverance – Sticking With It When It Sucks........................ 531
　　Why Faith Gets Hard: The Reality Check...................... 533
　　　1. The Emotion Fade..533
　　　2. Life Trauma and Disappointment........................534
　　　3. Unanswered Questions and Intellectual Doubts..... 535
　　　4. Community Disappointment...............................536
　　　5. The Daily Grind... 537
　　　6. Cultural Hostility...537
　　　7. Spiritual Warfare...538
　　The Biblical Case for Hanging On...................................539
　　　The Race Metaphor...539
　　　The Farming Analogy... 540
　　　The Refining Fire..541
　　　The Examples of the Faithful................................... 542
　　　The Direct Commands..543
　　Why Most People Quit: The Perseverance Killers.........543
　　　The Emotional Junkie... 544
　　　The Expectations Manager...................................... 545

    The Lone Ranger...545
    The Perfectionist Quitter.................................546
    The Minimum Viable Faith Person.........................547
    The Unrepentant Compromiser............................548
    The One-Crisis Quitter....................................548

The Perseverance Toolkit: Practical Ways to Keep Going. 549

    1. Develop Realistic Expectations........................549
    2. Build Sustainable Spiritual Rhythms..................550
    3. Leverage the Power of Micro-Commitments...... 551
    4. Create Accountability Structures........................ 552
    5. Remember Your "Why"..................................553
    6. Find Your Perseverance Community....................553
    7. Practice Strategic Remembering............................554
    8. Embrace Lamenting as Faith, Not Failure........... 555
    9. Adjust Rather Than Abandon...............................555
    10. Remember It's Not All About Feelings..............556

The Seven Seasons of Faith: Navigating Different Perseverance Challenges...557

    1. The Honeymoon Season...557
    2. The Wilderness Season.. 558
    3. The Deconstruction Season................................... 558
    4. The Crisis Season.. 559
    5. The Activist Season.. 560
    6. The Ordinary Season...561
    7. The Legacy Season..561

The 30-Day Perseverance Challenge............................ 562

    Week 1: Building Your Foundation.......................... 562
    Week 2: Counter-Conditioning Your Quitting Triggers... 564
    Week 3: Practicing While It's Easy........................... 566

  Week 4: Preparing for Long-Haul Faith.................. 568
  Week 5: Integration and Moving Forward..............570
 The Kick in the Pants: Quitting Is Easy—Finishing Is Worth It... 571

Conclusion..**576**
 So, Now What?..576
 What Real Growth Looks Like.....................................577
 The Rhythms, Not the Rules.. 579
 Pick Your Path, Not Your Performance.........................580
 Community, Not Just Personal Piety............................ 582
 When You Fail (Not If).. 584
 The Point of It All...586
 Now What?.. 588

A Letter to Myself in 10 Years....................................... **591**

Acknowledgments... **593**

Next Steps... **596**

Small Group Discussion Guide..................................... **599**
 How to Use This Guide...599
  Chapter 1: Prayer – Actually Talking to God................599
  Chapter 2: Bible Study – Knowing What You Claim to Believe..600
  Chapter 3: Fasting – Hunger as a Spiritual Alarm Clock... 601
  Chapter 4: Worship – Beyond the Music....................602
  Chapter 5: Solitude – Being Alone With God................ 603
  Chapter 6: Community – The People Who Keep You From Drowning..604
  Chapter 7: Confession – Bringing Your Crap Into the Light.. 604
  Chapter 8: Hospitality – Making Room for Outsiders. 605
  Chapter 9: Service – Getting Over Your Need to Be

  Important.. 606
  Chapter 10: Simplicity – Having Enough Without Having Everything... 607
  Chapter 11: Stewardship – Managing Your Sh*t........... 608
  Chapter 12: Humility – Getting Over Yourself.............. 609
  Chapter 13: Perseverance – Sticking With It When It Sucks.. 609
 Final Note to Group Leaders.. 610

Resources.. 611
 Bible Reading.. 612
 Prayer.. 613
 Accountability & Community.. 613
 Spiritual Discipline Tools... 614
 Final Note... 616

Introduction

Let's Be Honest About This Jesus Thing

If you've ever sat in church wondering if you're the only one who doesn't have this whole Christianity thing figured out, I have good news: you're not alone. The bad news? You're probably right—you don't have it figured out. But here's the secret nobody tells you at those shiny church welcome desks: nobody else does either.

We're all kind of winging it.

Sure, some people look like they've mastered the Christian life. They use phrases like "the Lord laid it on my heart" with a straight face. They seem to have Bible verses ready for every situation. They raise their hands at exactly the right moment in worship, and their Instagram feeds are an endless stream of coffee cups next to open Bibles with perfectly highlighted verses.

But behind the carefully curated Christian veneer, most of us are just trying to keep our spiritual pants on.

We check our phones before we check in with God each morning. We struggle to pray for five focused minutes but can binge-watch Netflix for five straight hours. We know more lyrics to Taylor Swift songs than we do Bible verses. We gossip right after church. We judge people for sins we committed last week. We worry about money and health and our kids as if God isn't actually in control.

And then we feel guilty about all of it because, well, shouldn't Christians be better at this stuff?

Here's the truth: following Jesus is hard. Not because Jesus makes it complicated, but because we do. We've turned discipleship into performance art. We've replaced relationship with religious achievement. We've swapped the revolutionary message of grace for an exhausting checklist of Christian duties that leaves us feeling like spiritual failures most of the time.

No wonder so many of us are secretly wondering if we suck at being Christians.

But what if the problem isn't that we're bad at Christianity? What if the problem is that we've misunderstood what Christianity is actually about?

Jesus didn't die so you could maintain a perfect quiet time streak. He didn't rise again so you could post inspirational Bible quotes on social media. He didn't send His Spirit so you could feel vaguely spiritual while essentially living like everyone else.

He came to transform you from the inside out. To bring you into genuine relationship with the living God. To make you more like Him in ways that actually matter.

And while that transformation is ultimately His work, not yours, there are specific practices that position you to experience it more fully. Habits that create space for God to do what only God can do. Disciplines that, when practiced consistently (not perfectly), gradually reshape how you think, feel, and live.

The early Christians understood this. So did believers throughout church history. But somewhere along the way, we've either forgotten these practices entirely or turned them into religious performances that drain life rather than produce it.

This book is about reclaiming these life-giving habits—not as items on a spiritual to-do list, but as proven pathways for becoming the kind of humans we were created to be. I've identified thirteen that seem particularly essential for not sucking at following Jesus in our distracted, disorienting modern world.

Fair warning: I'm not going to sugarcoat this. Some of these practices will feel uncomfortable. Some will expose areas where you're settling for a knockoff version of Christianity. Some might piss you off a little.

That's okay. Growth usually involves some discomfort.

But I promise not to pile on guilt or shame. This isn't about becoming the perfect Christian (spoiler alert: that person doesn't exist). It's about becoming more authentically who God created you to be—more loving, more present, more alive.

You don't need another book telling you to try harder at religion. You need practical ways to connect with Jesus that actually work in real life. You need grace-filled truth that challenges without crushing. You need someone to cut through the Instagram-perfect spirituality and talk about faith like a normal human being.

That's what I'm aiming for in these pages. No pretense. No performance. Just 13 straightforward practices that have helped followers of Jesus not suck at it for the past two thousand years.

You don't have to master all thirteen. You don't even have to be good at them. You just have to be willing to try them, fail at them, and keep showing up anyway.

Because here's the beautiful truth: Jesus isn't looking for your perfection. He's looking for your presence. And these practices are simply ways to show up consistently to the God who's always showing up for you.

So let's do this together. Not as spiritual superstars with all the answers, but as fellow travelers trying to follow Jesus one imperfect day at a time.

Chapter 1: A Grateful Heart – Learn to Say Thank You

Let's start with a truth bomb: most of us are ungrateful little shits.

Sorry for the language, but I'm not sorry for the honesty. Because here's what happens: we wake up in beds we didn't build, in homes we didn't design, breathing air we didn't create, with hearts that keep beating without our permission, and the first thing we do is grab our phones and complain about something on social media.

We step into hot showers with clean water—a luxury that billions of people on this planet would kill for—and spend those eight minutes thinking about all the things that might go wrong today. We drive cars that cost more than what most humans throughout history would earn in a lifetime, sit in climate-controlled offices, eat food we didn't have to hunt or grow, and still manage to bitch about our "hard lives."

I'm not saying your problems aren't real. I'm saying your perspective probably sucks.

And I'm including myself in this diagnosis. Because gratitude doesn't come naturally to any of us. We're wired for survival, which means we're wired to notice threats, problems, and shortcomings. We're not naturally wired to pause and appreciate what's going well or what we already have. That's why gratitude is a discipline—a spiritual practice—not just a feeling that shows up when good stuff happens.

This isn't just some self-help mumbo-jumbo either. Paul writes in 1 Thessalonians 5:18, "Give thanks in all circumstances; for this is the will of God in Christ Jesus for you." Did you catch that? ALL circumstances. Not just the Instagram-worthy moments. Not just when you get the promotion or when your kids behave or when your spouse remembers your anniversary. ALL circumstances.

That verse isn't suggesting gratitude as a nice option if you're feeling it. It's telling us this is God's will for our lives. As in, this is what God wants from you. As in, if you're not practicing gratitude, you're missing something fundamental about what it means to follow Jesus.

Why God Cares About Your Gratitude

Before we get into the nuts and bolts of how to actually become more grateful (because trust me, we'll get there), let's talk about why this matters so much to God. Why would an all-powerful deity care whether or not you're counting your blessings?

First, God knows that gratitude is the antidote to about a thousand spiritual diseases. Entitlement? Gratitude kills it. Self-pity? Gratitude destroys it. Materialism? Gratitude undermines it. Envy? Gratitude makes it impossible. Bitterness? Gratitude heals it.

Second, gratitude acknowledges reality. When you're grateful, you're admitting that you didn't create everything good in your life. You're confessing that you're not self-sufficient. You're recognizing that you're a recipient of grace, not just the product of your own awesomeness. This is called "truth," and God's pretty big on that.

In Psalm 100:4, we're told to "Enter his gates with thanksgiving, and his courts with praise!" This isn't because God has a fragile ego and needs our compliments. It's because approaching God without gratitude would be like showing up to a feast someone prepared for you and immediately complaining about the silverware placement. It's delusional. It misses what's actually happening. It fails to recognize reality.

Third, gratitude opens the door to joy. Not happiness—happiness comes and goes based on what happens. Joy is deeper. Joy can coexist with suffering. And joy, interestingly, almost always travels with gratitude. They're like conjoined twins. Where you find one, you typically find the other.

So when Paul says in Philippians 4:6, "Do not be anxious about anything, but in everything by prayer and supplication with thanksgiving let your requests be made known to God," he's not just giving us a formula for prayer. He's showing us how to replace anxiety with joy. Gratitude is the bridge that gets you there.

The Problem of Ingratitude

Before we talk about building gratitude, we need to admit how deep the problem of ingratitude goes. Because this isn't just about being rude or forgetting to write thank-you notes. This is about a fundamental orientation toward life that can poison everything.

The Bible's first story about human sin in Genesis 3 is essentially a story about ingratitude. Adam and Eve had paradise. They had perfect communion with

God. They had each other. They had responsibilities that matched their abilities. They had every tree in the garden except one.

And what did they focus on? The one thing they couldn't have. The one restriction. The one "no" in a garden full of "yes." That's what ingratitude does—it zooms in on what we lack rather than what we have. It magnifies restrictions and minimizes blessings.

Romans 1 goes even further, describing the downward spiral of humanity as beginning with a failure to give thanks. Paul writes that although people knew God, "they did not honor him as God or give thanks to him, but they became futile in their thinking, and their foolish hearts were darkened" (Romans 1:21). Notice the progression: lack of gratitude → futile thinking → darkened hearts → spiraling moral corruption.

That's not hyperbole. Ingratitude really does lead to a darkened heart—a perspective that can't see clearly, that misinterprets reality, that focuses on the wrong things. And from there, it's a short journey to all sorts of destructive behaviors and attitudes.

Think of the last time you were trapped in self-pity or bitterness. I'm guessing you weren't exactly making your best decisions during that period. I'm guessing your thoughts weren't particularly noble or true. I'm guessing your relationships probably suffered.

Ingratitude doesn't just make you unpleasant—it makes you unwise. It clouds your judgment.

The Gratitude Muscle

Here's where the rubber meets the road. Gratitude, like physical fitness, is primarily about practice, not knowledge. You don't get in shape by reading about workouts, and you don't become grateful by nodding along with inspirational quotes about thankfulness.

Gratitude is a muscle that grows stronger with use and atrophies with neglect. And just like physical exercise, it's going to feel unnatural and difficult at first. Your mind will resist. You'll feel fake or forced. You'll want to quit.

Do it anyway. Because what feels forced eventually becomes natural. What starts as discipline eventually becomes desire. Just like the person who hates running at first but eventually craves it, your gratitude habit can transform from obligation into inclination.

So how do we build this muscle? Let me give you some practical exercises:

1. The Gratitude Journal (But Not the Fluffy Kind)

You've probably heard of keeping a gratitude journal. It's good advice, but the way most people approach it is way too shallow. Writing "family, friends, food" every day isn't going to transform your perspective.

Instead, try this: Every day, write down three specific things you're grateful for, but with these rules:
- No repeating items for at least a month
- At least one item has to be something difficult or painful
- For each item, write one sentence about why you're grateful for it

That last rule is crucial. "I'm grateful for my job because it forces me to develop patience with difficult people" is much more powerful than just writing "my job." The why activates actual gratitude, not just a mental checklist.

And yes, you read that second rule correctly. Find something painful or difficult to be grateful for. The promotion you didn't get that forced you to develop new skills. The relationship that ended but taught you what you really need in a partner. The health scare that reminded you to prioritize what matters.

This isn't toxic positivity or putting on rose-colored glasses. It's developing the spiritual muscle to see how God works even through difficult circumstances.

It's taking Paul seriously when he says to give thanks in all circumstances—not for all circumstances, but in them.

2. The Gratitude Alarm

Set an alarm on your phone to go off three random times throughout the day. When it rings, stop whatever you're doing and find something to be grateful for in that exact moment.

This is harder than it sounds. If the alarm goes off during your commute when you're stuck in traffic, you have to find gratitude right there. If it goes off during an argument with your spouse, you have to find gratitude right there. If it goes off during a boring meeting or while changing a diaper or while waiting in line, you have to find gratitude right there.

This exercise trains your brain to find blessings in ordinary moments, not just during the highlight reel of your life. And over time, it helps you develop what the Puritans called "the sight of faith"—the ability to see beyond surface circumstances to the deeper reality of God's presence and provision.

3. The Gratitude Visit

This one comes from positive psychology research, and it's powerful. Think of someone who had a significant positive impact on your life whom you've never properly thanked. Write them a detailed letter explaining exactly what they did and how it affected you. Then—and this is the important part—arrange to visit this person and read the letter to them face-to-face.

If geography makes this impossible, do it via video call. The key is to watch their response as you express your gratitude directly to them.

This exercise does double duty: it cultivates your own gratitude while also blessing someone else. And research shows the positive effects on your wellbeing can last for months after just one gratitude visit.

For Christians, this has a spiritual dimension too. When you thank people specifically and sincerely for the ways they've blessed you, you're acknowledging that God often works through human instruments. You're recognizing the body of Christ in action.

4. Thankful Prayer First

Most of us approach prayer like a cosmic vending machine. We show up when we need something, insert our requests, and expect God to deliver.

Try flipping the script: Make it a rule that you cannot ask God for anything until you've spent at least two minutes thanking Him for what He's already given you. And not just the big obvious stuff. Thank Him for specific things from the last 24 hours.

This practice reshapes your entire relationship with God. It moves you from the entitled consumer to the grateful child. It reminds you that every request you bring is being brought to a God who has already been extraordinarily generous with you.

As Philippians 4:6 instructs, let your requests be made known to God with thanksgiving—not after thanksgiving, but with it. Gratitude doesn't just bookend your prayers; it infuses them.

5. The Gratitude Fast

This is the black diamond level of gratitude exercises. For 24 hours, commit to not complaining about anything. Not the weather, not politics, not your boss, not your spouse, not your kids, not your body, not traffic, not technology—nothing.

Every time you catch yourself about to complain (either out loud or in your head), replace the complaint with a statement of gratitude related to the situation.

About to complain about traffic? "I'm grateful I have a car and the means to maintain it."

About to complain about your spouse leaving dishes in the sink? "I'm grateful I have a partner to share my life with."

About to complain about work stress? "I'm grateful I have a job that provides for my needs."

This isn't about denying problems or suppressing genuine concerns. It's about breaking the habit of reflexive negativity that so many of us have developed. It's about training your mind to look for what's going right before fixating on what's going wrong.

And trust me, 24 hours will feel like an eternity the first time you try this. You'll be shocked at how many complaints are queued up in your mind at any given moment. But pushing through this exercise can create a fundamental shift in how you see your daily life.

The Hard Truth About Gratitude

Now, let me be clear about something: Practicing gratitude doesn't mean you'll never feel negative emotions. It doesn't mean you ignore injustice or pretend everything is fine when it isn't. Jesus himself experienced anger, grief, frustration, and disappointment. The Psalms are full of lament and complaint.

The difference is that gratitude gives these negative emotions proper context. It prevents them from becoming your primary lens for viewing life. It keeps them from hardening into bitterness or despair.

Think of it this way: Gratitude doesn't deny the darkness, but it insists that darkness isn't the whole story. It holds onto what's good even while acknowledging what's broken. It's the perfect balance of realism and hope.

And here's a truth that might be hard to swallow: Your level of gratitude has very little to do with your actual circumstances. Some of the most grateful people I've ever met were facing terminal illness, grinding poverty, or devastating loss. Some of the most entitled, ungrateful people I've known had every advantage and blessing life could offer.

Gratitude is a choice, not a feeling that descends when your life is Instagram-perfect. It's choosing to see and acknowledge what's good even when plenty isn't.

In Viktor Frankl's book "Man's Search for Meaning," he describes how even in Nazi concentration camps, some prisoners were able to maintain gratitude—for a sunset, for a crust of bread, for a moment of kindness.

If gratitude is possible in those circumstances, what's our excuse?

Gratitude When Life Actually Sucks

Let's address the elephant in the room. What about when life genuinely, objectively sucks? What about when you lose your job, get a scary diagnosis, or go through a painful divorce? What about when someone you love dies? What about chronic pain or mental illness?

Is gratitude still possible—or even appropriate—then?

The Bible's answer is yes. Remember Paul's instruction: "Give thanks in all circumstances." Not for all circumstances, but in them. There's a crucial difference.

Giving thanks for something terrible would be perverse. God doesn't expect you to be grateful for cancer or abuse or betrayal. But giving thanks in terrible circumstances? That's different. That's recognizing that even in your darkest valley, grace is still present.

The classic example is Job, who after losing his wealth, his health, and all ten of his children, still managed to say, "The LORD gave, and the LORD has taken away; blessed be the name of the LORD" (Job 1:21). That's not gratitude for tragedy. That's gratitude in tragedy.

Or consider Paul himself, writing his most joy-filled letter (Philippians) while in prison, facing possible execution. He wasn't thankful for his chains, but he found things to be thankful for while wearing them.

When your life falls apart, gratitude looks like:
- Thanking God for who He is, even when you can't thank Him for what's happening
- Noticing small mercies even in the midst of large pain
- Acknowledging the people who show up for you in your suffering
- Recognizing the strength you're developing through your struggle

In Habakkuk 3:17-18, the prophet writes: "Though the fig tree should not blossom, nor fruit be on the vines, the produce of the olive fail and the fields yield no food, the flock be cut off from the fold and there be no herd in the stalls, yet I will rejoice in the LORD; I will take joy in the God of my salvation."

That's not gratitude because everything's awesome. That's gratitude when everything is falling apart. That's the advanced class.

The Gratitude Challenge

Here's your 30-day challenge to jumpstart your gratitude practice:

Week 1: Gratitude Journal
Each day, write down three specific things you're grateful for (following the rules we discussed earlier). No repeats, at least one challenging thing, and explain why you're grateful for each.

Week 2: Gratitude Expressions
Each day, express specific gratitude to one person. This can be a text, email, phone call, or face-to-face conversation. Be detailed about what you appreciate about them or what they've done for you.

Week 3: Gratitude Prayer
Begin each prayer time with at least 5 minutes of thanksgiving before making any requests. Keep a running list of answered prayers to fuel your gratitude.

Week 4: Gratitude Perspective
Each day, identify one difficult situation in your life and write down three potential reasons to be grateful within that challenge. Not for the challenge itself, but for what God might be doing through it.

By the end of these 30 days, you won't have a perfect gratitude practice. But you will have begun to rewire your brain, and you'll have concrete evidence of how this discipline changes your perspective.

The Gratitude Effect

So what should you expect to change as you develop this gratitude muscle? Because if this is just about feeling warm fuzzies, it's probably not worth the effort.

First, gratitude will transform your relationship with God. When you begin to notice and name the specific ways God is working in your life, prayer becomes less transactional and more relational. You start to see God's character more clearly. You develop greater trust because you have concrete evidence of His faithfulness. You become less demanding and more receptive.

Second, gratitude will revolutionize your relationships. Grateful people are significantly less likely to keep score in relationships. They're less defensive. They're quicker to forgive. They notice and affirm the good in others rather than fixating on flaws. As you become more aware of how much grace you've received, you naturally extend more grace to others.

Third, gratitude will reshape your resilience. Grateful people bounce back faster from setbacks because they don't view problems as the whole story. They maintain perspective. They remember past difficulties they've overcome. They trust that good can come even from pain. This isn't naive optimism; it's biblical hope.

Fourth, gratitude will recalibrate your desires. One of the most insidious effects of our consumer culture is constant dissatisfaction—the nagging sense that you need more, better, newer things to be happy. Gratitude breaks this cycle. It helps you recognize the abundance you already have. It shifts your focus from what's missing to what's present.

Fifth, gratitude will refresh your witness. Let's be honest: Christians are often known more for what we're against than what we're for. We're perceived as judgmental, negative, and hypocritical. A life marked by genuine gratitude stands in stark contrast to this stereotype. It makes faith attractive. As Francis Schaeffer put it, gratitude is "the oil of relationships" that reduces friction and creates harmony.

The Choice Is Yours

At this point, you might be thinking, "This all sounds great, but my life really is harder than most people's. I have legitimate reasons to focus on what's wrong rather than what's right."

Maybe so. But here's the brutal truth: Your ingratitude isn't punishing the people who hurt you. It's not changing your circumstances. It's not impressing God with how serious your problems are. It's just making you miserable.

Gratitude is a choice available to you regardless of your circumstances. It's not about pretending everything is fine when it isn't. It's about refusing to let what's wrong blind you to what's right. It's about maintaining proper perspective. It's about acknowledging reality—the full reality, not just the painful parts.

As we wrap up this chapter, I want to be crystal clear: Developing gratitude won't make all your problems disappear. It won't give you a perfect life. It won't shield you from suffering.

What it will do is transform how you experience whatever life brings. It will give you resources to face difficulties without being destroyed by them. It will connect you more deeply to God and others. It will allow you to enjoy what you have instead of always craving what you lack.

The Kick in the Pants

So here's your kick in the pants: If you're not actively practicing gratitude, you're actively practicing entitlement. There's no neutral ground here.

Either you're training your mind to notice and appreciate the good, or you're training it to focus on what you think you deserve but don't have. Either you're developing the habit of thanksgiving, or you're developing the habit of criticism and complaint. Your mind is being shaped either way.

The writer Annie Dillard famously said, "How we spend our days is, of course, how we spend our lives." I'd add: How we train our attention is how we experience our days. If you train your attention toward what's lacking, missing, or wrong, that's primarily what you'll experience—even if your life is objectively blessed in countless ways.

Gratitude isn't just a nice spiritual add-on if you have time for it. It's not the cherry on top of an already-good Christian life. It's fundamental to your spiritual and emotional health. It's essential to your witness. It's commanded by God not because He needs your thanks, but because you need the transformation that comes through thanksgiving.

So stop waiting to feel grateful. Stop waiting for your circumstances to improve before you practice gratitude. Stop pretending that your ingratitude is justified by your problems.

Start the gratitude journal today. Set the gratitude alarm right now. Plan the gratitude visit this week. Begin your next prayer with thanksgiving. Try the gratitude fast tomorrow.

Because here's the truth: You don't need a better life to be grateful. You need a better perspective. And that perspective is available to you right now, regardless of your circumstances.

Start seeing what you have instead of obsessing over what you lack. Start noticing God's provision instead of focusing on your problems. Start appreciating the people around you instead of criticizing their flaws.

In other words, start being grateful. Not because everything is perfect, but because God is good even when life isn't.

Your life won't change overnight. Habits take time to form. But if you stick with this practice, six months from now, you'll look back and be amazed at how differently you see the world—and how differently the world sees you.

The choice is yours. Will you continue in the soul-sucking habit of ingratitude? Or will you begin the life-giving practice of thanksgiving?

As Joshua challenged the Israelites: "Choose this day whom you will serve" (Joshua 24:15). Will you serve your complaints, your sense of entitlement, your focus on what's wrong? Or will you serve the God who deserves your thanks regardless of circumstances?

I hope you choose gratitude. Not just because it's commanded, but because it's the pathway to the joy, peace, and perspective you're actually looking for.

Now close this book, grab a pen and paper, and write down the first five things you're genuinely grateful for. Your gratitude journey starts now.

Chapter 2:

Confession – Owning Your Crap

If there's one thing humans are exceptionally good at, it's avoiding the truth about ourselves.

We're masters of self-deception, Olympic-level mental gymnasts who can twist ourselves into pretzels trying to justify why we're right and everyone else is wrong. We've perfected the fine art of blame-shifting since the Garden of Eden, when Adam pointed at Eve and Eve pointed at the serpent, and nobody wanted to say those simple words: "I screwed up."

Sound familiar?

Let me guess: You picked up this book because you want to grow spiritually. You want to be a better Christian. You want to develop godly habits and live more like Jesus. That's awesome. But here's what you need to know right off the bat—nothing meaningful is going to change in your spiritual life until you get radically honest about what's broken in it.

Not what's broken in your spouse. Not what's broken in your church. Not what's broken in your parents or your boss or the government.

What's broken in YOU.

This is where confession comes in. Not the stuffy, ritualistic kind where you mumble a generic "forgive me" prayer before bed, but the gut-level, sometimes painful practice of dragging your specific sins into the light and owning them completely. No excuses. No "but you don't understand my situation." No "well, I wouldn't have done that if they hadn't..."

Just you, getting brutally honest about your crap.

And I know what you're thinking: "That sounds absolutely terrible. Why would I want to do that?"

Because it's the gateway to everything you actually want: freedom, growth, intimacy with God, authentic relationships, and a life not dominated by guilt, shame, and façades.

As James 5:16 puts it: "Therefore, confess your sins to one another and pray for one another, that you may be healed." Notice the connection there? Confession isn't just about getting forgiveness (though that's certainly part of it). It's about getting healed. It's medicine for your soul.

So let's talk about why we avoid confession like the plague, what we're missing when we do, and how to start practicing this life-changing discipline that's so much more than just admitting you're wrong.

The Confession-Avoidance Olympics

Before we get into the why and how of healthy confession, let's acknowledge the creative ways we avoid it. If avoiding confession were an Olympic sport, most of us would be gold medalists. Here are the events we've mastered:

The Blame Shift

This is the oldest avoidance technique in history, literally dating back to the first sin in Genesis 3. Adam blamed Eve. Eve blamed the serpent. Nobody just said, "I chose to disobey God." When confronted with his sin, Adam even managed to subtly blame God Himself: "The woman whom YOU gave to be with me..." Nice move, Adam.

We're still playing this game thousands of years later. "I wouldn't have a temper if my kids would just listen." "I wouldn't look at porn if my spouse was more interested in sex." "I wouldn't gossip if people didn't do such gossip-worthy things."

See how it works? The problem is never really me. It's always something or someone else that made me do it.

The Comparison Game

"Well, at least I'm not as bad as..." This is comparing yourself to people you think are worse to make yourself feel better about your sin. "Sure, I have road rage, but at least I'm not cheating on my spouse." "I may struggle with gossip, but at least I'm not one of those Christians who voted for [politician you hate]."

This is like saying your broken arm isn't a problem because your neighbor has cancer. One person's greater sin doesn't negate or diminish your need for confession and healing.

The Technicality Defense

This is where you redefine sin so narrowly that you can wiggle out on a technicality. "I didn't actually lie; I just didn't tell the whole truth." "It's not really lust if I don't click on the image." "It's not really gossip if I'm just sharing a prayer request."

Jesus called this out in the Sermon on the Mount. He was basically saying, "You think you haven't

57

committed adultery because you haven't physically cheated? Let's talk about what you're doing in your mind." The technicality defense doesn't work with God. He sees past our clever redefinitions.

The Justification Complex

"You don't understand my situation." This is where we present all the extenuating circumstances that make our sin understandable, even reasonable. "Anyone would have done what I did if they were in my shoes." "I had no choice." "You would have reacted the same way."

The problem is, sin is still sin even when it's understandable. Your difficult circumstances might explain your sin, but they don't justify it.

The Minimize and Dismiss

"It's not that big a deal." This is treating sin like it's no big thing. "Everyone struggles with this." "Nobody's perfect." "God has bigger things to worry about than my white lies."

This approach trivializes both sin and grace. If your sin is no big deal, then neither is God's forgiveness. You can't simultaneously claim that sin is trivial and that grace is amazing.

The Spiritual Bypass

This is using spiritual language to avoid dealing with specific sin. "I'm just a sinner saved by grace." "We're all broken people." "The ground is level at the foot of the cross."

These statements are theologically true but can be misused as get-out-of-confession-free cards. They're so general that they don't require any specific acknowledgment or change.

The Self-Flagellation Show

This might surprise you, but excessive self-criticism can actually be a way of avoiding true confession. When you beat yourself up dramatically—"I'm just the worst person ever!"—you're still controlling the narrative. You're still the director of your own moral performance, just playing the role of the villain instead of the hero.

Real confession isn't a performance. It's surrender.

Any of these sound familiar? Yeah, I thought so. We're all specialists in at least one of these techniques. The problem is, none of them lead to freedom. None of them lead to growth. And none of them reflect the kind of honesty that God calls us to.

Why We Run from Confession

So why do we work so hard to avoid confession? What are we really afraid of?

1. We're afraid of rejection

At our core, we fear that if people (or God) knew who we really are, they'd want nothing to do with us. So we present a carefully curated version of ourselves that's more acceptable, more put-together, more spiritual.

This fear isn't irrational. Some people will reject you if they know the real you. But that says more about them than it does about you. The incredible promise of the gospel is that God already knows the worst about you and loves you anyway.

Romans 5:8 tells us that "God shows his love for us in that while we were still sinners, Christ died for us." Not while we were getting our act together. Not while we were making progress. While we were still sinners. That's when He demonstrated His love most powerfully.

2. We're afraid of consequences

Let's be real: confession sometimes does come with consequences. If you confess to cheating on your spouse, that confession might lead to a painful process of rebuilding trust, or even the end of your marriage. If you confess to stealing from your workplace, you might lose your job.

But here's what we miss: the consequences of not confessing are ultimately far worse. They're just spread out and less visible. Unconfessed sin is like a slow poison that gradually corrupts your character, damages your relationships, and erodes your spiritual vitality.

Proverbs 28:13 puts it bluntly: "Whoever conceals his transgressions will not prosper, but he who confesses and forsakes them will obtain mercy." There's a natural law at work here: what stays hidden festers. What's exposed can be healed.

3. We're afraid of losing our image

For many of us, especially those of us who've been in church a long time, we've invested heavily in being seen as the "good Christian." We're the ones who have it together. We're the ones others come to for advice. We're the spiritual ones.

Confession threatens that identity. It means admitting we're not who we've presented ourselves to be. It means giving up the exhausting facade we've maintained.

But Jesus had harsh words for those who prioritized their religious image over authenticity. He called the Pharisees "whitewashed tombs"—beautiful on the outside but full of dead bones on the inside (Matthew 23:27). He wasn't impressed by their perfect religious performance. He was grieved by their lack of honesty.

4. We're afraid of feeling the full weight of our sin

Sometimes our avoidance isn't strategic; it's self-protective. We don't want to feel bad. We don't want to face the depth of our selfishness or the pain we've caused others. We don't want to sit with the uncomfortable reality of who we are apart from God's grace.

But here's the paradox: avoiding this discomfort doesn't make it go away. It just drives it underground where it morphs into anxiety, depression, addiction, or relational dysfunction. As the Psalmist wrote, "When I kept silent, my bones wasted away through my groaning all day long" (Psalm 32:3).

Feeling the appropriate weight of your sin isn't fun, but it's necessary for experiencing the true lightness of forgiveness. You can't know the heights of grace until you've acknowledged the depths of your need.

The Biblical Case for Confession

Now that we've identified our confession-avoidance techniques and the fears that drive them, let's look at what Scripture actually says about confession. Because this isn't just a useful psychological practice—it's a spiritual discipline with deep biblical roots.

1 John 1:8-9 lays it out clearly: "If we say we have no sin, we deceive ourselves, and the truth is not in us. If we confess our sins, he is faithful and just to forgive us our sins and to cleanse us from all unrighteousness."

There's a direct connection here between honesty about sin and experience of forgiveness. Self-deception blocks our ability to receive God's cleansing. Confession opens the floodgates for it.

In Psalm 32, David writes from personal experience about the misery of unconfessed sin and the liberation of bringing it into the light:

"Blessed is the one whose transgression is forgiven, whose sin is covered. Blessed is the man against whom the LORD counts no iniquity, and in whose spirit there is no deceit... I acknowledged my sin to you, and I did not cover my iniquity; I said, 'I will confess my transgressions to the LORD,' and you forgave the iniquity of my sin."

Note how he connects deceit—dishonesty about sin—with spiritual and emotional anguish. And note how confession is the turning point in his experience.

In the New Testament, James emphasizes the communal aspect of confession: "Therefore, confess your sins to one another and pray for one another, that you may be healed" (James 5:16). This goes beyond private confession to God; it includes being honest with other believers. Why? Because healing happens in community. Because we need others to speak truth to our blind spots, to pray for our weak areas, and to remind us of the gospel when we forget it.

Even Jesus, who had no sin of His own to confess, demonstrated the value of this discipline by submitting to John's baptism of repentance. He identified with sinful humanity not because He needed forgiveness but because He was establishing a pattern for us to follow.

The biblical vision of confession isn't about wallowing in guilt or engaging in a religious ritual. It's about living honestly before God and others. It's about refusing to hide in the shadows when God has called us into the light.

What Confession Is (And Isn't)

Before we get into the practical how-to of confession, let's clear up some misconceptions about what confession actually is. Because if we misunderstand the nature and purpose of this discipline, we'll either avoid it altogether or practice it in ways that harm rather than heal.

What Confession Isn't:

1. **Confession is not self-punishment.** The point isn't to beat yourself up or make yourself feel terrible as some kind of penance. Jesus already paid the full penalty for your sin on the cross. Confession acknowledges that payment; it doesn't try to supplement it.

2. **Confession is not a performance.** It's not about crafting the perfect, most eloquent admission of guilt. God doesn't grade your confession on style points. The tax collector in Jesus' parable simply said, "God,

be merciful to me, a sinner" (Luke 18:13). That was enough.

3. **Confession is not just saying "sorry."** It's not a formality or a social nicety. True confession involves genuine recognition of wrong, not just regret at being caught or facing consequences.

4. **Confession is not self-loathing.** Hating yourself is not the same as hating your sin. In fact, self-hatred often leads to more sin as we seek to escape the pain of our own contempt through addictive or destructive behaviors.

5. **Confession is not an end in itself.** The goal isn't just to get things off your chest. The goal is reconciliation with God and others, freedom from guilt and shame, and transformation into Christ's likeness.

What Confession Is:

1. **Confession is honest acknowledgment.** It's calling your sin what it actually is, without euphemisms or excuses. It's saying, "I lied," not "I wasn't entirely forthcoming." It's saying, "I lusted," not "I struggled with inappropriate thoughts."

2. **Confession is taking responsibility.** It's owning your actions and their impact, not minimizing or

deflecting. It's saying, "I hurt you with my words," not "You're too sensitive."

3. **Confession is an expression of sorrow.** Not just regret at consequences, but genuine grief over how your sin grieves God and harms others. As Paul writes in 2 Corinthians 7:10, "Godly grief produces a repentance that leads to salvation without regret."

4. **Confession is an act of trust.** When you confess, you're trusting that God's mercy is greater than your sin. You're trusting that His love for you isn't contingent on your performance. You're trusting that freedom is found in honesty, not in hiding.

5. **Confession is a pathway to change.** It's not just admitting what you've done wrong; it's the first step toward doing what's right. As John writes, "If we confess our sins, he is faithful and just to forgive us our sins and to cleanse us from all unrighteousness" (1 John 1:9). Forgiveness and cleansing go hand in hand.

With these clarifications in mind, let's talk about how to practically incorporate confession into your spiritual life.

The Practice of Confession: Getting Started

Confession isn't a one-time event but an ongoing practice, a regular rhythm in your relationship with God and others. Here's how to begin cultivating this life-changing discipline:

1. Establish a Daily Examination

The first step in confession is awareness. You can't confess what you don't recognize as sin. That's why the ancient spiritual practice of examination is so valuable.

At the end of each day, take 5-10 minutes to prayerfully reflect on your actions, words, and attitudes. Ask the Holy Spirit to show you where you've fallen short. Be specific. Don't just think, "I wasn't very Christ-like today." Ask:
- Did I speak with love and truthfulness?
- Did I act out of selfish ambition or vain conceit?
- Did I harbor anger, bitterness, or unforgiveness?
- Did I treat others as more important than myself?
- Did I give in to negative thought patterns?
- Did I misuse my time, talents, or resources?

This isn't about generating shame; it's about developing an accurate self-awareness. As Psalm 139:23-24 says, "Search me, O God, and know my heart... See if there be any grievous way in me."

For this examination to be effective, you need to approach it with both honesty and grace. Be ruthlessly honest about your sin, but always in the context of God's overwhelming grace toward you in Christ.

2. Confess Specifically to God

Based on what you've identified in your examination, bring specific sins before God in prayer. Don't just say, "Forgive all my sins." Name them: "Lord, I confess that I lied to my boss today to make myself look better." "God, I confess that I indulged in lustful thoughts about my coworker." "Father, I confess my anger at my children that came from selfishness, not love."

Why be so specific when God already knows everything? Because specificity is for your benefit, not God's. It prevents you from staying in vague generalities that don't lead to real change. It forces you to confront particular patterns and triggers in your life.

After confessing, take time to receive God's forgiveness afresh. Don't rush past this part. Let the reality of 1 John 1:9 sink in: "If we confess our sins, he is faithful and just to forgive us our sins and to cleanse us from all unrighteousness." God doesn't reluctantly forgive you; He faithfully and justly forgives because Jesus has paid the full price for your sin.

3. Develop Trusted Confession Relationships

Confession to God is essential, but it's not sufficient. James 5:16 calls us to "confess your sins to one another." Why? Because sin thrives in isolation. It loses power when dragged into the light of community.

Identify one or two trusted believers with whom you can be completely honest. This might be a spouse, a close friend, a small group, a mentor, or a pastor. The key qualities to look for are:
- Spiritual maturity
- Confidentiality
- Non-judgmental listening
- Commitment to both truth and grace

This doesn't mean you need to confess every sin to another person. But it does mean having someone who knows your ongoing struggles, your besetting sins, your areas of vulnerability. Someone who can ask you hard questions and remind you of the gospel when you forget it.

4. Practice Immediate Confession

Don't wait for your daily examination to confess obvious sin. When you recognize that you've sinned—whether against God or against another person—confess it immediately.

If you've sinned against someone else, go to them directly when possible. Jesus teaches in Matthew 5:23-24, "If you are offering your gift at the altar and there remember that your brother has something against you, leave your gift there before the altar and go. First be reconciled to your brother, and then come and offer your gift."

A good confession to another person includes:
- Clearly stating what you did wrong
- Acknowledging how it affected them
- Avoiding explanations that sound like excuses
- Asking for forgiveness (not just saying "I'm sorry")
- Committing to change

For example: "I spoke to you disrespectfully this morning. I was harsh and dismissive, and I know that was hurtful and undermining to you. I was stressed about work, but that's not an excuse for how I treated you. Will you forgive me? I'm working on managing my stress better so I don't take it out on you."

5. Embrace Regular Corporate Confession

Many church traditions include an element of corporate confession in their worship services. Whether your church does this formally or not, there's value in regularly confessing your sin alongside other believers.

This reminds us that we're not alone in our brokenness. It counters our tendency to think, "I'm the only one who struggles with this." It reinforces that the church is a community of the forgiven, not a showcase of the perfect.

If your church doesn't include corporate confession, you might incorporate elements of it in your small group or even simply by praying a prayer of confession (like Psalm 51) as part of your personal worship.

Common Roadblocks to Confession

Even with these practical steps, you'll encounter obstacles in your practice of confession. Here are some common roadblocks and how to overcome them:

Roadblock #1: "I don't feel bad enough about my sin."

Sometimes we don't confess because we don't feel the appropriate level of sorrow or conviction. We know intellectually that something is wrong, but emotionally we're not there.

Solution: Don't wait for feelings to lead. Obedience often precedes emotion. Confess based on what you know to be true from Scripture, not based on how you feel. As you practice confession, your emotional awareness of sin's seriousness will grow.

Also, ask God to give you a clearer vision of His holiness. When Isaiah saw God's holiness, his response was immediate: "Woe is me! For I am lost; for I am a man of unclean lips" (Isaiah 6:5). The more clearly we see God's perfect character, the more clearly we see our own sin by contrast.

Roadblock #2: "I've confessed this sin before, but I keep doing it."

Repeated confession of the same sin can feel futile or hypocritical. You think, "Why bother confessing again when I'll probably just repeat this sin next week?"

Solution: Remember that confession isn't just about getting forgiveness; it's about honesty in your relationship with God. Just as you wouldn't stop apologizing to your spouse for repeated offenses, don't stop confessing to God.

At the same time, repeated confession should be accompanied by concrete steps toward change. This might include:
- Identifying and avoiding triggers
- Establishing accountability
- Seeking professional help if needed
- Addressing root issues behind the behavior

Roadblock #3: "I'm afraid of what others will think if I confess."

The fear of others' judgment can be paralyzing, especially in church cultures that value having the appearance of spiritual success.

Solution: Start small with one trusted person rather than a large group. Choose someone who has demonstrated grace in their own life, someone who understands the gospel deeply enough to know that we're all dependent on mercy.

Also, remember that vulnerability usually breeds vulnerability. Your honest confession often gives others permission to be equally honest about their struggles. You might be the catalyst for creating a more authentic community.

Roadblock #4: "I can't forgive myself, even if God forgives me."

Sometimes we confess to God but continue to punish ourselves, unable to accept the forgiveness He offers.

Solution: Recognize that refusing to forgive yourself is, at its root, a form of pride. It's saying that your standards are higher than God's, that the blood of Jesus is sufficient for others but not for you.

Preach the gospel to yourself: If you've confessed your sin to God, it is forgiven. Period. Not because you deserve forgiveness, but because Jesus paid for it. Colossians 2:14 says He has "canceled the record of debt that stood against us... nailing it to the cross." Your job is not to forgive yourself but to accept the forgiveness already secured by Christ.

Roadblock #5: "God seems distant despite my confession."

Sometimes you confess sincerely but still feel disconnected from God. You wonder if your confession "worked."

Solution: Remember that feelings are not always reliable indicators of spiritual reality. God's forgiveness is a fact based on Christ's work, not a feeling based on your emotional state.

That said, if persistent sin has damaged your spiritual sensitivity, restoration takes time. Just as a broken bone doesn't heal instantly even after it's properly set, your spiritual and emotional connection to God may need time to recover even after genuine confession.

Keep showing up in prayer, Scripture reading, and worship, trusting that God is at work even when you can't feel it. As Psalm 51:10-12 models, ask God to "create in me a clean heart" and "restore to me the joy of your salvation."

Beyond Confession: The Full Picture

Confession is essential, but it's only part of the process of spiritual transformation. To fully experience the freedom and growth God intends, confession must be connected to these related practices:

Repentance

Confession acknowledges sin; repentance turns away from it. The Greek word for repentance, metanoia, literally means "to change your mind." It's a fundamental shift in thinking that leads to a change in behavior.

Jesus repeatedly called people to "repent and believe the gospel" (Mark 1:15). This isn't just feeling sorry for sin but actively moving in a different direction.

Practical repentance might look like:
- Deleting apps that lead to temptation
- Establishing boundaries in relationships that have become inappropriate
- Creating new habits to replace destructive ones
- Making restitution where possible (like Zacchaeus in Luke 19)

Receiving Forgiveness

It's one thing to confess; it's another to truly receive the forgiveness God offers. Many Christians live with a vague cloud of guilt hanging over them because they've never fully embraced the radical nature of God's grace.

Micah 7:19 says God will "cast all our sins into the depths of the sea." Psalm 103:12 says, "as far as the east is from the west, so far does he remove our transgressions from us." This isn't partial or probationary forgiveness; it's complete and irreversible.

Receiving this forgiveness means:
- Refusing to continue punishing yourself

- Believing that God's view of you is now based on Christ's righteousness, not your sin
- Living from acceptance rather than for acceptance

Walking in the Spirit

Long-term freedom from sin requires more than willpower; it requires the ongoing work of the Holy Spirit in your life. As Paul writes in Galatians 5:16, "Walk by the Spirit, and you will not gratify the desires of the flesh."

Walking in the Spirit includes:
- Daily surrender to God's control
- Regular time in Scripture and prayer
- Ongoing awareness of the Spirit's presence
- Dependence on His power rather than your own strength

Community Support

The Christian life was never meant to be lived alone. We need others to encourage us, hold us accountable, and remind us of the gospel.

Hebrews 3:13 instructs us to "exhort one another every day... that none of you may be hardened by the deceitfulness of sin." Sin is deceptive, and we need other perspectives to see clearly where we're being deceived.

This is why regular participation in a local church and smaller community groups is essential. It's not just about fellowship; it's about spiritual survival.

Confession and Mental Health

It's important to address how the practice of confession relates to mental health issues like clinical depression, anxiety disorders, or trauma.

If you struggle with excessive guilt, scrupulosity (religious OCD), or overwhelming shame that doesn't respond to normal spiritual practices, please consider seeking professional mental health support alongside your spiritual disciplines. Sometimes our brains get stuck in unhealthy patterns that need specialized care.

Confession should lead to freedom, not to an intensification of shame or despair. If your experience of confession consistently leads to the latter, that may indicate either a misunderstanding of the gospel or an underlying mental health concern that needs attention.

A good therapist, especially one who understands and respects your faith, can be an invaluable partner in your spiritual growth. Seeing a therapist doesn't mean your faith is weak or that spiritual disciplines have failed. It simply means you're using all the resources God has provided for your wellbeing.

The Transformative Power of Confession

When practiced consistently in the context of God's grace, confession becomes not a burden but a pathway to profound transformation. Here's what you can expect as this discipline takes root in your life:

Freedom from Shame

Shame thrives in secrecy. It whispers, "If people knew who you really are, they would reject you." Confession directly challenges this lie by bringing sin into the light and experiencing acceptance anyway.

As you practice confession and experience God's unwavering love despite your worst sins, shame begins to lose its power. You internalize the truth that your identity is not determined by your failures but by Christ's perfect righteousness credited to you.

Deeper Intimacy with God

Hidden sin creates distance in relationships, including your relationship with God. Not because God withdraws—He doesn't—but because hiding requires holding parts of yourself back.

Confession removes these barriers. It allows for unfiltered communication, honest prayer, and a sense of being fully known and fully loved. As Psalm 32:1-2 describes, there is a profound blessedness in being transparent before God.

More Authentic Relationships

The vulnerability of confession spills over into all your relationships. As you become more honest about your struggles and weaknesses, you create space for others to do the same.

This leads to friendships characterized by depth rather than performance, by mutual support rather than mutual impression. You'll find yourself drawn to people who value authenticity over appearance, substance over style.

Greater Compassion for Others

It's easy to judge others harshly for sins you've never struggled with. But when you regularly confront your own brokenness through confession, you develop greater empathy for others in their weakness.

This doesn't mean excusing sin, but it does mean approaching others with the same grace you've received. As Jesus said to the self-righteous religious leaders, "Let him who is without sin among you be the first to throw a stone" (John 8:7).

Accelerated Spiritual Growth

Confession speeds up your spiritual development by short-circuiting the cycles of denial, rationalization, and self-deception that keep you stuck. It creates a feedback loop: as you become more aware of specific sins through confession, you become more sensitive to the Holy Spirit's conviction, which leads to more specific confession, and so on.

Over time, this increased awareness and honesty allows for targeted growth in precisely the areas where you most need it.

A 30-Day Confession Challenge

If you're ready to experience the transformative power of this discipline, here's a 30-day plan to get you started:

Days 1-10: Daily Examination and Private Confession

Each evening, spend 10 minutes in quiet reflection. Ask the Holy Spirit to show you where you've sinned that day. Write down what comes to mind, being as specific as possible. Then confess these sins directly to God, thanking Him for His forgiveness through Christ.

Days 11-20: Scripture-Guided Confession

For these days, use Scripture to guide your confession. Read one of the following passages each day, letting it illuminate areas of sin in your life:
- Psalm 51
- Romans 12:9-21
- Galatians 5:19-26 (works of the flesh vs. fruit of the Spirit)
- Ephesians 4:25-32
- Philippians 2:1-11
- Colossians 3:5-17
- James 3:1-12 (on taming the tongue)
- James 4:1-10
- 1 Peter 2:1-3
- 1 John 2:15-17

After reading, confess the specific ways you've fallen short in these areas.

Days 21-30: Communal Confession

Identify a trusted Christian friend and ask if they'd be willing to be a confession partner for this period. Arrange to meet (in person or virtually) three times over these ten days.

Before each meeting, prayerfully identify one area of ongoing struggle that you'll share with them. During the meeting:
- Share honestly about your struggle
- Ask them to pray with you
- Receive their reminder of God's grace
- Discuss practical steps toward change

This graduated approach eases you into the discipline of confession, starting with the more comfortable practice of private confession before moving to the more vulnerable practice of communal confession.

The Kick in the Pants: Stop Hiding, Start Healing

Let me be blunt: You can't be healed from what you won't admit you have.

You wouldn't go to a doctor, list half your symptoms, lie about your lifestyle, and expect an accurate diagnosis and effective treatment. So why do you think your spiritual life will improve if you're not honest about what's really going on?

Your carefully constructed Christian persona isn't fooling God. He sees past the spiritual hashtags, the Bible verse phone backgrounds, and the worship songs on your playlist. He knows what websites you visit at 2 AM. He hears what you say about others when they're not around. He witnesses your thought life in full HD.

And here's the miracle that should blow your mind daily: He loves you anyway. Not the sanitized version of you that you present at church. The real you. The messy you. The struggling you.

When Christ died on the cross, He didn't die for theoretical sins. He died for your actual sins—the embarrassing ones, the repetitive ones, the ones you hope no one ever discovers. He already paid for them in full.

So what exactly are you hiding? And why?

Your sin does not surprise God. It doesn't disqualify you from His love. The only thing that's accomplished by your hiding is the delay of your own healing and the limitation of your own freedom.

Jesus said, "You will know the truth, and the truth will set you free" (John 8:32). That starts with being truthful about who you really are—both the good and the bad. It starts with dragging your sin out of the shadows where it grows like a fungus and into the light where it can be properly dealt with.

No, confession isn't comfortable. Neither is chemotherapy. But both can save your life.

So here's your challenge: Stop managing your image and start tending to your soul. Stop worrying about what others think and start caring about what's true. Stop pretending to be whole and admit where you're broken.

Because God's grace is big enough for your mess—but you've got to admit it's yours.

Freedom starts where denial ends. And a lifetime of spiritual growth is waiting for you on the other side of those three difficult words:

"I have sinned."

Not "I made a mistake." Not "Mistakes were made." Not "I'm only human." But the clear, unequivocal admission: "I have sinned."

Say it to God. Say it to yourself. And when necessary, say it to others.

Then watch as the God who loves honesty begins to transform you from the inside out—not into a better-behaved version of your false self, but into your true self, the person He created you to be all along.

This is the paradox at the heart of the gospel: only by admitting that you're broken can you begin to become whole. Only by confessing your darkness can you fully experience the light. Only by acknowledging your sin can you fully embrace your identity as God's beloved child.

So what are you waiting for? Your confession journey starts now. Not tomorrow when you feel more spiritual. Not next week when your life settles down. Now.

Because now is when you need God's grace. Now is when you need freedom. Now is when healing can begin.

Stop hiding. Start healing.

Your Father is waiting.

Chapter 3:

Celebration – Finding Joy in the Mundane

Let's be honest right out of the gate: your life is probably pretty boring most of the time.

I don't mean that as an insult. My life is boring too. Most people's lives are. We wake up, brush our teeth with the same toothbrush, drive the same route to work, see the same faces, eat the same lunch, answer the same emails, scroll through the same social media apps, watch the same shows, and then do it all again tomorrow.

Even if you have kids (which, let's face it, can be both incredibly meaningful and mind-numbingly tedious), you're still wiping the same butts, making the same mac and cheese, and reading the same bedtime story for the 437th time.

This is normal human existence. Not the highlight reel we see on Instagram, but the actual day-to-day grind where most of us spend 99% of our lives.

And here's the problem: most of us have bought into the idea that joy is what happens when something "celebration-worthy" occurs—a promotion, a graduation, a wedding, a vacation. We treat joy like it's the rare dessert after a long stretch of eating boring vegetables. It's the thing we get to have only after we've endured enough mundane moments.

We're waiting for our next dopamine hit, our next Instagram-worthy experience, our next reason to feel alive.

But what if I told you this approach is completely backward? What if celebration isn't just the response to special occasions but a discipline that shapes how you experience every day? What if learning to celebrate—intentionally, regularly, even in ordinary circumstances—is actually essential to your spiritual health?

In Philippians 4:4, Paul writes, "Rejoice in the Lord always; again I will say, rejoice." Always. Not just when you feel like it. Not just when circumstances are awesome. Always.

And in case you missed it, he repeats himself. "Again I will say, rejoice." It's like he knows we're going to think, "Surely he doesn't mean ALWAYS always," so he doubles down. Yes, always.

But here's the thing: Paul wasn't writing this from a beach vacation or after some major ministry success. He was in prison. Literally chained to a wall. Facing possible execution. And he's telling people to rejoice always.

Was Paul delusional? Engaging in toxic positivity? Spiritually bypassing the reality of his situation?

Not at all. He understood something most of us miss: celebration isn't primarily a response to circumstances; it's a discipline that shapes our perspective regardless of circumstances. It's not about denying reality but about seeing a bigger reality—one that includes God's presence, promises, and purposes even in the most ordinary or difficult moments.

This is what we're going to explore in this chapter: celebration as a spiritual discipline—a practice we choose rather than a feeling we chase. We'll look at why it matters, what makes it so hard, and how to get better at it (without becoming one of those creepy Christians with the permanent fake smile).

Why Celebration Matters

Before we dive into the how-to, let's talk about why celebration matters in the first place. Because if you're anything like me, you might be thinking, "With everything wrong in the world, shouldn't we be more focused on serious things like justice or evangelism or not being a jerk to people?"

Those things definitely matter. But here's why celebration deserves a spot on your spiritual disciplines list:

1. Celebration is an act of spiritual warfare

You read that right. In a world bent toward despair, choosing joy is an act of rebellion. Celebration declares that despite evidence to the contrary, God is still on the throne, still good, and still working things toward redemption.

The enemies of your soul want you discouraged, cynical, and defeated. When you choose celebration—not as denial but as defiant hope—you're essentially giving the middle finger to darkness. You're saying, "You don't get the final word here."

Nehemiah understood this when he told the Israelites, "Do not be grieved, for the joy of the Lord is your strength" (Nehemiah 8:10). Joy isn't just a nice feeling; it's spiritual strength. It's the fuel that sustains you through difficulty. It's what keeps you in the fight when everything in you wants to quit.

2. Celebration trains your attention

Your brain has a negativity bias. It's wired to notice threats, problems, and what's wrong more readily than what's right. This made sense for our ancestors (the ones who noticed the lion hiding in the grass survived to reproduce), but it creates a distorted view of reality.

Deliberate celebration is like training your brain's attention muscles to notice what's good, what's working, and where God is active. It's not pretending problems don't exist; it's refusing to let problems monopolize your awareness.

Over time, this changes your default perception. You start naturally noticing God's fingerprints in ordinary moments rather than just dwelling on what's broken. As Paul instructs in Philippians 4:8, "Whatever is true, whatever is honorable, whatever is just, whatever is pure, whatever is lovely, whatever is commendable, if there is any excellence, if there is anything worthy of praise, think about these things."

3. Celebration honors God

When you celebrate, you're essentially saying, "God, I notice and value what you're doing." It's acknowledging that every good gift comes from Him

(James 1:17) and that He's worthy of recognition even in small blessings.

Think about it: If you spent hours preparing a meal for someone you love, and they wolfed it down without comment while scrolling on their phone, you'd feel unappreciated. But if they savored each bite, commented on the flavors, and thanked you specifically for your effort, you'd feel seen and valued.

God doesn't need our validation, but celebration is still a form of worship that honors Him. It says, "I see what you're doing, and I'm grateful."

4. Celebration sustains community

Have you noticed how shared celebration bonds people together? Whether it's a sports victory, a wedding, or just a good meal, celebrating together creates connection that helps sustain relationships through harder times.

The early church understood this. In Acts 2:46-47, we read that they "broke bread in their homes and ate together with glad and sincere hearts, praising God and enjoying the favor of all the people." Their regular celebration was part of what made their community attractive to others.

In contrast, communities without celebration become dry, functional, and eventually burn out. The same is true for individuals. We need the rhythm of celebration to sustain us for the long haul.

5. Celebration reminds us of our future

Christians are people who believe in a future where everything sad comes untrue, where death is defeated, tears are wiped away, and celebration becomes the permanent state of reality. When we celebrate now, we're practicing for eternity. We're giving the world a taste of what's coming.

This is why Revelation describes heaven with imagery of a feast, a wedding, music, and celebration. It's why Jesus' first miracle was turning water into wine at a wedding celebration. God is not anti-fun or anti-pleasure. He invented celebration. And our small celebrations now are appetizers for the eternal feast to come.

Why Celebration Is So Damn Hard

If celebration is so important, why do most of us suck at it? Why does joy often feel like a distant acquaintance rather than a constant companion? Here are some real obstacles we face:

1. We're chronically exhausted

Let's be real: it's hard to celebrate when you can barely keep your eyes open. Between work demands, family responsibilities, financial pressure, and the constant noise of technology, many of us are running on fumes. Celebration takes energy we often don't feel like we have.

This is why disciplines like rest and Sabbath are so interconnected with celebration. You can't consistently experience joy when you're burned out. Sometimes the most spiritual thing you can do is take a nap.

2. We're distracted by comparison

Nothing kills joy faster than comparing your ordinary life to someone else's highlight reel. And in the age of social media, we're doing this constantly, often without realizing it.

While you're washing dishes, you're scrolling through photos of your friend's European vacation. While you're sitting in traffic, you're reading about someone else's book deal. While you're dealing with your teenager's attitude, you're seeing perfectly coordinated family photos with everyone smiling.

Comparison is the thief of joy, and our phones have made comparison easier than ever.

3. We're addicted to outrage

Let's face it—being angry is oddly satisfying. It gives us a sense of moral clarity and righteousness. It provides an adrenaline hit. It bonds us with others who share our outrage. And in a world with legitimate injustices, anger can seem like the only appropriate response.

The problem is, outrage is addictive. Our brains get rewired to look for things to be mad about. And the algorithms that govern our media consumption are more than happy to feed this addiction, serving us an endless stream of content designed to keep us angry and engaged.

This makes celebration feel trivial or even inappropriate. "How can I celebrate when [insert latest outrage] is happening?" becomes our default response.

4. We're waiting for permission

Many of us subconsciously believe we need to earn the right to celebrate—by achieving enough, working hard enough, or suffering enough. We treat joy like it's a limited resource that must be rationed carefully rather than an abundant gift to be embraced regularly.

This mindset is often reinforced by religious messaging that emphasizes sacrifice and service to the exclusion of celebration. We develop a vague sense that serious Christians should be, well, serious—focused on weighty spiritual matters rather than experiencing delight.

5. We misunderstand what celebration is

Perhaps the biggest obstacle is that we've reduced celebration to parties, achievements, and special occasions. We think it requires elaborate preparation, perfect circumstances, or significant milestones.

But biblical celebration is much broader and more accessible. It can be as simple as pausing to notice a beautiful sunset, savoring a good cup of coffee, or expressing gratitude for a small kindness. It's less about the scale of the event and more about the attitude of the heart.

Celebration as a Discipline (Not Just a Feeling)

So how do we overcome these obstacles? By recognizing that celebration isn't primarily about feeling happy—it's about choosing to notice and honor what's good even when we don't feel like it.

In Psalm 118:24, the psalmist writes, "This is the day that the LORD has made; let us rejoice and be glad in it." Note that this is a decision, not just an emotional response. "Let us rejoice" is an invitation to action regardless of how we feel.

The discipline part comes in making this choice consistently, especially when it doesn't come naturally. It's like going to the gym—you don't do it because you already feel strong; you do it to become strong. Similarly, you don't practice celebration because you already feel joyful; you practice it to cultivate joy.

This isn't fake it till you make it. It's not about plastering on a smile while dying inside. It's about training your attention to notice God's presence and gifts in all circumstances, and choosing to honor those gifts through deliberate acts of celebration.

Over time, this discipline reshapes your default perception. You become more attuned to goodness, more resistant to cynicism, and more capable of experiencing joy even amid difficulties.

Practical Ways to Celebrate the Ordinary

Alright, enough theory. Let's get practical. Here are specific ways to practice celebration as a discipline, especially in the mundane moments of everyday life:

1. The Daily Joy List

At the end of each day, write down three specific things that brought you joy, delight, or satisfaction. Not just generic blessings like "family" or "health," but particular moments: the way the light hit the trees during your morning commute, the satisfying click of finishing a difficult task, the taste of a perfectly ripe peach.

The key is to be specific and to look for small, ordinary pleasures rather than just big events. This trains your brain to notice these moments throughout the day, knowing you'll be recording them later.

For extra impact, review your list periodically. Over time, you'll build an impressive record of God's goodness in everyday moments that can sustain you through darker seasons.

2. Sacred Interruptions

Schedule regular "celebration interruptions" throughout your day. Set an alarm on your phone for random times, and when it goes off, pause whatever you're doing to notice and celebrate something good in that exact moment.

Maybe it's the comfort of your chair, the fact that your lungs are working, or the privilege of having meaningful work. Maybe it's simply that God is present, even if you can't feel Him.

This practice breaks the spell of autopilot living and creates small islands of awareness and gratitude in your day.

3. Meal as Celebration

For most of us, meals have become utilitarian—something to rush through while watching TV or scrolling on our phones. But eating can be one of the most accessible forms of daily celebration.

Try this: For one meal each day, put away all devices. Set the table, even if you're eating alone. Light a candle. Say a prayer of thanks that specifically mentions the food in front of you. Then eat slowly, actually tasting each bite.

This isn't about fancy food (though that's nice sometimes). It's about receiving ordinary food as a gift and treating it with appropriate honor.

Jesus spent so much time eating with people that his critics called him a glutton (Luke 7:34). He understood that sharing food is a profound act of celebration and communion. The Last Supper wasn't a coincidence; it was consistent with how Jesus lived.

4. Sabbath Celebration

Sabbath isn't just about rest; it's about celebration. It's setting aside time to delight in God, creation, and the simple gift of being alive.

Try setting aside one 24-hour period each week as a "delight day." This isn't about religious rules but about protecting space for joy. During this time:

- Disconnect from productivity (no work emails, house projects, or task lists)
- Engage in activities that bring genuine pleasure (not just numbing entertainment)
- Connect with people you enjoy
- Spend time noticing and appreciating God's creation

- Express gratitude through prayer, journaling, or conversation

As Isaiah 58:13-14 describes, there's blessing in calling the Sabbath a delight rather than a burden. It's a day to celebrate God's sufficiency and our limits, to remember that the world continues to turn even when we step off the productivity treadmill.

5. Celebration Triggers

Identify everyday actions that can serve as triggers for mini-celebrations. For example:

- Every time you stop at a red light, take a deep breath and notice something beautiful around you
- Whenever you wash your hands, say a quick thank you for running water
- Each time you get a notification on your phone, pause to name one thing you're grateful for before checking it
- When you walk through a doorway, remember that God is with you in the next space

These triggers help embed celebration into your existing routines rather than adding one more thing to your to-do list.

6. The Celebration Circle

Find a small group of friends (2-4 is ideal) who will commit to being your "celebration circle." Meet regularly (in person or virtually) with the explicit purpose of sharing what you're celebrating in your lives.

Set ground rules:
- No venting or problem-solving during this time
- Each person shares 2-3 specific things they're celebrating since you last met
- Others respond with genuine delight rather than comparison or one-upmanship
- End by praying thanks together

This social reinforcement helps sustain celebration when individual motivation wanes. Plus, hearing others' celebrations often helps you notice similar gifts in your own life.

7. Declaring Good News

Make it a daily practice to share good news with at least one person. This could be a small personal win, something you're grateful for, or a broader piece of positive news from the world (yes, good things still happen!).

This isn't about toxic positivity or denying problems. It's about correcting the imbalance created by our negativity-focused information ecosystem. Most of us consume and share far more bad news than good news, creating a distorted view of reality.

By intentionally spreading good news, you're not just practicing celebration yourself; you're creating ripples that help others do the same.

8. Celebration Through Creativity

Creative expression is a powerful form of celebration. It honors God as Creator by reflecting His creative nature in us. You don't have to be "talented" to do this—the joy is in the process, not the product.

Try setting aside 15-30 minutes each week for creative celebration:
- Draw or paint something beautiful you observed
- Write a haiku about an ordinary blessing
- Take photos that capture everyday grace
- Make music, even if it's just drumming on the dashboard
- Dance in your kitchen to a song that lifts your spirit
- Cook a meal with full presence and creativity

These activities engage your senses and help you participate in beauty rather than just observing it.

9. Celebration Memorials

The Israelites often built physical memorials to remember God's faithfulness. You can create your own modern versions:

- Keep a jar where you drop notes about moments worth celebrating
- Create a digital photo album specifically for "ordinary beautiful moments"
- Make a playlist of songs that help you celebrate God's goodness
- Set up a physical space in your home dedicated to reminders of things worth celebrating

These tangible reminders become especially valuable during difficult seasons when celebration doesn't come naturally.

10. Celebrating Through Others

Sometimes it's easier to celebrate with and for others than for ourselves. When you're struggling to find joy, try these approaches:

- Send a text celebrating something specific you appreciate about a friend
- Write a positive online review for a local business you value

- Congratulate someone on a recent achievement, no matter how small
- Participate enthusiastically in others' celebrations, even when you don't feel celebratory

This outward focus often rekindles your own capacity for joy while blessing others in the process.

Celebrating in Hard Seasons

Let's address the elephant in the room: What about when life genuinely sucks? What about when you're dealing with chronic illness, grief, financial stress, or relationship breakdown? Is celebration still possible—or even appropriate—then?

The biblical answer is yes, but with important qualifications.

Ecclesiastes 3:4 acknowledges that there is "a time to weep, and a time to laugh; a time to mourn, and a time to dance." Forced celebration that denies genuine pain is not spiritual maturity—it's emotional dishonesty.

Jesus himself wept (John 11:35). Paul speaks of being "sorrowful, yet always rejoicing" (2 Corinthians 6:10), suggesting that sorrow and joy can coexist rather than one replacing the other.

So how do we practice celebration authentically during genuinely difficult seasons?

1. Celebrate smaller

In hard times, scale back your expectations for celebration. Look for tiny moments of grace: a pain-free hour, a friend's text, a warm cup of tea, a moment of clarity. These small celebrations don't negate your suffering; they provide pinpricks of light in the darkness.

2. Celebrate honestly

Include lament as part of your practice. Many of the Psalms begin with raw expressions of pain before moving toward praise. This isn't failure; it's biblical integrity. Start where you are, not where you think you should be.

A prayer like, "God, today was awful, but I thank you that you were present even when I couldn't feel you" can be a profound act of faithful celebration.

3. Celebrate in community

When you can't find the strength to celebrate, let others hold hope for you. This is why church communities gathering weekly for worship matters—sometimes you go not because you feel like celebrating but because you need to borrow faith from those who do.

4. Celebrate the unseen

In the hardest seasons, celebration often focuses not on present circumstances but on unseen realities: God's unchanging character, His promises for the future, the internal work He's doing even when external circumstances are painful.

As Paul writes in 2 Corinthians 4:16-18, "So we do not lose heart. Though our outer self is wasting away, our inner self is being renewed day by day. For this light momentary affliction is preparing for us an eternal weight of glory beyond all comparison, as we look not to the things that are seen but to the things that are unseen."

5. Celebrate past faithfulness

When you can't see God working now, recall how He's worked before. The Israelites repeatedly recounted the exodus story when facing new challenges. This isn't just nostalgia; it's reminding yourself of God's proven character as fuel for present hope.

The Celebration Challenge

Ready to get serious about celebration as a spiritual discipline? Try this 30-day challenge to jumpstart your practice:

Week 1: Notice

For the first week, focus on simply noticing what's already worth celebrating in your daily life:
- Day 1: Physical pleasures (tastes, textures, sensations)
- Day 2: Beauty in your environment
- Day 3: Relationships and connections
- Day 4: Your own abilities and strengths
- Day 5: Evidence of God's provision
- Day 6: Small wins and progress
- Day 7: Moments of meaning or purpose

Each day, write down at least three specific observations.

Week 2: Express

During the second week, add expression to your noticing:
- Day 8: Tell someone what you appreciate about them
- Day 9: Share something you're celebrating on social media (as an alternative to the usual complaints)
- Day 10: Write a thank-you note for an ordinary service (to your mail carrier, barista, etc.)
- Day 11: Make or share a meal with intentional gratitude
- Day 12: Create something (art, music, food, etc.) as a response to something good
- Day 13: Physically move your body in celebration (dance, raise your hands, take a gratitude walk)
- Day 14: Pray specifically about what you're celebrating, not just what you need

Week 3: Disrupt

For week three, intentionally disrupt your normal patterns to create space for celebration:
- Day 15: Take a different route to work and notice new beauty
- Day 16: Eat a meal without technology, focusing fully on the experience
- Day 17: Spend 30 minutes in nature without your phone
- Day 18: Listen to music without doing anything else

- Day 19: Reach out to someone you haven't connected with in a while to share appreciation
- Day 20: Try a new food or experience with full presence
- Day 21: Take a full Sabbath day for rest and delight

Week 4: Deepen

In the final week, focus on deeper forms of celebration:
- Day 22: Celebrate something difficult in your life and what it's teaching you
- Day 23: Celebrate someone you find challenging by identifying their strengths
- Day 24: Practice celebration first thing in the morning, before checking your phone
- Day 25: Celebrate something about yourself that you normally criticize
- Day 26: Find something to celebrate in a current global or cultural challenge
- Day 27: Celebrate God's character through focused worship
- Day 28: Identify one celebration practice to continue beyond this challenge
- Days 29-30: Reflect on what's changed in your perspective and create a sustainable celebration rhythm going forward

Overcoming Celebration Blockers

Even with the best intentions, certain mindsets can consistently block our ability to celebrate. Here are some common celebration blockers and how to address them:

The Perfectionist

If you're waiting for the perfect circumstances to celebrate, you'll be waiting forever. Perfectionism kills celebration by constantly moving the goalposts. "I'll be happy when..." becomes a perpetual future state that never arrives.

Antidote: Practice "good enough" celebrations. Set a timer for 5 minutes and celebrate something within those constraints. No elaborate preparations, no perfect execution—just simple, imperfect acknowledgment of what's good.

The Productivity Addict

If you measure your worth by what you accomplish, celebration feels like wasted time. You might rush through or entirely skip moments of joy because they don't contribute to your to-do list.

Antidote: Reframe celebration as productive—because it is. It builds resilience, strengthens relationships, and sustains energy for the long haul. Schedule it as you would any other important task, and notice how it actually enhances your effectiveness over time.

The Expected Celebrator

Sometimes our celebration muscles atrophy because we only use them for culturally prescribed occasions—birthdays, major holidays, graduations. We forget how to notice and honor the extraordinary in ordinary days.

Antidote: Create personal celebrations for non-traditional milestones. Did you finally finish that book that's been on your nightstand for months? Make a small ceremony of it. Did you navigate a difficult conversation with grace? Light a candle to mark the moment.

The Anxious Anticipator

If you're constantly bracing for the next problem, celebration feels naïve or even dangerous, as if enjoying the present might somehow jinx the future.

Antidote: Practice containment—mentally placing your worries in a container for a defined period so you can fully experience the present good. Tell yourself, "I'll return to that concern at 4pm, but for these 15 minutes, I'm going to fully engage with what's good right now."

The Cynical Observer

If you pride yourself on seeing through positive spin or identifying what's wrong with everything, celebration can feel intellectually dishonest. You might even see joy as something for less perceptive, less sophisticated people.

Antidote: Challenge yourself to apply the same analytical skills to identifying what's genuinely good. Make it an intellectual exercise if necessary: "What's one truly positive thing about this situation that even my critical mind can't dispute?"

Signs You're Growing in Celebration

How do you know if you're making progress in this discipline? Here are some indicators that celebration is becoming more integrated into your spiritual life:

1. You notice good things without trying. Your default attention is shifting toward grace rather than having to force yourself to look for it.

2. Your prayer life includes more thanksgiving, not just requests. You naturally talk to God about what you're celebrating, not just what you need.

3. You bounce back faster from disappointments. While you still feel appropriate negative emotions, they don't define or derail you as much as before.

4. You're less prone to envy when scrolling social media. You can genuinely celebrate others' good news without immediately comparing it to your own situation.

5. Your physical body shows signs of reduced stress. Celebration literally changes your physiological state, potentially improving sleep, digestion, and immune function.

6. Others comment on changes they notice in your outlook or presence. You may become known as someone who brings perspective and joy rather than criticism or complaint.

7. You find yourself spontaneously sharing good news with others rather than primarily venting or problem-solving.

8. You experience more frequent moments of genuine delight—not forced positivity, but authentic appreciation for what's in front of you.

The Relationship Between Celebration and Other Disciplines

Celebration doesn't exist in isolation from other spiritual practices. In fact, it's deeply interconnected with many of the disciplines we'll explore throughout this book:

- **Gratitude** provides the foundation for celebration. It's hard to celebrate what you haven't first noticed and appreciated.

- **Sabbath** creates space for celebration to flourish. When you step off the productivity treadmill, you have room to delight in what already is rather than striving for what isn't yet.

- **Community** amplifies celebration. Joy shared is joy multiplied.

- **Simplicity** removes distractions that often prevent us from noticing what's worth celebrating.

- **Presence** (mindfulness) enables celebration by bringing us fully into the moment rather than being lost in regrets about the past or worries about the future.

As you develop these related disciplines, you'll find that celebration becomes more natural and accessible.

The Kick in the Pants: Stop Waiting for the Big Stuff

Let me be blunt: If you're waiting for life to get amazing before you start celebrating, you're going to waste most of your existence.

The highlight reel moments—the promotions, the weddings, the vacations, the achievements—are rare. They're the peaks that rise up occasionally from the vast plains of ordinary days. If you reserve joy only for those peaks, you'll spend most of your life joyless.

What a waste. What a tragic misreading of what God intends for you.

Scripture doesn't say "Rejoice when circumstances are Instagram-worthy." It says "Rejoice in the Lord always." The Lord is always present. Always working. Always worthy of celebration, even in—especially in—the mundane Tuesday afternoons of your life.

Your problem isn't that your life lacks celebration-worthy moments. Your problem is that you've been trained to miss them, to discount them, to scroll past them while waiting for something bigger and better.

Stop it. Stop postponing joy. Stop treating celebration like it's a rare luxury rather than daily bread.

Joy isn't what you feel when life finally gets better; it's what you choose so you can survive life as it actually is. It's not the dessert you earn after eating your vegetables; it's the vitamin that keeps you healthy enough to keep going.

The ability to find and create celebration in ordinary moments isn't just nice; it's necessary. It's how you refuel for the work God has given you. It's how you maintain perspective when problems loom large. It's how you resist the cultural current of cynicism and despair.

As C.S. Lewis observed, "Joy is the serious business of heaven." When you practice celebration—even in small ways, even when you don't feel like it, even when the world seems to be falling apart—you're participating in that serious business. You're declaring that darkness doesn't get the final word. You're aligning yourself with the ultimate reality of God's kingdom, where celebration isn't just an occasional event but the permanent state of affairs.

So tomorrow morning, when you wake up to the same alarm, in the same bed, facing the same commute and the same job and the same challenges—make a different choice. Choose to notice what's good. Choose to honor what's beautiful. Choose to celebrate what's working.

Not because everything is perfect, but because the God who loves you is at work even in imperfection. Not because problems don't exist, but because they don't deserve to monopolize your attention. Not because celebration comes naturally, but because the discipline of joy is worth the effort it requires.

The world doesn't need more cynics who pride themselves on seeing what's wrong with everything. It needs more celebrators who've trained themselves to detect grace in unexpected places.

Which will you be?

Life is happening right now, in all its ordinary glory. Celebration is available right now, if you'll only reach for it.

So what are you waiting for?

Chapter 4:

Submission – Letting Go of Control

Let's be honest right out of the gate: the word "submission" probably makes you cringe.

I get it. In our culture, submission sounds like weakness. It sounds like being a doormat. It sounds like giving up your voice, your power, your autonomy. Nobody puts "excellent at submitting" on their resume or dating profile.

And if we're really being honest, the church hasn't always helped. Some toxic versions of "Christian submission" have been used to keep people (especially women) in harmful situations, to silence questions, and to maintain unhealthy power dynamics.

So if you're approaching this chapter with some hesitation, I don't blame you. But here's what I want you to know: true biblical submission isn't what you think it is. It's not about being weak—it's about recognizing where true strength comes from. It's not about being passive—it's about actively placing your trust in the right place.

Think of it this way: submission isn't surrendering to defeat; it's surrendering to a greater victory than the one you could win on your own.

Here's the blunt truth most of us don't want to admit: we are control freaks. We white-knuckle our way through life, desperately trying to manage outcomes, people, circumstances, and even God Himself. We think if we just work hard enough, plan well enough, or worry thoroughly enough, we can guarantee the results we want.

How's that working out for you?

If you're like most humans I know (myself included), all that controlling behavior isn't bringing you peace. It's bringing you anxiety, exhaustion, and strained relationships. Because the dirty little secret of control is that it's mostly an illusion anyway. The more desperately you try to grasp it, the more it slips through your fingers.

That's why submission is such a vital spiritual discipline. Not because God has some weird power trip where He needs you to grovel, but because letting go of your death grip on control is the only way to actually live with freedom and peace.

As Jesus said in Matthew 16:25, "For whoever would save his life will lose it, but whoever loses his life for my sake will find it." There's a paradox here that most of us spend our whole lives trying to avoid: the way to truly gain your life is to stop clutching it so tightly.

So in this chapter, we're going to explore what real submission looks like (and what it doesn't), why it matters, and how to practice it without becoming a religious weirdo or losing your authentic self in the process. Because the truth is, you were never meant to carry the burden of being in control of everything—and letting go might be the most freeing thing you ever do.

What Submission Actually Is (And Isn't)

Before we go any further, let's clear up some misconceptions. Because if we're working with a warped definition of submission, we'll end up with a warped practice of it.

What Submission IS NOT:

1. **Submission is not blind obedience.** God never asks you to turn off your brain. Jesus himself engaged with Scripture thoughtfully and asked questions.

Blind following is a characteristic of cults, not Christianity.

2. **Submission is not staying in abusive situations.** Nothing in Scripture indicates that God wants people to endure ongoing abuse in the name of submission. In fact, the Bible repeatedly shows God delivering people from oppression, not calling them to remain in it.

3. **Submission is not a personality type.** You don't have to be naturally passive, quiet, or compliant to practice this discipline well. Some of the Bible's greatest examples of submission were strong-willed individuals with fierce personalities.

4. **Submission is not the absence of boundaries.** Healthy submission to God often requires setting clear boundaries with people. Jesus himself regularly set boundaries around his time, energy, and purpose.

5. **Submission is not approval-seeking.** The goal isn't to make yourself small so others will like you or to perform spiritual gymnastics to impress God. It's about trusting God's goodness and wisdom above your own.

What Submission IS:

1. **Submission is recognizing reality.** It's acknowledging that you are not God, not all-knowing, not all-powerful—and that's actually a good thing. It's admitting that your perspective is limited and your control is partial at best.

2. **Submission is trust in action.** As Proverbs 3:5-6 puts it, "Trust in the LORD with all your heart, and do not lean on your own understanding. In all your ways acknowledge him, and he will make straight your paths." Submission is what happens when your trust in God becomes more than just a nice idea—it changes how you actually live.

3. **Submission is strength under authority.** It's not weakness; it's placing your strength under the direction of someone stronger and wiser. Think of a powerful horse that allows itself to be directed by its rider—the horse doesn't become less powerful by submitting; it becomes more purposeful.

4. **Submission is freedom from ultimate responsibility.** When you stop trying to be the god of your own life, you're freed from the crushing weight of having to figure everything out, control every outcome, and fix every problem.

5. **Submission is aligning with reality instead of fighting it.** Much of our stress comes from refusing to accept things as they actually are. Submission

allows us to stop wasting energy fighting reality and start working with God in the midst of it.

Now that we have a clearer picture of what we're talking about, let's look at why this matters so much.

The Control Addiction

If you're a human being in the 21st century, chances are you have a control problem. Our entire culture is built around the myth that with enough effort, technology, and determination, we can control just about everything.

We try to control our image through carefully curated social media. We try to control our bodies through fitness trackers and diet apps. We try to control our future through retirement accounts and five-year plans. We try to control other people through manipulation, guilt, or force of personality.

Even our approach to spirituality can become just another control mechanism. We follow certain formulas or say certain prayers thinking we can control God's response. "If I just have enough faith, if I just use the right words, if I just avoid these sins, then God will have to give me what I want."

This addiction to control manifests in various ways:

The Overthinking Trap

You know this one—you replay conversations in your head, analyze decisions to death, and create elaborate mental simulations of future scenarios. You think if you just think enough about something, you can somehow guarantee it will go well.

But Ecclesiastes 11:4 reminds us, "He who observes the wind will not sow, and he who regards the clouds will not reap." Sometimes all that overthinking just prevents you from taking action at all.

The Worry Cycle

You may have convinced yourself that worrying is productive—like it's a form of problem-solving or preparation. If you worry thoroughly enough about something bad happening, maybe you can prevent it.

Jesus directly challenged this control mechanism in Matthew 6:27: "And which of you by being anxious can add a single hour to his span of life?" Worry creates the illusion of control while actually draining you of the energy you need to deal with real problems.

The Perfectionism Pattern

This is control disguised as excellence. If you can just do everything perfectly—be the perfect parent, the perfect employee, the perfect Christian—then maybe you can guarantee the outcomes you want and the approval you crave.

But perfectionism is exhausting and ultimately impossible. As James 3:2 plainly states, "We all stumble in many ways." The pursuit of perfect control leads to constant disappointment.

The Manipulation Game

This is when you try to control others through subtle (or not-so-subtle) tactics: guilt trips, passive-aggressive comments, conditional love, or even spiritual language. "God told me that you should..."

This approach damages relationships and violates the dignity of others. It's the opposite of 1 Peter 5:3's instruction to lead "not domineering over those in your charge, but being examples to the flock."

The Planning Obsession

While planning itself is wise, planning obsession happens when you think having enough backup plans will guarantee you never face uncertainty. Your Google Calendar is a color-coded masterpiece, and any deviation sends you into a tailspin.

Proverbs 16:9 offers a reality check: "The heart of man plans his way, but the LORD establishes his steps." Planning is good; thinking your plans are bulletproof is delusional.

Sound familiar? These control mechanisms aren't just annoying habits—they're symptoms of a deeper spiritual issue. At their core, they reveal a fundamental mistrust in God's goodness, wisdom, and power. Each one says, "I don't really believe God has this under control, so I'd better handle it myself."

And that, my friends, is the opposite of submission.

The Biblical Case for Submission

You might be thinking, "Okay, control issues are bad, but why is submission the answer? Why can't I just work on being less anxious while still maintaining my independence?"

Because submission isn't just a helpful self-help technique—it's at the very heart of what it means to follow Jesus. Consider these biblical foundations:

Jesus Modeled Submission

If anyone had the right to assert control, it was Jesus. Yet his entire life was characterized by submission to the Father's will.

In John 5:19, Jesus explained, "The Son can do nothing of his own accord, but only what he sees the Father doing." He didn't come up with his own agenda or execute his own plan. He consistently aligned himself with the Father's purposes.

Most powerfully, in the garden of Gethsemane, facing torture and death, Jesus prayed, "Not my will, but yours, be done" (Luke 22:42). This wasn't passive resignation; it was active trust and alignment with God's redemptive plan, even when that plan included profound suffering.

If Jesus—who, unlike us, actually had the wisdom and power to control things effectively—chose submission, who are we to insist on maintaining control?

Submission Shows Up Throughout Scripture

From Genesis to Revelation, the Bible continually calls God's people to trust and submit rather than grasp for control:

- Abraham left his homeland without knowing the destination, submitting to God's direction (Genesis 12).
- Joseph interpreted his years of suffering as part of God's larger plan, not a situation he needed to control (Genesis 50:20).
- Moses had to learn submission through 40 years in the wilderness before he was ready to lead.
- David refused to take matters into his own hands by killing Saul, choosing instead to wait for God's timing (1 Samuel 24).
- The prophets called Israel to stop trusting in military alliances and political maneuvering and return to trusting God.
- Paul, formerly self-sufficient and controlling, came to see his weakness as the venue for God's strength (2 Corinthians 12:9-10).

Creation Itself Reflects This Design

The universe functions through a kind of built-in submission. Plants submit to the seasons. Animals submit to their instincts. The planets submit to the laws of physics. Everything in creation has its proper place and function.

Humans are the only creatures who consistently rebel against this design, insisting on our autonomy and control even when it damages us and others. We're like fish who think we can decide for ourselves whether to breathe water or air—and then wonder why we're gasping and dying on the shore.

As Psalm 19:1-4 observes, "The heavens declare the glory of God, and the sky above proclaims his handiwork... There is no speech, nor are there words, whose voice is not heard." Creation silently models submission to its Creator, while we humans rage against our proper place.

The Alternative Is Pride—And It Doesn't End Well

The Bible consistently identifies pride—the refusal to submit—as the root of sin and the path to destruction.

Proverbs 16:18 warns that "Pride goes before destruction, and a haughty spirit before a fall." James 4:6 reminds us that "God opposes the proud but gives grace to the humble." And Isaiah 14 describes

Lucifer's fall as the result of saying, "I will ascend... I will be like the Most High."

The consistent message is clear: when we refuse to acknowledge God's authority and insist on maintaining control, we set ourselves against the grain of reality itself. And reality tends to win those contests.

The Freedom of Letting Go

Here's the paradox: submission, properly understood, doesn't diminish you—it liberates you.

Think about it. The burden of trying to control everything is exhausting. You were never designed to carry it. When you let go, you're not giving up something valuable; you're putting down something that was crushing you.

1 Peter 5:6-7 captures this beautifully: "Humble yourselves, therefore, under the mighty hand of God so that at the proper time he may exalt you, casting all your anxieties on him, because he cares for you."

Notice how submission (humbling yourself under God's hand) is directly connected to relief from anxiety. You can cast your worries onto God precisely because you've acknowledged that He's in charge, He's mighty, and He cares for you.

This doesn't mean life becomes perfect when you submit. It means you stop carrying the impossible weight of thinking everything depends on you. You're freed to live within your actual capabilities and limitations as a human being, trusting God with what's beyond them.

In Matthew 11:28-30, Jesus offers this invitation: "Come to me, all who labor and are heavy laden, and I will give you rest. Take my yoke upon you, and learn from me, for I am gentle and lowly in heart, and you will find rest for your souls. For my yoke is easy, and my burden is light."

Jesus isn't saying, "Submit to me, and I'll make you do hard things." He's saying, "The yoke you're currently wearing—the yoke of self-reliance and control—is breaking your back. My yoke—the yoke of submission to God—is actually designed for human flourishing. It fits properly. It distributes the weight correctly."

When you stop trying to be the god of your own life, you can finally start being the human you were created to be. And it turns out that's a much better, much freer way to live.

Practical Submission: How to Actually Let Go

So how do we move from the theory of submission to the practice of it? How do we loosen our white-knuckled grip on control and start living in the freedom of trust? Here are some practical approaches:

1. The Open-Handed Prayer Practice

Most of us pray with clenched fists, metaphorically if not literally. We come to God with our demands, our timelines, and our solutions already determined. We're not really asking for His intervention; we're asking for His stamp of approval on our plans.

Try this instead: When you pray, physically open your hands, palms up. This simple posture reminds you that you're releasing control, not grasping for it. You're receiving what God gives rather than demanding what you want.

Instead of saying, "God, here's what I need you to do by this deadline," try, "God, here's the situation. I trust you to work in it according to your wisdom and timing. Show me my part, and help me accept what I cannot change."

This doesn't mean you can't bring specific requests to God. It means you hold those requests loosely, trusting that God might have better plans than the ones you've devised.

2. The "Not My Job" Discernment

A key part of submission is clarity about what is and isn't your responsibility. Many of us suffer from responsibility confusion—we take ownership of things that aren't actually ours to control.

Make a three-column list:
- Things that are my responsibility (my actions, my responses, my words)
- Things that are someone else's responsibility (their choices, their feelings, their growth)
- Things that are God's responsibility (outcomes, timing, other people's hearts, the future)

When you find yourself stressed and controlling, check which column the issue belongs in. If it's not in your column, practice releasing it to the appropriate party.

As Philippians 2:12-13 balances, "Work out your own salvation with fear and trembling, for it is God who works in you, both to will and to work for his good pleasure." You have your part; God has His. Submission means respecting that distinction.

3. The Obedience Experiment

Sometimes submission is less about your attitude and more about your actions. When you know what God is asking you to do (through Scripture, wise counsel, and the Spirit's guidance), but you're hesitating because you're afraid of the outcome or don't understand the reasoning, try a simple obedience experiment.

Commit to obeying in this one area for a defined period—say, two weeks. Tell God you're willing to set aside your doubts and fears temporarily to see what happens when you simply trust and obey. Approach it with curiosity rather than dread.

This approach honors Psalm 34:8: "Oh, taste and see that the LORD is good!" Sometimes you have to taste before you can see. You have to experience the results of submission before you fully understand its value.

4. The Reality Acceptance Practice

Much of our controlling behavior stems from our refusal to accept reality as it actually is. We waste enormous energy fighting against circumstances we cannot change rather than working within them.

When facing a difficult situation, try this three-step practice:
1. Name the reality without judgment: "This is what's happening."
2. Identify what you can and cannot change about it.
3. Pray for grace to accept what cannot be changed and wisdom to change what can.

This echoes the famous Serenity Prayer and aligns with Paul's testimony in Philippians 4:11-13: "I have learned in whatever situation I am to be content... I have learned the secret of facing plenty and hunger, abundance and need. I can do all things through him who strengthens me."

Contentment isn't passive resignation; it's active submission to reality as it is while trusting God to work within it.

5. The Control Inventory

Most of us have specific triggers or areas where our control issues flare up most intensely. Take time to identify yours:
- Do you micromanage at work?
- Try to control your spouse's behavior?
- Obsess over your children's success?
- Manage your image on social media?
- Panic when plans change?
- Need to drive in every group situation?

Once you've identified your control hot spots, you can practice targeted submission in those specific areas. Start with something small but meaningful—perhaps letting someone else choose the restaurant or route, not correcting someone when they're slightly wrong, or allowing a project to unfold without your constant oversight.

6. The "Fast from Control" Challenge

Just as fasting from food makes you more aware of your dependence on God for sustenance, fasting from control reveals your addiction to being in charge.

Choose one day a week to deliberately practice not being in control:
- Don't check the weather forecast.
- Let someone else plan the day's activities.
- Refrain from checking work email outside office hours.
- Say "whatever you think" when asked for your preference.
- Don't look at your investment accounts.

Pay attention to the anxiety that arises when you can't check, manage, or direct things. That discomfort reveals how much you've been depending on control rather than on God.

7. The Sabbath Submission

The biblical practice of Sabbath is fundamentally an exercise in submission. By stopping your work for a day, you're acknowledging that the world will continue to turn without your constant effort. You're admitting that you are not indispensable. You're trusting God to hold things together while you rest.

As Mark Buchanan writes in "The Rest of God," Sabbath is "a day of profound alignment with God's created order."

Try practicing a true Sabbath—24 hours where you completely disengage from productivity, control, and management of life. No work emails, no home improvement projects, no planning sessions. Just presence, enjoyment, and rest.

This honors the Fourth Commandment and aligns you with God's rhythm for creation. It's submission in practice, not just in theory.

Submission in Key Relationships

The discipline of submission doesn't just affect your relationship with God; it transforms how you relate to others. Let's look at how submission plays out in key relationships:

Authority Structures

Romans 13:1 instructs, "Let every person be subject to the governing authorities. For there is no authority except from God, and those that exist have been instituted by God."

This doesn't mean blind obedience to unjust rulers. It does mean recognizing that part of submitting to God involves respecting the legitimate authority structures He's established for ordered society. This includes government, workplace leadership, and church authority.

Submission in these contexts means:
- Following laws and regulations unless they clearly contradict God's commands
- Respecting the office even when you disagree with the officeholder
- Working through proper channels for change rather than simply ignoring rules you don't like
- Giving leaders the benefit of the doubt rather than assuming the worst

When Peter and John were ordered by the religious authorities to stop preaching about Jesus, they respectfully but firmly replied, "Whether it is right in the sight of God to listen to you rather than to God, you must judge" (Acts 4:19). This shows the balance—they acknowledged the leaders' position but recognized God's higher authority.

Marriage Relationships

Few topics in Christianity generate more heat than submission in marriage. Ephesians 5:21-33 calls for mutual submission between spouses, with a specific call for wives to submit to husbands and husbands to love their wives sacrificially as Christ loved the church.

Whatever your interpretation of these verses, healthy submission in marriage is never about one person dominating the other. It's about both partners putting the relationship above their individual preferences and seeking what best serves their union and family.

Submission in marriage means:
- Listening to understand, not just to respond
- Being willing to yield on matters of preference rather than insisting on your way
- Honoring your spouse's wisdom and perspective
- Making decisions together whenever possible
- Supporting each other's callings and gifts

The goal isn't for one spouse to control the other but for both to align themselves with God's purposes for their marriage.

Friendship and Community

Ephesians 5:21 calls believers to be "submitting to one another out of reverence for Christ." This mutual submission creates healthy Christian community.

In friendships and church relationships, submission looks like:
- Being willing to be corrected and challenged (Proverbs 27:17)
- Considering others' needs above your own (Philippians 2:3-4)
- Respecting different perspectives rather than insisting you're always right
- Allowing others to use their gifts even when they do things differently than you would
- Compromising on non-essential matters for the sake of unity

True submission in community doesn't mean you never express your views or preferences. It means you hold them loosely, valuing relationship above being right or getting your way.

Common Roadblocks to Submission

If submission were easy, we'd all be doing it already. But several significant obstacles often stand in our way:

Fear

Perhaps the biggest roadblock to submission is fear. We're afraid that if we let go of control:
- We'll be taken advantage of
- Bad things will happen
- Our needs won't be met
- We'll lose our identity
- We'll make the wrong choice

This fear reveals a fundamental mistrust of God's character. We don't really believe He's good, wise, and powerful enough to take care of us if we submit to Him.

The antidote to this fear is repeatedly focusing on God's nature and promises. As 2 Timothy 1:7 reminds us, "God gave us a spirit not of fear but of power and love and self-control." The more you meditate on who God actually is, the less frightening submission becomes.

Past Wounds

If you've been hurt by authority figures who abused their power or by religious leaders who weaponized the concept of submission, you may have legitimate trauma around this topic.

Submission to an abusive person or system isn't godly—it's harmful. If your resistance to submission stems from past wounds, it's important to:
- Acknowledge the legitimate hurt you experienced
- Recognize that abusive leadership is a perversion of God's design, not an example of it
- Work with trusted counselors to heal from these experiences
- Start with small, safe acts of submission to rebuild trust

God is patient with your healing process. He doesn't demand that you jump immediately from trauma to complete trust.

Misunderstanding God's Character

Many of us struggle with submission because we fundamentally misunderstand who God is:
- If you see God primarily as a harsh judge, submission feels like surrendering to punishment.
- If you see God mainly as distant and uninvolved, submission seems pointless.

- If you view God as capricious or unpredictable, submission feels dangerous.

The remedy is to immerse yourself in Scripture's full portrait of God's character—His justice and mercy, His transcendence and immanence, His constancy and creativity. As your understanding of God expands, submission becomes not just safer but actually desirable.

Cultural Conditioning

We live in a culture that worships autonomy, self-determination, and individual rights. From childhood, we're taught that freedom means doing whatever we want whenever we want. The idea of voluntarily placing ourselves under authority runs counter to everything our culture celebrates.

Recognizing this conditioning is the first step to overcoming it. Romans 12:2 calls us to be "transformed by the renewal of your mind," which includes questioning the cultural assumptions we've absorbed about control, freedom, and authority.

True freedom isn't the absence of constraints; it's functioning according to your design. A train is most free when it stays on its tracks, not when it jumps them in the name of autonomy.

Discerning Healthy vs. Unhealthy Submission

Not all calls for submission are legitimate. Discernment is crucial for distinguishing healthy submission from its unhealthy counterfeits. Here are some key differences:

Healthy Submission:

1. **Is given freely, not coerced.** True submission is a voluntary choice, not something extracted through manipulation, force, or fear.

2. **Preserves dignity and agency.** Healthy submission respects your identity, gifts, and voice. You're still fully yourself, just aligned under proper authority.

3. **Is based on trust and respect.** You submit because you trust the wisdom and goodness of the authority, not because you're afraid of punishment.

4. **Aligns with God's revealed will.** Legitimate authorities will never ask you to violate clear biblical commands or principles.

5. **Promotes growth and flourishing.** Over time, healthy submission should lead to greater wholeness, not diminishment.

Unhealthy Submission:

1. **Is demanded or manipulated.** If someone has to threaten, guilt, or force you into submission, something is wrong with their authority.

2. **Erases individuality.** If submission requires you to abandon your God-given identity, gifts, or conscience, it's not biblical submission.

3. **Is rooted in fear or shame.** If your primary motivation is avoiding punishment or earning approval, you're in an unhealthy dynamic.

4. **Contradicts Scripture.** Anyone who asks you to lie, cheat, harm others, or violate your conscience is not exercising legitimate authority.

5. **Leads to diminishment.** If submission consistently makes you smaller, weaker, or more dependent rather than helping you flourish, it's likely toxic.

When facing a questionable call to submit, ask:
- Does this align with Scripture?
- Does this honor the image of God in me?

- Does this promote true flourishing?
- Would wise, godly counselors affirm this direction?

Remember Acts 5:29: "We must obey God rather than men." God's authority always trumps human authority when the two conflict.

The Submission Paradox

Here's the beautiful paradox of submission: the more fully you surrender control to God, the more you become who you were truly created to be.

This isn't just spiritual theory; it's how reality works. Think about it:
- A musician submits to musical theory and practice, and gains freedom to truly express themselves.
- An athlete submits to training regimens and team strategy, and becomes capable of extraordinary performance.
- A writer submits to the constraints of grammar and genre, and finds their unique voice.

In every domain, true mastery and freedom come not from rejecting all constraints but from submitting to the right ones.

The same principle applies spiritually. By submitting to God's design for your life, you don't lose your unique identity—you discover it. You find out who you were meant to be all along, before your insistence on control warped and limited your development.

As C.S. Lewis observed, "The more we get what we now call 'ourselves' out of the way and let Him take us over, the more truly ourselves we become... It is when I turn to Christ, when I give myself up to His Personality, that I first begin to have a real personality of my own."

This is the great reversal at the heart of the gospel: the way up is down. The path to true selfhood runs through surrender. The road to freedom passes through submission.

Jesus expressed this paradox in Mark 8:35: "For whoever would save his life will lose it, but whoever loses his life for my sake and the gospel's will save it." The more desperately you cling to control of your life, the more it slips through your fingers. But when you release it to God, you receive it back more vibrant and purposeful than before.

The 7-Day Submission Challenge

Ready to put this into practice? Here's a week-long challenge to help you develop the discipline of submission in your daily life:

Day 1: Acknowledge Reality

Spend 15 minutes reflecting on these questions:
- What are you currently trying to control that is actually beyond your control?
- How are these control efforts affecting your peace, relationships, and spiritual life?
- Write a simple prayer acknowledging the limits of your control and asking God for the courage to trust Him more.

Day 2: Morning Surrender

Before checking your phone or starting your day, spend 5 minutes in surrender:
- Physically open your hands as a symbol of releasing control
- Pray, "Lord, this day is yours. Guide my steps, direct my path, and help me trust your leading even when it differs from my plans."
- Identify one specific area where you'll practice letting go of control today.

Day 3: Schedule Interruption

Deliberately allow an interruption to your plans:
- Leave a 30-minute block unscheduled and ask God to fill it as He wishes
- When unexpected changes arise, respond with "This is God's day, not mine" rather than frustration
- Notice how you feel when plans change—this reveals your attachment to control

Day 4: Authority Check

Reflect on your relationship with legitimate authorities in your life:
- Is there an authority figure (boss, pastor, government official) you consistently resist or criticize?
- How might respectful submission look in this relationship, even if you disagree on some matters?
- Take one concrete step toward more respectful engagement with this authority.

Day 5: Relationship Submission

Practice mutual submission in an important relationship:
- Ask a spouse, friend, or family member what would make their day better
- Do something their way instead of your way, without commentary or complaint

- Look for opportunities to put their preferences above your own as an act of love

Day 6: Outcome Release

Identify a situation where you're anxiously trying to control the outcome:
- Write down your fears about what might happen if things don't go your way
- Counter each fear with a truth about God's character and promises
- Physically enact a "release ritual"—write your concerns on paper and then burn it, bury it, or place it in a "God box" as a symbol of giving it to Him

Day 7: Sabbath Submission

Practice a full day of submission through Sabbath:
- Refrain from productivity, planning, and problem-solving for 24 hours
- Resist the urge to check work communications or "just handle one thing"
- When control urges arise, replace them with a breath prayer like "Your will, not mine" or "I trust you, Lord"
- End the day by reflecting on what you learned about yourself and God through this practice

This challenge isn't about perfection; it's about progress. Each small act of letting go trains your submission muscles and builds your capacity to trust God more fully.

The Kick in the Pants: Control Is Killing You

Let's get real for a moment: your white-knuckled grip on control is slowly suffocating your soul.

That constant background anxiety? It's the sound of you trying to be God. That chronic tension in your shoulders? It's the weight of carrying burdens you were never designed to bear. That distance you feel in your relationships? It's the inevitable result of treating people as variables to be managed rather than hearts to be known.

Control doesn't deliver what it promises. It doesn't make you safer—it makes you smaller. It doesn't give you peace—it gives you ulcers. It doesn't earn you respect—it drives people away.

And here's the kicker: most of what you're trying so desperately to control is outside your control anyway. You're exhausting yourself fighting battles you can't win.

Your obsessive planning can't prevent a market crash or a cancer diagnosis. Your helicopter parenting can't guarantee your kids will make good choices. Your image management can't make everyone like you. Your religious rule-following can't earn God's love.

Jesus didn't fight God's will—He submitted to it. And that's what saved the world.

When He prayed, "Not my will, but yours, be done" in Gethsemane, He wasn't surrendering to defeat. He was aligning Himself with a victory bigger than any He could achieve by asserting His own preferences.

The invitation is clear: Put down the burden of playing God. It's crushing you, and you're not very good at it anyway.

Submission doesn't mean you're weak—it means you trust Someone stronger. It doesn't mean you stop caring—it means you start caring about the right things. It doesn't mean you become less—it means you become who you were created to be.

The great irony is that the freedom you're looking for isn't found in being in control; it's found in trusting the One who is.

So loosen your grip. Take a deep breath. Open your hands.

The God who formed galaxies and knows when a sparrow falls is perfectly capable of handling your career path, your love life, your health concerns, and your future. And unlike you, He can see around corners. He knows what's coming. He's working with complete information and perfect wisdom.

Wouldn't it be a relief to stop pretending you've got it all figured out? Wouldn't it be freeing to admit you're not the center of the universe? Wouldn't it be life-giving to trust that God's got this, even when "this" is messy and confusing?

That's the invitation of submission. Not to become nothing, but to become fully the something God created you to be—a beloved child who trusts their Father rather than an exhausted actor trying to direct the play while performing in it.

The weight of control is slowly crushing you. Put it down.

Exchange it for the "easy yoke" Jesus offered—the paradoxical freedom that comes from being under His authority rather than frantically asserting your own.

Your tight grip isn't keeping your life from falling apart; it's keeping you from falling into the hands of the God who loves you.

Let go. He's got you.

Chapter 5:

Service – Doing the Dirty Work

Let's be honest: when most of us think about "serving others," we picture ourselves doing something that makes us look good.

We imagine serving at a soup kitchen on Thanksgiving—while someone conveniently captures the perfect candid photo for our Instagram. We think about going on mission trips to exotic locations—where we can pose with adorable children and collect experiences that make for great small group testimonies. We envision ourselves on stage, using our talents for God's glory—while an audience applauds our sacrifice.

I hate to burst your bubble, but that's not what Jesus had in mind.

When Jesus talked about service, He wasn't thinking about your personal brand or your spiritual resume. He was talking about getting your hands dirty doing thankless work that nobody notices—and finding joy in it anyway.

In the upside-down economy of God's kingdom, true greatness doesn't come from being in the spotlight. It comes from being willing to do what others won't do. It comes from choosing the lowest position instead of angling for the highest. It comes from serving when there's absolutely nothing in it for you.

Mark 10:42-45 captures this perfectly. When His disciples were arguing about who would get the best positions in His kingdom, Jesus said: "You know that those who are considered rulers of the Gentiles lord it over them, and their great ones exercise authority over them. But it shall not be so among you. But whoever would be great among you must be your servant, and whoever would be first among you must be slave of all. For even the Son of Man came not to be served but to serve, and to give his life as a ransom for many."

Did you catch that? Jesus—the Creator of the universe, the King of kings, the one being in history who actually deserved to be served—came to serve others. And not just in comfortable, convenient ways. He gave His life. He did the ultimate dirty work.

So in this chapter, we're not talking about service that boosts your ego or builds your platform. We're talking about the kind that costs you something. The kind that goes against your self-interest. The kind that sometimes, let's be honest, straight-up sucks—but transforms you and reflects Christ in a way nothing else can.

What Real Service Looks Like

Before we dig into the how-to, let's get clear on what we're talking about. Because there's service, and then there's SERVICE.

What Service Is NOT:

1. **Service is not a performance.** If you're doing it primarily to be seen, praised, or applauded, it's not service—it's self-promotion. Jesus had harsh words for those who "do all their deeds to be seen by others" (Matthew 23:5).

2. **Service is not a transaction.** If you're keeping score, expecting payback, or serving only those who can return the favor, you're just engaging in marketplace exchange, not Christlike service. Jesus taught, "When you give a feast, invite the poor, the crippled, the lame, the blind, and you will be blessed, because they cannot repay you" (Luke 14:13-14).

3. **Service is not a spiritual merit badge.** If you see it as earning points with God or checking a box on

your Christian to-do list, you've missed the heart of service. Service flows from grace, not guilt.

4. **Service is not just doing what you enjoy.** While using your gifts is important, limiting your service to only what feels good, convenient, or aligned with your "passion" isn't the full picture. Sometimes true service means doing what's needed, not what's fun.

What Service IS:

1. **Service is meeting real needs, not just doing nice things.** It addresses actual needs that matter to the other person, not just what you think they should want. Jesus didn't wash the disciples' feet because it was symbolic; He did it because their feet were legitimately dirty in a foot-travel culture, and nobody else was willing to do this necessary but lowly task.

2. **Service is often inconvenient.** It interrupts your schedule, disrupts your comfort, and demands your energy when you'd rather be doing something else. Think of the Good Samaritan, who stopped his journey, changed his plans, and spent his own resources to help a bleeding stranger (Luke 10:25-37).

3. **Service is frequently unseen.** Much of the most important service happens behind the scenes, with no audience and no recognition. Jesus taught, "When you give to the needy, do not let your left hand know

what your right hand is doing, so that your giving may be in secret. And your Father who sees in secret will reward you" (Matthew 6:3-4).

4. **Service often involves doing things beneath your perceived status.** It requires setting aside your sense of importance, education, or position to do work that might seem "beneath you." This is exactly what Jesus did when He, the Teacher and Lord, took on the role of the lowest household servant by washing feet (John 13:1-17).

5. **Service centers the other person, not you.** It's focused on their needs, their dignity, their flourishing—not on how serving makes you feel or what it does for your reputation. As Philippians 2:4 directs, "Let each of you look not only to his own interests, but also to the interests of others."

With these distinctions in mind, let's look at why service matters so much in the Christian life.

Why Service Is Non-Negotiable

Service isn't just a nice add-on for especially spiritual Christians. It's fundamental to following Jesus. Here's why:

1. Jesus Modeled It Himself

The most compelling reason to serve others is that Jesus himself made service central to His life and mission. He didn't just talk about serving—He embodied it.

John 13:3-5 describes one of the most powerful scenes in the Gospels: "Jesus, knowing that the Father had given all things into his hands, and that he had come from God and was going back to God, rose from supper. He laid aside his outer garments, and taking a towel, tied it around his waist. Then he poured water into a basin and began to wash the disciples' feet and to wipe them with the towel that was wrapped around him."

Note the context: Jesus, fully aware of His divine identity and authority ("knowing that the Father had given all things into his hands"), didn't use that status as an excuse to avoid menial service. Instead, He deliberately chose the role of the lowest household servant.

Washing feet wasn't a cute symbolic gesture in first-century Palestine. It was dealing with the grime and stink of feet that had walked dusty roads in sandals. It was the job nobody wanted. And Jesus—with full awareness of who He was—chose to do it.

If service was not beneath Jesus, what possible justification do we have for thinking any task is beneath us?

2. Service Transforms Us

Service isn't just about what we accomplish for others; it's about what happens inside us. Few spiritual practices are as effective at killing our ego, reshaping our priorities, and aligning our hearts with Christ's.

When you serve—especially in ways that offer no external reward—you're directly confronting your self-centeredness. You're practicing putting others first. You're developing the mind of Christ described in Philippians 2:5-7: "Have this mind among yourselves, which is yours in Christ Jesus, who, though he was in the form of God... emptied himself, by taking the form of a servant."

Service is one of God's primary tools for making you more like Jesus. It's spiritual formation disguised as helping others.

3. Service Demonstrates the Gospel

The gospel isn't just something we believe or proclaim—it's something we embody. And few things demonstrate the gospel's reality more powerfully than sacrificial service.

When you serve with no expectation of return, you're illustrating God's grace in tangible form. When you serve those who can't repay you, you're showing what it means that God loved us while we were still sinners (Romans 5:8). When you serve in ways that cost you something, you're reflecting the sacrificial love of Christ.

In a world obsessed with getting ahead and looking out for number one, selfless service stands out like a neon sign pointing to a different way of being human.

4. Service Is How the Church Functions

The New Testament consistently describes the church as a body where each member serves the others according to their gifts. Service isn't an optional ministry track; it's how the body of Christ operates.

1 Peter 4:10 makes this clear: "As each has received a gift, use it to serve one another, as good stewards of God's varied grace." Every believer has received gifts, and those gifts are given for service, not self-promotion or personal fulfillment.

Similarly, Ephesians 4:16 describes the church growing "when each part is working properly"—not just the paid staff, not just those with platform gifts, but each and every member serving according to their function.

A non-serving Christian is as contradictory as a non-wet water or a non-flying bird. Service isn't what some Christians do; it's what makes someone recognizable as a follower of Christ.

5. Service Is an Antidote to Cultural Toxicity

We live in a culture saturated with entitlement, self-importance, and status-seeking. Service directly counters these poisonous influences.

When you regularly do thankless tasks for others, it's hard to maintain an inflated sense of your own importance. When you serve people who can't enhance your social standing, you break free from the status games that dominate our society. When you choose the lowest position instead of angling for recognition, you're practicing a countercultural way of being.

Service is revolutionary in a me-first world. It's not just good for others; it's liberation from the exhausting pursuit of self-importance that leaves so many people burned out and empty.

The Different Types of Service

Service comes in many forms, and they all have their place in the Christian life. Let's look at some different categories of service and what makes each valuable:

Planned vs. Spontaneous Service

Planned service involves committing to regular, scheduled ways of serving others—like volunteering weekly at a food bank, teaching Sunday school, or maintaining a church building. This type of service builds consistency and allows you to develop skills and relationships over time.

Spontaneous service means responding to needs as they arise, without prior planning—like helping a neighbor move furniture, picking up a shift for a sick coworker, or stopping to help a stranded motorist. This type of service develops your attentiveness and flexibility.

Both are necessary. If you only serve when you feel like it or when a need happens to cross your path, you may miss the character development that comes from committed, ongoing service. But if you only serve in structured, planned ways, you may become rigid and miss daily opportunities to show Christ's love in ordinary moments.

As Galatians 6:10 encourages, "So then, as we have opportunity, let us do good to everyone, and especially to those who are of the household of faith." Note the phrase "as we have opportunity"—this covers both the opportunities we create through commitments and those that unexpectedly arise.

Public vs. Hidden Service

Public service happens where others can see it—leading worship, teaching a class, serving meals at a community event. This type of service often uses visible gifts and may receive recognition.

Hidden service occurs behind the scenes, with few or no witnesses—cleaning bathrooms after church, anonymously paying someone's bill, praying for others in private. This type of service directly counters our desire for recognition and approval.

Both have their place, but hidden service provides a unique spiritual training ground. Jesus emphasized this in Matthew 6:1: "Beware of practicing your righteousness before other people in order to be seen by them, for then you will have no reward from your Father who is in heaven."

Hidden service purifies your motives and trains you to seek God's approval rather than human recognition. It's a powerful antidote to the social media mindset that asks, "If no one sees it, did it even happen?"

Comfortable vs. Stretching Service

Comfortable service uses your natural abilities, aligns with your personality, and feels relatively easy—like the tech-savvy person running the church sound system or the extrovert greeting newcomers.

Stretching service pushes you beyond your comfort zone, natural inclinations, or perceived abilities—like the introvert visiting shut-ins or the impatient person mentoring a child with behavior challenges.

Both matter. Using your natural gifts honors how God designed you. But stretching service often produces the most growth and prevents you from limiting your service to only what feels good.

Romans 12:6-8 acknowledges our differing gifts for service, but the surrounding context makes clear we're all called to things like "outdoing one another in showing honor," "contributing to the needs of the saints," and "showing hospitality" (Romans 12:10, 13)—regardless of whether these align with our natural gifts.

Individual vs. Collective Service

Individual service happens when you personally meet a need—like driving someone to an appointment, writing an encouraging note, or helping with a project.

Collective service involves joining with others to accomplish what none could do alone—like serving on a disaster relief team, participating in a community building project, or contributing to a group effort to support a family in need.

Both expressions reflect Christ's love. Individual service often allows for personal connection and immediate response. Collective service reminds us we're part of a body and can accomplish more together than separately.

As Ecclesiastes 4:9-10 observes, "Two are better than one, because they have a good reward for their toil. For if they fall, one will lift up his fellow. But woe to him who is alone when he falls and has not another to lift him up." Some needs simply require collaborative service.

The Heart of Service: Love, Not Duty

While service often involves doing things you don't particularly feel like doing, the motivation matters enormously. Service that flows from obligation or guilt is fundamentally different from service that flows from love.

This distinction is captured perfectly in 1 Corinthians 13:3: "If I give away all I have, and if I deliver up my body to be burned, but have not love, I gain nothing." You can perform extraordinarily sacrificial acts of service, but without love as the motivating force, they profit you nothing spiritually.

So how do you cultivate love as your motivation rather than duty? A few thoughts:

1. **Remember how you've been served.** Reflect regularly on how Christ has served you through His incarnation, life, death, and resurrection. Meditate on how others have served you throughout your life. Gratitude for service received naturally fuels a desire to serve others.

2. **See Christ in those you serve.** Jesus taught that when we serve "the least of these," we're serving Him (Matthew 25:40). Try to look past external appearances to see the image of God in each person you serve.

3. **Pray for love where it's lacking.** Be honest with God when you're serving out of obligation rather than

love. Ask Him to give you His heart for the person or situation. Sometimes love follows action rather than preceding it.

4. **Start where love already exists.** If you're struggling to serve from love, begin with serving people or causes you already care about deeply. As serving from love becomes a habit in these areas, it can spread to other contexts.

5. **Remember that emotions follow actions.** Sometimes you won't feel loving at first. That's okay. Start serving anyway, and often the emotions catch up with the actions. Mother Teresa noted that she didn't always feel love for those she served, but she chose to act with love, trusting the feelings would follow.

The Real-World Cost of Service

Let's get practical about what service costs, because pretending it's all joy and fulfillment isn't honest or helpful. Real service—the kind that genuinely reflects Christ—often involves:

Time You Don't Have

Service frequently requires giving time you feel you can't spare. In our chronically busy culture, time might be the most precious resource of all, which makes it one of the most meaningful things to give.

When the Good Samaritan stopped for the wounded traveler, he gave up time that would have advanced his own journey. When you drive an elderly neighbor to appointments, babysit for a single parent, or stay after an event to clean up, you're sacrificing time you could spend on your own priorities.

Jesus never seemed rushed, despite having the most important mission in history. He made time for interruptions, for children, for the sick, for individual conversations. He knew that people matter more than efficiency.

Energy You'd Rather Conserve

Service often demands your energy when you're already tired. It asks you to give from your mental, emotional, and physical reserves when they feel depleted.

Think about Jesus feeding the 5,000. The context in Mark 6 is important: Jesus and the disciples had been so busy they "had no leisure even to eat" (v. 31). Jesus had invited them to come away to rest, but the crowds followed them. Despite His own fatigue, "he had compassion on them" (v. 34) and spent the day teaching and ultimately feeding them.

When you help someone move on your day off, listen to a friend in crisis when you're already emotionally drained, or take on an additional responsibility at church during a busy season at work, you're giving energy you'd rather conserve.

Comfort You'd Like to Keep

Service regularly disrupts your comfort, requiring you to engage with situations, environments, or people outside your comfort zone.

Jesus left the perfect comfort of heaven for the constraints of human existence. He engaged with people across social boundaries that made His disciples uncomfortable—touching lepers, speaking with Samaritans, welcoming children, dining with tax collectors.

When you welcome a refugee family with different customs, serve in a neighborhood unlike your own, care for someone with a difficult health condition, or open your home to a person in crisis, you're sacrificing comfort for the sake of others.

Status You'd Prefer to Maintain

Perhaps most challenging of all, true service often means voluntarily taking a lower position than the one you feel entitled to occupy.

The foot-washing scene in John 13 is so powerful precisely because Jesus deliberately stepped down from His rightful status as Teacher and Lord to take the lowest servant's position. This wasn't just about getting feet clean; it was a dramatic enactment of Philippians 2's description of Christ emptying Himself and taking the form of a servant.

When you do work that feels "beneath" your education level, clean up messes you didn't make, take the blame for a team failure even when it wasn't your fault, or set aside your preferences to honor someone else's, you're practicing status-lowering service that directly counters our culture's status-seeking default.

Practical Ways to Serve (That Actually Help)

Let's get super practical. Here are some ways to serve others that genuinely meet needs rather than just making you feel good:

In Your Home

1. **Do the chores no one else wants.** Every household has them—cleaning hair from the shower drain, taking out the trash on a rainy night, unclogging the toilet. Without comment or complaint, start doing these tasks before anyone else has to.

2. **Notice what's running low before others do.** Be the one who replaces the empty toilet paper roll, refills the ice tray, or buys more milk before the last drop is gone. These small acts of attentiveness communicate care.

3. **Create space for others to flourish.** This might mean handling childcare so your spouse can pursue a hobby, keeping the house quiet during a roommate's important call, or adjusting your schedule to accommodate someone else's needs.

4. **Be the first to apologize.** Even when the conflict isn't mostly your fault, be the first to say "I'm sorry for my part in this." This breaks the cycle of blame and creates space for healing.

In Your Church

1. **Volunteer for the unglamorous, ongoing needs.** Churches always need people to clean bathrooms, change light bulbs, shovel snow, update databases,

and perform maintenance. These behind-the-scenes roles rarely get recognition but are essential.

2. **Show up when extra hands are needed.** Be the person who consistently helps set up before events and clean up afterward. Be reliable for the mundane tasks that make ministry possible.

3. **Step in during leadership gaps.** When a ministry leader moves away or steps down, volunteer to help during the transition, even if it's not your passion area. Preventing ministry disruption serves the whole body.

4. **Make room for others to serve.** If you've been in a visible role for a long time, consider stepping back to create space for others to develop their gifts. Mentoring a replacement can be a profound form of service.

In Your Workplace

1. **Do quality work even when it goes unnoticed.** Serving well means doing your job with integrity and excellence even when the boss isn't looking—because ultimately, as Colossians 3:23 reminds us, "Whatever you do, work heartily, as for the Lord and not for men."

2. **Take on unassigned responsibilities that serve the team.** Be the person who makes coffee when it's empty, organizes the shared workspace, or updates the outdated procedure document that's frustrating everyone.

3. **Give credit away.** When a project succeeds, highlight others' contributions before mentioning your own. Look for opportunities to celebrate colleagues' work, especially those who are often overlooked.

4. **Mentor others without self-interest.** Share your knowledge, skills, and connections to help others advance, even if there's no obvious benefit to you. Be generous with what you've learned.

In Your Community

1. **Adopt an elderly or homebound neighbor.** Offer to pick up groceries, mow their lawn, or just visit regularly. These consistent, practical forms of care can make the difference between someone staying in their home or having to leave.

2. **Support parents of young children.** Offer specific help like babysitting on a regular schedule, dropping off a meal during a tough week, or taking an older child for an activity to give parents focused time with a new baby.

3. **Notice and meet practical needs.** Keep your eyes open for opportunities to help—the neighbor who's struggling with heavy packages, the person at the grocery store who's short on cash, the family who could use help with home repairs they can't afford.

4. **Show up consistently for unglamorous community needs.** Volunteer to pick up litter in public spaces, serve at the local food bank during non-holiday times, or help with administrative tasks at a community organization. These roles are crucial but often have volunteer shortages.

Common Barriers to Serving (And How to Overcome Them)

Even when we understand the importance of service, several barriers can keep us from actually doing it. Let's address some common obstacles:

"I Don't Have Time"

This is probably the most frequent barrier people cite. With work, family, and other commitments, adding service feels impossible.

How to overcome it:

1. Start small. Even 30 minutes a week is meaningful if it's consistent.
2. Integrate service into existing activities. Invite a lonely neighbor to join your family dinner, or serve alongside your children as a bonding activity.
3. Examine your time honestly. Most of us spend hours on social media, streaming services, or other leisure activities. Reallocating some of that time to service doesn't mean you can't rest—it just changes how you allocate your time.
4. Remember that service often multiplies effectiveness. When the disciples gave Jesus their small lunch in John 6, He multiplied it to feed thousands. Similarly, the time you give in service often produces fruit beyond what seems mathematically possible.

"I'm Too Tired/Stressed/Overwhelmed"

Many people are running on empty, making the energy requirements of service seem impossible.

How to overcome it:
1. Recognize that some forms of service can actually be energizing rather than depleting, especially when they align with your gifts.
2. Start by serving in ways that require presence more than action—like listening to someone who needs to talk or providing companionship to someone who's isolated.

3. Be honest about your limitations, but don't use them as a permanent excuse. Maybe you can't serve in high-energy ways right now, but you can write encouragement notes or pray for specific needs.

4. Consider whether stress is coming from trying to control outcomes that aren't yours to control. Sometimes service provides relief by focusing outward rather than inward.

"I Don't Know What to Do"

Many people want to serve but feel paralyzed by not knowing where to start or what needs exist.

How to overcome it:

1. Ask leaders in your church about specific needs that match your availability.

2. Talk to friends who are actively serving and ask if you can join them.

3. Look for existing structures that make serving straightforward, like established ministries or community organizations with volunteer programs.

4. Start by meeting a need you personally observe, even if it's small. This builds the habit of service while you discern longer-term directions.

"I'm Afraid I'll Do It Wrong"

Fear of inadequacy or making mistakes prevents many people from serving, especially in areas outside their expertise.

How to overcome it:
1. Remember that willingness matters more than expertise. Most service needs require a good heart more than specialized skills.
2. Start serving alongside someone more experienced who can provide guidance.
3. Be honest about your limitations. Say, "I'm new at this, but I'd like to help" rather than pretending to know more than you do.
4. Recognize that imperfect service is better than no service. The people you're helping would rather have your imperfect assistance than be left with no help at all.

"I've Been Hurt in Past Service Situations"

Some people have had negative experiences with service—being taken for granted, facing criticism, or serving in toxic environments.

How to overcome it:
1. Acknowledge the hurt rather than minimizing it. It's real, and it matters.
2. Start with time-limited, clearly bounded service until trust rebuilds.

3. Serve alongside healthy, balanced people who model sustainable service.

4. If necessary, serve in a completely different context than where the hurt occurred until healing progresses.

5. Remember that your service is ultimately unto the Lord, not dependent on how others receive or recognize it.

The Savior Complex: When Service Goes Wrong

An important warning: service can become toxic when it stems from unhealthy motivations or patterns. Here are some signs that your approach to service has gone sideways:

Signs of a Savior Complex

1. **You feel indispensable.** You believe the ministry/family/organization would collapse without you. This indicates you've made service about your importance rather than others' needs.

2. **You resent not being appreciated enough.** While everyone likes acknowledgment, if you're bitter about lack of recognition, you're probably serving for the wrong reasons.

3. **You can't say no even when you should.** Healthy service includes boundaries. If you can't decline any request, you may be serving from people-pleasing or a need to feel needed rather than from love.

4. **You feel superior to those you serve.** If you subtly look down on those you help, seeing them as projects rather than people of equal worth, your service has become about your ego rather than their dignity.

5. **You've neglected your primary responsibilities.** If your service to others has led to neglect of your family, health, or direct callings from God, you've crossed into unhealthy territory.

6. **You're chronically exhausted but can't slow down.** Burnout in service often stems from trying to be God to others rather than serving as His instrument, recognizing your limitations.

The Antidote to a Savior Complex

1. **Remember there's only one Savior, and it's not you.** Jesus said, "I will build my church" (Matthew 16:18)—not "You will build my church." Your role is important but limited.

2. **Serve from sufficiency, not scarcity.** True Christian service flows from the overflow of Christ's love in you, not from desperate attempts to earn worth or approval.

3. **Practice receiving service, not just giving it.** Jesus not only washed feet but also allowed His own feet to be washed with expensive perfume. Letting others serve you acknowledges your humanity and need.

4. **Take regular Sabbaths from service.** Even Jesus withdrew regularly to rest and pray. Constant service without renewal isn't sustainable or godly.

5. **Check your language.** If you frequently use phrases like "my ministry" or "my people," you might be over-identifying with your role. Practice saying "the ministry I get to participate in" or "the people God has allowed me to serve."

6. **Celebrate when others succeed without you.** A true servant rejoices when the work continues even in their absence. If this threatens you, your ego is too tied to your service.

Service as a Lifestyle, Not Just an Activity

The goal isn't just to add service activities to your schedule but to develop a servant's heart that infuses everything you do. Here's how to move toward service as a lifestyle:

1. Start Where You Already Are

You don't need to join a new program or sign up for a mission trip to begin serving. Look at your existing relationships and responsibilities:

- How can you serve your spouse/roommate/family members more intentionally?
- What would make your coworkers' lives easier that's within your power to do?
- Who in your existing circles (church, neighborhood, friend group) has a need you could meet?

Service as a lifestyle begins with bringing a servant's mindset to your current situations rather than compartmentalizing service as a separate category of life.

2. Make Service a Reflex, Not a Decision

Work toward service becoming your default response rather than something you have to deliberate about each time:

- When you see trash, pick it up without analyzing whose job it is.
- When someone looks lost, offer help before they have to ask.
- When a task needs doing, step up without waiting to see if someone else will.
- When you notice a need you can meet, meet it without calculating what's in it for you.

Jesus didn't have committee meetings to decide whether to heal someone or help someone. He saw needs and responded with compassion as His natural reflex. We can grow toward this same instinctive responsiveness.

3. Examine Your Use of Power and Privilege

All of us have some forms of power or privilege—whether from our position, education, wealth, connections, abilities, or demographic factors. A servant's mindset asks, "How can I use what I have to benefit others, not just myself?"

This might look like:
- Using your professional skills pro bono for a nonprofit
- Leveraging your connections to help someone get a job interview
- Speaking up for someone who isn't being heard in a meeting

- Sharing access to resources you have that others don't

1 Peter 4:10 reminds us that we are "stewards of God's varied grace"—meaning the advantages we have aren't for hoarding but for dispensing to others.

4. Integrate Service Into Your Identity

Rather than seeing service as something you do, begin to see it as who you are. This identity-level change happens through:

- Regularly meditating on Christ's servanthood and your identification with Him
- Practicing the language of servanthood ("How can I help?" rather than "That's not my job")
- Celebrating examples of service you observe in others
- Finding joy in service rather than viewing it as a burden or obligation

As this servant identity takes root, you'll find yourself naturally looking for ways to serve without having to consciously decide each time.

The 30-Day Service Challenge

Ready to develop your service muscles? Try this 30-day challenge designed to help you build a habit of service across different contexts:

Days 1-10: Home and Inner Circle

For the first ten days, focus on serving those closest to you:

1. Make a list of the tasks everyone in your household dislikes. Do one each day without comment.
2. Write a specific note of encouragement to someone in your immediate circle.
3. Prepare a favorite meal or treat for your family/roommates without being asked.
4. Take on a household responsibility that normally belongs to someone else.
5. Ask a family member or close friend, "What's one thing I could do that would make your week better?" Then do it.
6. Look around your living space for something that's been broken or neglected. Fix it.
7. Create space for someone close to you to pursue something they enjoy without interruption.
8. Think of something a family member or friend has mentioned wanting. Surprise them with it if possible.
9. Spend 30 minutes fully engaged with a family member in an activity of their choosing.
10. Apologize for something you've done that hurt someone close to you, even if it was unintentional.

Days 11-20: Community and Church

For the second ten days, expand your service to your broader community:

11. Contact your church and ask about a behind-the-scenes need you could help with.
12. Write a thank-you note to someone whose service usually goes unnoticed (custodian, administrative staff, etc.).
13. Bring a meal or care package to someone going through a difficult time.
14. Offer to run errands for an elderly or homebound neighbor.
15. Stay after an event to help clean up without being asked.
16. Donate items in good condition to a local shelter or assistance program.
17. Offer to babysit for a single parent or couple who rarely get a break.
18. Make a financial contribution to meet a specific need, preferably anonymously.
19. Volunteer for a task at church that regularly goes unfilled.
20. Reach out to someone who is new to your community or church and invite them to coffee or a meal.

Days 21-30: Stretch Zone

For the final ten days, push beyond your comfort zone:

21. Research organizations addressing a need in your community. Sign up for one volunteer shift.
22. Initiate a conversation with someone you normally avoid or overlook.
23. Identify a cause you care about and take one concrete action to support it.
24. Look for someone being excluded or marginalized in a group setting and deliberately include them.
25. Offer help to someone you find difficult to like or get along with.
26. Volunteer for a service role that uses skills you're still developing rather than ones you've mastered.
27. Give up something you enjoy for a day (coffee, social media, etc.) and donate the time or money to serving others.
28. Share credit or praise that came to you with someone who contributed but wasn't recognized.
29. Do something kind for someone who has hurt or offended you.
30. Reflect on the past 29 days and choose one form of service to continue as an ongoing commitment.

Throughout this challenge, keep a simple journal noting:
- What you did
- How it felt (both challenges and rewards)

- What you learned about yourself and others
- How your perspective on service is changing

This isn't about checking boxes but about developing new eyes to see needs and new reflexes to meet them.

Service That Transforms You

If you approach service as primarily about what you accomplish for others, you'll eventually burn out. But if you recognize service as a two-way street—something that not only helps others but forms you into Christ's likeness—you'll discover sustainable joy in it.

Here are some of the transformative effects of regular, Christ-centered service:

Your Ego Shrinks to a Healthy Size

Nothing deflates an inflated sense of self-importance like regularly doing tasks that society deems lowly or insignificant. When you clean toilets, change diapers (literal or metaphorical), or do work that goes completely unnoticed, you can't maintain the illusion that you're too important for mundane responsibilities.

This isn't about developing low self-esteem; it's about right-sizing your ego. You matter tremendously to God, but you're not the center of the universe. Service helps you internalize this truth on a gut level, not just intellectually.

Your Compassion Grows

Regular service puts you in contact with the reality of others' lives in ways that expand your capacity for empathy. You begin to see beyond stereotypes and assumptions to the complex humanity of each person.

Jesus consistently moved beyond demographic labels to see individuals—not just "a Samaritan" but a Samaritan woman with a specific story; not just "a tax collector" but Zacchaeus with particular struggles and hopes. Service helps you develop this same granular compassion.

Your Self-Sufficiency Diminishes

Ironically, serving others reveals how much you yourself need help and grace. You bump into your own limitations—your impatience, your judgment, your finitude. You realize you're not the hero of the story, swooping in to save the day, but a fellow broken human being whom God is using despite your flaws.

This growing awareness of your own need creates space for deeper dependence on God and greater receptivity to help from others—both essential for spiritual growth.

Your Joy Deepens

Despite the real costs of service, committed servers consistently report a profound joy that those focused on self-fulfillment rarely experience. As Jesus taught, "It is more blessed to give than to receive" (Acts 20:35).

This isn't just nice spiritual language; it's a psychological reality. Numerous studies show that regular altruistic service increases happiness and life satisfaction more effectively than self-focused pursuits of pleasure.

The joy of service isn't always immediate—sometimes you have to push through fatigue, resistance, or thanklessness to experience it. But it's deeper and more lasting than the fleeting happiness of self-indulgence.

The Kick in the Pants: Get Over Yourself and Grab a Towel

Let's be brutally honest: if you think certain tasks are beneath you—if you're too important to clean a toilet, sit with a difficult child, visit a smelly nursing home, or serve someone who can't enhance your social status—you have fundamentally misunderstood what it means to follow Jesus.

The Son of God washed dirty feet. He touched lepers. He allowed a woman with a bleeding condition to touch Him. He spent time with people who could offer Him nothing but their need.

If service was not beneath Jesus, what possible justification do you have for thinking any task is beneath you?

Your reluctance to serve in unglamorous ways reveals how much of your identity is still tied to worldly status rather than kingdom values. Your hesitation to help without recognition shows how addicted you still are to others' approval. Your careful calculation of what's "fair" or "reasonable" for you to do demonstrates how transaction-based your understanding of love remains.

Don't misunderstand me—this isn't about burning yourself out or enabling dysfunctional relationships.

It's about honestly confronting the entitlement, self-importance, and status-seeking that keep you from experiencing the freedom and joy of Christ-like service.

Church philosopher Gordon Fee put it bluntly: "You can tell a lot about a person's relationship with God by how they treat those who can do nothing for them."

What does your service (or lack thereof) say about your relationship with God?

Here's the good news: you don't need more guilt about not serving enough. You need a profound encounter with the God who "did not come to be served but to serve" (Mark 10:45). You need to experience His servant love for you so deeply that it naturally overflows to others.

The solution isn't to grit your teeth and serve more. It's to fall more deeply in love with the Servant King who loved you when you had nothing to offer Him but your need.

So start there. Meditate on Christ washing feet. Reflect on Him touching the untouchable. Consider Him giving His life for people who would deny, betray, and abandon Him.

Then pick up your towel—not out of obligation, but out of the overflow of having received this scandalous, status-reversing love yourself.

You don't need a platform—you need a towel. You don't need a stage—you need a servant's heart. You don't need more recognition—you need more of Christ's love flowing through you.

In God's upside-down kingdom, the path to greatness runs through the valley of service. As Jesus said, "Whoever would be great among you must be your servant, and whoever would be first among you must be slave of all" (Mark 10:43-44).

So get over yourself. Roll up your sleeves. Do the dirty work no one else wants to do. And discover there—in the lowly, thankless tasks—the unmistakable presence of the One who became a servant for you.

Chapter 6:

Worship – More Than Sunday Mornings

Let me start with a confession: I've faked worship more times than I can count.

I've stood in church with my hands raised, singing words about surrender while mentally making my grocery list. I've closed my eyes during the "emotional" part of the song to look spiritual while actually wondering if the Falcons won yesterday. I've judged the worship leader's skinny jeans while pretending to be lost in the presence of God.

Sound familiar? If not, you're either lying or you're Jesus. (Spoiler alert: you're not Jesus.)

Here's the uncomfortable truth most of us don't want to face: much of what we call "worship" is actually just religious performance—a Christian version of going through the motions. We confuse emotional experiences with spiritual encounters. We mistake music preferences for theological convictions. We treat worship like a concert where God is the entertainment and we're the critics.

But what if that's got it completely backward? What if worship isn't primarily a Sunday morning activity but a way of living? What if it's less about what happens in a building with a band and more about what happens in every moment of your life?

In Romans 12:1, Paul writes, "I appeal to you therefore, brothers, by the mercies of God, to present your bodies as a living sacrifice, holy and acceptable to God, which is your spiritual worship." Notice he doesn't say "present your voices as a singing sacrifice" or "present your Sunday mornings as a church-attending sacrifice." He says present your bodies—your whole self, your entire existence—as worship.

This chapter is about blowing up our tiny, constrained definition of worship and rediscovering what it means to live a life that genuinely glorifies God. Because if your worship starts and stops with a playlist, you're missing the whole point—and probably annoying the crap out of the God you claim to be praising.

What Worship Really Is (And Isn't)

Before we dive into practical applications, we need to get clear on what worship actually is, because our understanding has been severely distorted by church culture.

What Worship IS NOT:

1. **Worship is not just music.** This is the most common misconception. We literally call the singing part of church the "worship time," as if the rest isn't worship. But music is just one expression of worship, not its definition.

2. **Worship is not an emotional state.** While worship can absolutely involve emotions, equating worship with "feeling something" creates a dangerous standard. Some days you'll feel nothing while genuinely worshiping, and other days you'll feel tingles that have more to do with the bass guitar than the Holy Spirit.

3. **Worship is not a church activity.** Limiting worship to what happens in a sacred building for a designated hour contradicts everything the New Testament teaches about worship being a whole-life response to God.

4. **Worship is not a performance for God.** God doesn't need your talent, your perfect pitch, or your raised hands. He's not impressed by your awesome harmony or how many Bible verses you can quote. He sees straight through the show to the heart behind it.

5. **Worship is not about your preferences.** Whether you like hymns or hip-hop, organs or electric guitars, is completely irrelevant to whether something constitutes genuine worship. Making worship about your style preferences is actually a form of self-worship disguised as God-worship.

What Worship IS:

1. **Worship is acknowledging God's worth and responding appropriately.** The word "worship" comes from the Old English "worthship"—declaring and responding to the worth of something. True worship recognizes who God is and responds with appropriate honor, submission, and love.

2. **Worship is surrender.** At its core, worship is about yielding control, laying down your rights and preferences, and saying, "Not my will, but yours." This can happen during a song, but it can also happen while changing diapers, sitting in traffic, or doing your taxes.

3. **Worship is reorienting your attention.** To worship is to deliberately shift your focus from yourself, your problems, and your desires to God's character, promises, and purposes. It's choosing to see reality from God's perspective rather than your own limited viewpoint.

4. **Worship is offering.** In worship, you're presenting something to God—your time, attention, resources, talents, obedience, or gratitude. As David said in 2 Samuel 24:24, "I will not offer burnt offerings to the LORD my God that cost me nothing." Real worship involves sacrifice.

5. **Worship is a lifestyle, not an event.** As Paul makes clear in Romans 12:1, authentic worship encompasses your entire existence. It's a moment-by-moment choice to honor God with your thoughts, words, actions, and attitudes in every sphere of life.

Once we expand our understanding of worship to include all of life, the implications are both liberating and challenging. Liberating because worship becomes accessible in every moment, not just when the band plays. Challenging because it means nothing in your life is neutral—everything either glorifies God or something else.

The Biblical Foundation for Whole-Life Worship

This isn't some trendy, new interpretation of worship. It's deeply rooted in Scripture.

In John 4, Jesus has a fascinating conversation with a Samaritan woman about worship. She brings up the debate about where proper worship should happen—on the Samaritans' mountain or in Jerusalem. Jesus' response is revolutionary: "God is spirit, and those who worship him must worship in spirit and truth" (John 4:24).

In other words, authentic worship isn't defined by location but by the engagement of your spirit with God's Spirit, grounded in the truth of who He is. This completely decouples worship from any physical space or ritual.

Throughout the Old Testament, God consistently tells His people that He's not impressed by their religious performances when their daily lives contradict their worship songs. In Isaiah 1:13-14, God declares, "I cannot endure iniquity and solemn assembly... My soul hates your new moons and your appointed feasts; they have become a burden to me; I am weary of bearing them." Ouch.

The prophet Micah clarifies what God actually wants: "He has told you, O man, what is good; and what does the LORD require of you but to do justice, and to love kindness, and to walk humbly with your God?" (Micah 6:8). That's whole-life worship, not just religious observance.

In the New Testament, this understanding gets even clearer. Beyond Romans 12:1, Paul writes in 1 Corinthians 10:31, "So, whether you eat or drink, or whatever you do, do all to the glory of God." Eating, drinking, whatever—all of it can be worship when done with the right heart.

Colossians 3:23-24 extends this to our work: "Whatever you do, work heartily, as for the Lord and not for men, knowing that from the Lord you will receive the inheritance as your reward. You are serving the Lord Christ." Your job—whether you're a pastor, plumber, parent, or programmer—is a worship opportunity.

Even the mundane act of eating can be worship, as Paul notes in 1 Timothy 4:4-5: "For everything created by God is good, and nothing is to be rejected if it is received with thanksgiving, for it is made holy by the word of God and prayer." That sandwich can be a sacred act when eaten with gratitude to the God who provided it.

The biblical picture is clear: worship isn't compartmentalized to certain times, places, or activities. It's a continuous posture of honoring God with your entire existence.

The Idolatry of Sunday-Only Worship

When we reduce worship to what happens on Sunday mornings, we create a dangerously bifurcated life: "sacred" activities where God gets our attention, and "secular" activities where we're on our own. This division isn't just incorrect—it's actually a form of idolatry.

Why? Because it implies that God only deserves or desires a small portion of our lives. It treats Him like a weekly appointment rather than the Lord of every moment. It creates the illusion that we can give God His designated time slot and then live the rest of our lives according to our own preferences and priorities.

This Sunday-only approach produces Christians who sing passionately about surrender while living Monday through Saturday in ways that directly contradict those lyrics. We become masters of compartmentalization, experts at religious performance, and terrible at genuine worship.

Jesus had harsh words for this kind of disconnected religiosity: "This people honors me with their lips, but their heart is far from me; in vain do they worship me" (Matthew 15:8-9). Lip service without life alignment is vain worship—empty, worthless, accomplishing nothing.

The irony is that our Sunday "worship experiences" often become idols themselves. We become more passionate about the style of music, the quality of the production, or the emotional experience than about the God we're supposedly worshiping. We shop for churches based on the "worship vibe" rather than looking for places that will shape us into genuine worshipers in every area of life.

If you find yourself more concerned about the drums being too loud, the songs being too repetitive, or the leader wearing the wrong outfit than about whether your life throughout the week reflects God's character and values, you might be worshiping worship instead of worshiping God.

The Trinity of False Worship

While we're on the topic of idolatry, let's talk about the things we actually worship instead of God. Because here's the uncomfortable truth: you're always worshiping something. The question isn't whether you worship, but what you worship.

As humans, we tend to fall into worshiping three main categories of idols:

1. Comfort and Pleasure

This idol says, "Life should be easy, pain-free, and pleasant." Its worshipers make decisions based on what feels good rather than what honors God. They avoid difficult conversations, challenging commitments, and sacrificial service. They use people and love things, rather than loving people and using things.

You might be worshiping comfort and pleasure if:
- Your primary goal for each day is to avoid discomfort
- You regularly choose what feels good over what you know is right
- You resent God when life gets difficult
- You spend more time and money enhancing your comfort than helping others

Jesus directly confronted this idolatry when He said, "If anyone would come after me, let him deny himself and take up his cross daily and follow me" (Luke 9:23). The cross wasn't comfortable—it was an instrument of suffering and death. Jesus called His followers not to maximize pleasure but to embrace self-denial for the sake of something greater.

2. Success and Achievement

This idol says, "Your worth comes from what you accomplish and how others perceive your achievements." Its worshipers are driven by career advancement, social status, academic credentials, or measurable outcomes. They gauge their value by comparing themselves to others and constantly feel they need to do more or be more.

You might be worshiping success and achievement if:
- You feel worthless when you're not producing something
- Your identity is wrapped up in your job title, income, or accomplishments
- You're terrified of failure because it feels like a statement about your value
- You use metrics (followers, sales, growth, etc.) to determine if you're "winning" at life

God addressed this idolatry through the prophet Jeremiah: "Thus says the LORD: 'Let not the wise man boast in his wisdom, let not the mighty man boast in his might, let not the rich man boast in his riches, but let him who boasts boast in this, that he understands and knows me'" (Jeremiah 9:23-24). Your achievements aren't the point; knowing God is.

3. Approval and Acceptance

This idol says, "Being liked, included, and validated by others is essential for wellbeing." Its worshipers adjust their behavior, opinions, and even core beliefs to maintain others' approval. They're devastated by criticism, obsessed with their reputation, and perpetually anxious about what others think of them.

You might be worshiping approval and acceptance if:
- You regularly compromise your convictions to avoid conflict
- You feel devastated rather than merely disappointed when someone criticizes you
- You carefully curate your social media to present an idealized version of yourself
- You can't make decisions without consulting multiple people about what they think you should do

Jesus confronted this idol when He asked, "How can you believe, when you receive glory from one another and do not seek the glory that comes from the only God?" (John 5:44). The pursuit of human approval makes true faith impossible because it competes with seeking God's approval.

These false gods demand our worship but give nothing of lasting value in return. They promise fulfillment but leave us empty. They require constant sacrifice but never provide peace. They look appealing but ultimately destroy what matters most.

True worship of the living God, by contrast, often requires sacrificing comfort, success, and approval in the short term—but leads to genuine fulfillment, purposeful living, and lasting peace. As Jesus promised, "Whoever loses his life for my sake will find it" (Matthew 16:25).

Practical Ways to Worship Beyond Sunday

So what does whole-life worship actually look like in practice? How do we move from compartmentalized Sunday performances to authentic, integrated worship in everyday life? Here are some practical approaches:

1. The Morning Consecration

Start each day with a deliberate act of dedication. Before checking your phone or diving into responsibilities, take 30 seconds to pray: "God, I offer this day to you. Everything I do today—from the important to the mundane—I dedicate as worship to you. Help me glorify you in all of it."

This simple practice sets the tone for the day, reminding you that everything that follows can be an act of worship. It frames your entire day as an offering to God rather than just a series of tasks to complete.

King David modeled this approach in Psalm 5:3: "O LORD, in the morning you hear my voice; in the morning I prepare a sacrifice for you and watch." He began his day by preparing an offering for God and then lived expectantly, watching for God's presence and activity.

2. Work as Worship

Most of us spend the majority of our waking hours working, whether at a paid job, raising children, studying, or maintaining a home. This isn't time away from worship; it's one of your primary worship venues.

Transform your work into worship by:
- Seeing your work as service to God, not just to an employer or family
- Pursuing excellence not to impress others but to honor God with your best
- Maintaining integrity even when it costs you
- Using your skills to benefit others, not just yourself
- Expressing gratitude for the ability to contribute through your labor

Paul addressed slaves (the ancient equivalent of employees) with this perspective: "Whatever you do, work heartily, as for the Lord and not for men, knowing that from the Lord you will receive the inheritance as your reward" (Colossians 3:23-24). Your ultimate boss is God, not your human supervisor.

3. Gratitude Triggers

Intentionally link common daily experiences to gratitude. For example:
- Every time you stop at a red light, thank God for something specific
- Each time you wash your hands, express appreciation for clean water
- Whenever you eat, acknowledge God as the ultimate provider
- When you enter or exit your home, thank God for shelter
- As you get into bed, identify three gifts from the day

These triggers help transform routine moments into worship opportunities. They train you to see God's goodness throughout your day rather than just when prompted in a church service.

Gratitude is a form of worship because it acknowledges that "every good gift and every perfect gift is from above, coming down from the Father of lights" (James 1:17). When you thank God, you're recognizing His provision and expressing appropriate appreciation.

4. Sacred Listening

Most of us listen to something during our day—music, podcasts, audiobooks, radio. Transform this time into worship by deliberately including content that directs your attention toward God, shapes your thinking according to truth, or helps you love others better.

This doesn't mean you can only listen to Christian content. A thoughtful interview, a well-crafted story, or even instrumental music can direct your mind toward truth, beauty, and goodness—all of which reflect God's character.

The key is listening with discernment and intention, not passive consumption. As Paul instructs, "Finally, brothers, whatever is true, whatever is honorable, whatever is just, whatever is pure, whatever is lovely, whatever is commendable, if there is any excellence, if there is anything worthy of praise, think about these things" (Philippians 4:8). What enters your mind shapes your worship.

5. Relational Worship

Your interactions with others can be profound acts of worship when approached with the right heart. Practice seeing each person you encounter as a divine image-bearer worthy of dignity and respect, regardless of whether they're pleasant, useful, or agreeable.

Specific ways to worship through relationships include:
- Listening attentively without planning your response
- Showing patience with difficult people
- Speaking truth with kindness rather than harshness
- Forgiving instead of harboring resentment
- Serving without expecting recognition

Jesus directly connected our treatment of others with our worship of God: "As you did it to one of the least of these my brothers, you did it to me" (Matthew 25:40). How you treat people is how you treat Jesus—which means every human interaction is a worship opportunity.

6. Creation Appreciation

The natural world constantly declares God's glory (Psalm 19:1), but we're often too distracted to notice. Intentionally pause to observe and appreciate creation as an act of worship:
- Watch a sunrise or sunset with full attention
- Notice the intricate design of a flower, insect, or leaf
- Feel the rain, wind, or sunshine on your skin
- Listen to birds, flowing water, or rustling leaves
- Gaze at the night sky and contemplate its vastness

These moments of wonder naturally evoke worship as you recognize the power, creativity, and artistry of God displayed in what He's made. As Romans 1:20 notes, "His invisible attributes, namely, his eternal power and divine nature, have been clearly perceived, ever since the creation of the world, in the things that have been made."

7. Physical Worship

Your body itself can be an instrument of worship beyond just singing or raising hands in church. Romans 12:1 explicitly calls us to present our bodies as living sacrifices.

Ways to worship with your body include:
- Caring for your health as stewardship of God's temple (1 Corinthians 6:19-20)
- Using physical discipline as a spiritual training ground
- Employing your strength to serve others in practical ways
- Practicing self-control in eating, sleeping, sexuality, etc.
- Resting appropriately as an acknowledgment of your limitations and God's sufficiency

This concept of bodily worship challenges our tendency to separate the physical from the spiritual. In God's economy, how you treat and use your physical self is inherently spiritual.

8. Financial Worship

How you earn, spend, save, and give money reveals what you truly value and trust. Transform your financial life into worship by:
- Giving generously and joyfully, not grudgingly
- Earning honestly, even when dishonesty might be profitable
- Spending thoughtfully, recognizing God's provision
- Saving wisely, neither hoarding out of fear nor neglecting stewardship
- Contentment with what you have rather than constant craving for more

Jesus said, "Where your treasure is, there your heart will be also" (Matthew 6:21), directly connecting our financial choices with our spiritual orientation. Your bank statement and credit card bill are theological documents—they show what you actually worship, not just what you say you worship.

Transforming Sunday Worship Too

While we've been emphasizing that worship extends far beyond Sunday mornings, that doesn't mean corporate worship gatherings aren't important. They absolutely are—just not in the way many of us think.

The purpose of gathered worship isn't primarily emotional experience, musical enjoyment, or religious obligation. It's about the people of God encouraging one another, aligning themselves with truth, and practicing together what they're called to live individually.

Here's how to transform your approach to Sunday worship:

1. Prepare Your Heart

Don't just show up at church and expect to instantly engage in meaningful worship. Take time beforehand to prepare your heart:
- Get adequate rest the night before (seriously, this matters)
- Pray before you arrive, asking God to make you receptive
- Confess any known sin that might hinder your communion with God
- Resolve conflicts with others when possible (Matthew 5:23-24)
- Review the past week, noticing where God has been at work

This preparation helps you transition from the scattered attention of daily life to the focused engagement of corporate worship. It recognizes that meaningful worship requires intentionality, not just attendance.

2. Participate, Don't Consume

Many of us approach church with a consumer mindset: "What am I going to get out of this?" Instead, ask, "How can I fully participate in what God is doing here?"

Active participation might include:
- Singing wholeheartedly, even if you don't like the song or can't carry a tune
- Engaging mentally with the Scripture reading and sermon, not just letting the words wash over you
- Praying along with corporate prayers rather than mentally checking out
- Noticing and encouraging others in the congregation
- Arriving on time and staying until the end as a sign of respect and commitment

Hebrews 10:24-25 frames gathering together not as a spectator event but as mutual encouragement: "Let us consider how to stir up one another to love and good works, not neglecting to meet together, as is the habit of some, but encouraging one another."

3. Focus on God, Not Just Experience

It's easy to evaluate worship based on how it made you feel—whether the music moved you emotionally or the sermon resonated with your situation. But authentic worship focuses primarily on God's character and actions, not your experience.

Even when you don't feel emotionally engaged, you can still offer true worship by:
- Declaring God's attributes and actions regardless of your emotional state
- Expressing gratitude for specific ways God has been faithful
- Submitting your will to His, especially when you don't feel like it
- Remembering and affirming the truth of the gospel
- Offering your attention as a gift, even when your mind wants to wander

Job exemplified this when he declared, "The LORD gave, and the LORD has taken away; blessed be the name of the LORD" (Job 1:21). He worshiped not because he felt good—he had just lost everything—but because God remained worthy of worship despite his circumstances.

4. Connect Sunday to Monday

Don't treat Sunday worship as disconnected from the rest of your life. Intentionally bridge these worlds by:
- Taking notes during the sermon about specific applications
- Discussing with others how the worship themes apply to daily living
- Selecting one song lyric or Scripture verse to meditate on throughout the week
- Identifying a truth from the gathering that addresses a current challenge
- Building relationships with other worshipers that continue beyond Sunday

James warns against being "hearers only, deceiving yourselves" and calls us instead to be "doers of the word" (James 1:22-25). Sunday worship should equip and inspire your daily worship, not stand apart from it.

When Worship Feels Impossible

Let's get real: sometimes worship is the last thing you feel like doing. When you're exhausted, disappointed, angry, or suffering, lifting your hands (literally or figuratively) can feel impossible or even hypocritical.

The psalms give us permission to be honest about these struggles. Many psalms begin with raw expressions of pain, confusion, or anger before moving toward praise. This pattern teaches us that genuine worship doesn't require denying your actual feelings or pretending everything is fine when it's not.

Here's how to approach worship in difficult seasons:

1. Start with Honesty

Don't begin with forced praise if that's not where you are. Start by telling God exactly how you feel—your doubts, disappointments, frustrations, and fears. This honesty isn't disrespectful; it's relational intimacy.

Psalm 13 begins with "How long, O LORD? Will you forget me forever? How long will you hide your face from me?" The psalmist doesn't sugarcoat his experience of divine absence. Yet remarkably, the same psalm ends with "I will sing to the LORD, because he has dealt bountifully with me." Honesty creates the pathway to authentic praise.

2. Worship from Memory, Not Just Feeling

When you can't see God's goodness in your current circumstances, worship based on what you remember of His character and past faithfulness.

The psalmist models this approach in Psalm 42:4-6: "These things I remember, as I pour out my soul: how I would go with the throng and lead them in procession to the house of God with glad shouts and songs of praise... Why are you cast down, O my soul, and why are you in turmoil within me? Hope in God; for I shall again praise him, my salvation and my God."

He acknowledges his current emotional turmoil while intentionally recalling past experiences of God's presence. The memory becomes a foundation for hope when immediate experience seems empty.

3. Borrow Faith When Necessary

When your own faith feels weak or absent, lean on the faith of others—through Scripture, worship music written by believers who've weathered similar storms, or present-day friends who can believe on your behalf until your faith revives.

This isn't fake or secondhand faith; it's participating in the communion of saints described in Hebrews 12:1—being "surrounded by so great a cloud of witnesses" who testify to God's faithfulness even when you struggle to see it.

4. Offer Minimal Worship

Sometimes the best worship you can offer is very small—a whispered "help," a moment of stillness, a single tear, a brief glance heavenward. This isn't inferior worship; it might be the most costly and precious worship you ever give.

Jesus affirmed the value of minimal offerings when He praised the widow's two small coins above the large donations of the wealthy (Luke 21:1-4). It's not the size of the offering but the heart behind it that matters to God.

5. Remember That Lament Is Worship

Biblical lament—the honest expression of pain, confusion, and complaint to God—is itself a form of worship. It demonstrates trust that God is listening, that He cares about your suffering, and that He's the appropriate recipient of your deepest pain.

Approximately one-third of the psalms are laments, suggesting that expressions of sorrow and questioning have a legitimate place in the worship life of believers. Lament honors God by refusing to turn away from Him in pain, instead bringing that pain directly to Him.

The Worship Experiment: 7 Days of Intentional Worship

Ready to expand your understanding and practice of worship beyond Sunday mornings? Try this seven-day experiment designed to help you integrate worship into all areas of life:

Day 1: Work Worship

Focus on transforming your primary work (job, studies, homemaking, etc.) into conscious worship:
- Before beginning, specifically dedicate your work to God
- Set hourly reminders to pause and remember who you're ultimately working for
- Look for ways your work reflects God's character (creating, ordering, nurturing, restoring, etc.)
- Identify and pray for the people who will benefit from your labor
- At the end of the day, offer your work to God as a completed sacrifice, regardless of results

Reflect: How did consciously working for God rather than primarily for yourself or others change your experience?

Day 2: Body Worship

Focus on honoring God through your physical existence:
- Thank God for specific aspects of your body's design and function
- Make one healthy choice explicitly as an act of stewardship, not vanity
- Use your physical strength or ability to serve someone else
- Practice being fully present in physical sensations (taste, touch, sight, sound, smell)
- Notice and appropriately respond to your body's needs for rest, movement, nourishment

Reflect: How does treating your body as a worship instrument rather than just a physical vehicle change your relationship with it?

Day 3: Relationship Worship

Focus on making your interactions with others acts of worship:
- Before each significant conversation, silently pray, "Help me see and serve this person as you would"
- Practice really listening instead of just waiting to speak
- Look for specific evidences of God's image in each person you encounter

- Choose patience in a situation where you'd normally be irritated
- Express specific appreciation to at least three people

Reflect: How does viewing relationships as worship opportunities change how you approach interactions?

Day 4: Creation Worship

Focus on recognizing and responding to God through His creation:
- Spend at least 10 minutes outside with no phone or distractions, simply noticing natural beauty
- Learn something new about the natural world and let it prompt awe
- Thank God for something in creation that directly benefits your life
- Care for some aspect of creation as an act of stewardship (plants, animals, natural resources)
- Use creation as a prayer prompt (let weather, animals, plants, etc. guide your prayers)

Reflect: How does intentionally engaging with creation as a worship venue affect your awareness of God's presence and character?

Day 5: Resource Worship

Focus on honoring God through how you use money and possessions:
- Identify one way to be more generous today
- Make one purchasing decision based primarily on ethical considerations, not just price or convenience
- Express gratitude for three material provisions you typically take for granted
- Evaluate one area where discontentment might be affecting your relationship with God
- Choose simplicity in one small way as a statement of trust in God's sufficiency

Reflect: How does seeing your resources as worship tools rather than just personal assets change your relationship with money and possessions?

Day 6: Challenge Worship

Focus on finding God in difficulties and challenges:
- Identify a current struggle and look for how God might be working within it
- Express gratitude for something difficult that shaped you positively in the past
- Practice trusting God with an outcome you can't control
- Reflect on how dependence on God during challenges itself honors Him
- Respond to one difficult person or situation with grace rather than resentment

Reflect: How does approaching challenges as worship contexts rather than just problems to solve change your perspective?

Day 7: Sabbath Worship

Focus on honoring God through rest and celebration:
- Set aside regular activities for a designated period (even a few hours if a full day isn't possible)
- Disconnect from technology that demands your attention
- Engage in activities that bring genuine delight, seeing enjoyment as a form of worship
- Reflect on the previous six days, noticing where God has been present
- Practice being rather than doing, acknowledging that your value comes from who you are in Christ, not what you produce

Reflect: How does intentional rest and celebration honor God in ways that activity and productivity cannot?

After completing this experiment, consider which forms of worship felt most natural and which were most challenging. This reveals both your worship strengths and growth areas. Choose one challenging form to continue practicing regularly, allowing God to expand your worship vocabulary beyond what comes easily.

Signs of Growth in Worship

How do you know if you're growing as a worshiper? Here are some indicators that worship is becoming more integrated into your entire life:

1. **You're increasingly aware of God's presence in ordinary moments,** not just during overtly religious activities or emotional experiences.

2. **Your decision-making process naturally includes consideration of what honors God,** not just what benefits you or pleases others.

3. **You find yourself responding to beauty, goodness, and truth with gratitude to their Source,** rather than just enjoying them for their own sake.

4. **Your emotional relationship with God has more texture and range,** including not just positive feelings like joy and peace but also holy anger at injustice, godly sorrow over sin, and appropriate fear of the Lord.

5. **You're becoming more attentive to idolatry in your own life,** noticing when good things (work, relationships, comfort, etc.) start functioning as ultimate things.

6. **Sunday worship feels more like a continuation of your ongoing worship life rather than a disconnected religious event.**

7. **Your worship is increasingly about God's glory rather than your emotional satisfaction,** though you may paradoxically experience deeper joy as a result.

8. **You're more able to worship authentically in difficult circumstances,** not denying the pain but finding God within it.

Notice that none of these growth indicators involve how many worship songs you know, how intensely you feel during worship sets, or how stylistically contemporary or traditional your worship preferences are. Real worship growth transforms your entire orientation toward life, not just your religious expressions.

Common Worship Blockers (And How to Overcome Them)

Even with the best intentions, certain habits, mindsets, and circumstances can block your ability to worship. Here are some common worship blockers and strategies for addressing them:

1. Distraction

In our notification-saturated world, sustained attention has become increasingly difficult. Yet worship requires focused attention on God rather than fragmented awareness.

Strategies for overcoming distraction:
- Create technology boundaries (no-phone zones/times, notification settings, digital Sabbaths)
- Practice single-tasking instead of multitasking
- Use physical postures that help focus (sitting upright, closing eyes, etc.)
- Prepare physical spaces that minimize distractions
- Train attention through contemplative practices like Lectio Divina or centering prayer

Jesus understood the challenge of distraction when He taught, "When you pray, go into your room and shut the door and pray to your Father who is in secret" (Matthew 6:6). Creating boundaries around potential distractions supports focused worship.

2. Hurry

Worship requires a pace that allows for awareness, reflection, and response. When you're constantly rushing from one thing to the next, worship becomes challenging if not impossible.

Strategies for overcoming hurry:
- Build margin into your schedule rather than booking every minute
- Say no to good opportunities that would overload your life
- Practice arriving early rather than rushing in late
- Schedule buffer time between activities for mental/spiritual transition
- Set a sustainable pace for your life rather than constantly sprinting

Jesus never rushed despite having the most important mission in history. He maintained an unhurried pace that allowed for interruptions, connection, and presence with God and others.

3. Unconfessed Sin

Persistent, unaddressed sin creates a barrier in your relationship with God that hinders worship. As Isaiah 59:2 says, "Your iniquities have made a separation between you and your God, and your sins have hidden his face from you so that he does not hear."

Strategies for addressing unconfessed sin:
- Practice regular self-examination and confession
- Establish accountability with trusted believers
- Respond promptly to the Holy Spirit's conviction rather than rationalizing

- Receive God's forgiveness fully rather than continuing to punish yourself
- Take practical steps toward repentance, not just feeling sorry

The good news is that confession immediately removes this barrier. As 1 John 1:9 promises, "If we confess our sins, he is faithful and just to forgive us our sins and to cleanse us from all unrighteousness."

4. Comparison and Competition

When worship becomes performance-oriented or comparison-driven, its true nature is corrupted. Focusing on how you appear to others or how your worship compares to theirs removes God from the center.

Strategies for overcoming comparison:
- Close your eyes during corporate worship to reduce visual distractions
- Practice hidden forms of worship that no one else will ever see
- Celebrate the diverse expressions of worship in Scripture and church history
- Identify and confess competitive attitudes in spiritual contexts
- Focus on God's unique relationship with you rather than how you measure up to others

Jesus condemned those who practiced their spirituality to be seen by others (Matthew 6:1-18). Authentic worship is directed toward God, not human observers.

5. Worship Consumerism

When you approach worship primarily asking "What do I get out of this?" rather than "What can I give to God?", you've adopted a consumer mindset that fundamentally distorts worship.

Strategies for overcoming consumerism:
- Shift your language from "I liked/didn't like that worship" to "That worship honored God"
- Stay with a church through seasons when the worship style isn't your preference
- Engage fully even with songs or liturgical elements you wouldn't choose
- Focus on giving to God through worship rather than receiving an experience
- Prepare to worship rather than expecting leaders to generate your participation

True worship transforms you from a consumer to a contributor, from audience to participant, from critic to offerer.

The Kick in the Pants: Worship or Worthless Ship?

Let's get brutally honest for a moment. Most of what passes for worship in our lives—both inside and outside church—is actually worthless ship. It's an empty vessel that looks like it might float but has no real substance.

We sing songs about surrender while white-knuckling control of our lives. We raise hands to lyrics about God being enough while our calendars and bank accounts scream that we're trusting in everything but Him. We belt out "break my heart for what breaks yours" while scrolling past human suffering without a second thought. We claim "I'll give you everything" while calculating the minimum we can give and still feel spiritual.

This disconnect between our worship words and worship life isn't just hypocritical—it's exactly what God said He hates: "This people honors me with their lips, but their heart is far from me" (Matthew 15:8).

God doesn't want your Sunday morning performance. He doesn't need your raised hands, your emotional tears, or your perfect attendance record. He wants your Monday morning choices. Your Thursday afternoon priorities. Your Saturday night decisions. He wants worship that costs you something, that changes how you live, that realigns what you value.

If your worship stops when the music ends, you're doing it wrong. If your worship is limited to a building or an event, you've missed the whole point. If your worship doesn't transform how you spend your time, money, and attention, it's not worship at all—it's religious entertainment.

The question isn't whether you worship. Everyone worships something. The question is whether what you worship is worthy of your life's devotion. Is it big enough to build your life around? Is it true enough to stake your eternity on? Is it good enough to transform you into something beautiful?

Comfort and convenience won't cut it. Success and achievement will eventually disappoint. Human approval evaporates like morning dew. These false gods demand everything but deliver nothing that lasts.

Only the living God—the Creator who spoke galaxies into existence, the Redeemer who died to reconcile you to Himself, the Sustainer who holds every atom together by His power—is worthy of true worship. Only He deserves the devotion of your entire existence, not just your religious compartment.

So here's your challenge: Stop treating worship like a Sunday activity and start recognizing it as a life orientation. Stop confusing emotional experiences with spiritual reality. Stop saying you surrender while living like you're in charge.

Start seeing every moment as a worship opportunity. Every decision as a declaration of what you truly value. Every action as a statement of what you really believe.

Because worship isn't about the song—it's about the surrender. It's not about feeling something—it's about giving everything. It's not about what happens in a service—it's about what happens in a life.

What are you really worshiping? Your comfort? Your reputation? Your autonomy? Your pleasures? Your achievements? Or the God who made you, redeemed you, and calls you His own?

The answer isn't found in what you say. It's found in how you live.

So live like He's really on the throne. Live like His opinion matters more than human approval. Live like His promises are more reliable than your plans. Live like worship isn't just what you do sometimes but who you are always.

Because that's what worship really is. Not a performance, but a life surrendered. Not a feeling, but a commitment. Not a moment, but a lifetime of declaring, through both lips and life, that God alone is worthy.

Start now. Start where you are. Start with whatever you have. But for heaven's sake, start worshiping for real.

Chapter 7:

Guidance – Seeking Wisdom Without the BS

Let's be honest: most of us treat God like a divine GPS that we only check when we're completely lost, the road looks scary, or we're about to make a life-altering turn.

The rest of the time? We're cruising along, making decisions based on what feels good, what other people think we should do, or what seems least likely to mess up our comfortable little lives. Then we have the audacity to wonder why we keep ending up in spiritual dead ends and emotional ditches.

This approach to divine guidance is about as effective as checking Google Maps once a year and expecting to navigate daily commutes, road trips, and cross-country moves without a single wrong turn. It's not just ineffective—it's delusional.

But what's the alternative? It's certainly not the weird, hyper-spiritualized approach where people claim "God told me" about everything from their coffee order to their career path, often without having spent more than five distracted minutes in prayer that month. You know the type—they've got a direct line to the Almighty for parking spot selection but somehow missed the memo about loving their neighbor and caring for the poor.

Here's the deal: God does want to guide you. He's not playing cosmic hide-and-seek with His will, sadistically watching as you stumble around in the dark. As James 1:5 plainly states, "If any of you lacks wisdom, let him ask God, who gives generously to all without reproach, and it will be given him."

But guidance from God is a relationship, not a transaction. It's a daily walking-together, not an occasional emergency hotline. It's about developing the ability to recognize His voice amid all the noise—which happens through consistent connection, not crisis-only contact.

In this chapter, we're going to cut through both the passive negligence and the pseudo-spiritual nonsense to get at what seeking God's guidance actually looks like in real life. Not the Instagram-worthy spiritual moments, but the everyday, unsexy work of learning to hear God's voice and follow His lead—even when (especially when) it contradicts your carefully laid plans or deeply held desires.

Why We Suck at Seeking Guidance

Before we dive into how to get better at this, let's get real about why most of us are so terrible at seeking God's direction in the first place. Understanding these barriers is crucial because they'll keep sabotaging your efforts unless you identify and address them.

1. Pride: "I Got This"

The most fundamental barrier to seeking guidance is the delusion that we don't really need it. We might not say this out loud (especially in church circles), but our actions reveal our true beliefs. We think we're smart enough, experienced enough, or intuitive enough to figure life out on our own.

Proverbs 3:5-6 directly confronts this mindset: "Trust in the LORD with all your heart, and do not lean on your own understanding. In all your ways acknowledge him, and he will make straight your paths."

Notice it doesn't say, "Don't use your brain" or "Understanding is bad." It says don't LEAN on your own understanding. Don't put your weight on it. Don't make it your primary support. Because your understanding, no matter how impressive, is woefully incomplete.

Think about it: You don't know what will happen tomorrow. You can't see all the factors at play in any situation. You're blind to your own biases and blind spots. You're influenced by cultural assumptions you're not even aware of. And yet you think you can navigate life's complexity without guidance from the One who sees it all? That's not confidence—that's arrogance.

2. Impatience: "I Need Answers NOW"

We live in an instant society. We can get same-day delivery, stream any movie on demand, and get angry when a webpage takes more than three seconds to load. This impatience infects our spiritual lives too. We want God to operate at our speed, providing immediate, clear answers to our questions.

But divine guidance rarely works that way. More often, it unfolds gradually, requiring patience and persistent seeking. As Psalm 27:14 instructs, "Wait for the LORD; be strong, and let your heart take courage; wait for the LORD!"

When we're unwilling to wait, we typically default to one of two equally problematic approaches: we either make impulsive decisions based on minimal information, or we invent "signs" to convince ourselves God has spoken when He hasn't. Both lead to disaster.

3. Fear: "What If I Don't Like the Answer?"

Sometimes we avoid seeking guidance because, deep down, we're afraid of what we might hear. We have a sneaking suspicion God's direction might contradict our desires, require uncomfortable changes, or lead us into challenging territory.

Jesus highlighted this reality in John 3:19-20: "The light has come into the world, and people loved the darkness rather than the light because their works were evil. For everyone who does wicked things hates the light and does not come to the light, lest his works should be exposed."

While this passage speaks specifically about sin being exposed, the principle applies broadly: we avoid light (including the illuminating guidance of God) when we suspect it will reveal things we'd prefer to keep hidden—even from ourselves. We don't want to confront our selfish motives, comfortable idolatries, or misplaced priorities.

So instead of sincerely asking, "God, what should I do?" we either don't ask at all, or we ask while already having decided what answer we want to hear.

4. Confusion: "How Do I Even Know It's God?"

A legitimate barrier for many sincere Christians is uncertainty about how to recognize God's voice among the many competing voices in their heads and lives. They genuinely want guidance but aren't confident they can distinguish divine direction from their own thoughts, cultural conditioning, or even deceptive influences.

Jesus addressed this in John 10:27: "My sheep hear my voice, and I know them, and they follow me." The implication is clear: His followers can learn to recognize His voice. But like any voice recognition, this is a skill developed through regular exposure and attentive listening, not an automatic ability.

Without this skill development, people either become paralyzed (afraid to move without 100% certainty) or presumptuous (claiming divine authority for what are essentially personal preferences).

5. Compartmentalization: "God for Sundays, Me for Mondays"

Many Christians have unconsciously divided their lives into "spiritual matters" (where they might seek God's input) and "secular matters" (where they rely entirely on conventional wisdom or personal judgment).

They'll pray about which church to attend or whether to lead a small group, but wouldn't think to seek God's guidance about their career, finances, relationships, entertainment choices, or political views. These areas they reserve for their own autonomous decision-making.

This artificial division has no biblical basis. Colossians 3:17 instructs, "Whatever you do, in word or deed, do everything in the name of the Lord Jesus, giving thanks to God the Father through him." Everything means everything—not just the parts you've labeled "spiritual."

The Foundations of True Guidance

Now that we've identified the barriers, let's establish a more solid understanding of how God actually guides His people. There are four primary channels of divine guidance, and they work together like instruments in an orchestra—each with its distinct contribution, but creating harmony when properly aligned.

1. Scripture: The Authoritative Foundation

The Bible is the bedrock of divine guidance, the standard against which all other perceived guidance must be measured. As Psalm 119:105 states, "Your word is a lamp to my feet and a light to my path."

This doesn't mean you'll find a verse that specifically tells you whether to take that job in Seattle or marry that person you're dating. But Scripture does provide:

- Clear commands that eliminate certain options (If that "opportunity" requires dishonesty, Scripture has already ruled it out)
- Principles that apply across situations (Love your neighbor, pursue unity, forgive as you've been forgiven)
- Values that should shape your decisions (Justice, mercy, faithfulness, generosity)
- Wisdom for navigating life's complexity (Particularly in books like Proverbs, Ecclesiastes, and James)
- Examples of how God has led others (Both positive models to follow and cautionary tales to avoid)

The problem is that many Christians expect Scripture to function like a crystal ball or direct hotline when it's more like a comprehensive worldview that shapes how you see and respond to everything. It's not just an answer book; it's a lens through which you interpret life and a compass that orients your direction.

2 Timothy 3:16-17 explains that Scripture is "profitable for teaching, for reproof, for correction, and for training in righteousness, that the man of God may be complete, equipped for every good work." Notice the comprehensive language—"complete" and "equipped for every good work." The Bible provides the essential foundation and framework for all divine guidance.

2. The Holy Spirit: The Internal Guide

While Scripture provides the objective standard, the Holy Spirit offers personalized, moment-by-moment guidance as we navigate specific situations. Jesus promised in John 16:13, "When the Spirit of truth comes, he will guide you into all the truth."

The Spirit's guidance typically manifests through:

- Internal promptings (A sense of being drawn toward or away from particular choices)
- Conviction (Clear awareness of right and wrong in specific situations)
- Illumination (Suddenly understanding Scripture or a situation with new clarity)
- Peace or disquiet (What Colossians 3:15 calls letting "the peace of Christ rule in your hearts")
- Spiritual gifts (Particularly wisdom, discernment, and sometimes prophecy)

It's important to note that the Spirit's guidance never contradicts Scripture. God doesn't send mixed messages. The same Spirit who inspired the Bible (2 Peter 1:21) won't lead you to violate its teaching. This is a crucial test for distinguishing genuine spiritual guidance from emotional impulses or deceptive influences.

The Spirit's guidance also typically aligns with the fruit of the Spirit described in Galatians 5:22-23: "love, joy, peace, patience, kindness, goodness, faithfulness, gentleness, self-control." If what you perceive as "guidance" leads toward anger, division, pride, or impulsivity, it's probably not from the Holy Spirit.

3. Community: The External Confirmation

God rarely intends us to discern His will in isolation. He's established the church as a community of mutual guidance, correction, and confirmation. Proverbs 11:14 wisely notes, "Where there is no guidance, a people falls, but in an abundance of counselors there is safety."

The community aspect of guidance includes:

- Direct advice from mature believers who know you well
- The collective wisdom of church tradition and teaching

- Confirmation of personal leadings through others independently sensing the same direction
- Loving correction when you're veering off course
- Accountability for following through on direction received

Think of community as a safeguard against self-deception. We all have blind spots, biases, and the capacity for remarkable self-justification. Other believers can see things in us and our situations that we cannot see ourselves.

Acts 13:1-3 provides an excellent example of communal guidance. The direction for Barnabas and Saul to be set apart for mission work came not through their private prayer alone, but was confirmed and commissioned by the church community as they worshiped and fasted together.

4. Circumstances: The Providential Alignment

While not as directly authoritative as the other channels, circumstances often serve as supporting evidence of God's guidance. Open and closed doors, timing, resources, and opportunities can all be part of how God directs our paths.

Romans 8:28 assures us that "for those who love God all things work together for good, for those who are called according to his purpose." This doesn't mean everything that happens is good, but that God can work through all circumstances—even difficult ones—to accomplish His purposes and guide His people.

Circumstantial guidance might include:

- Unexpected opportunities that align with Spirit-led desires
- Closed doors that redirect your path
- Providential connections with specific people at just the right time
- Resources becoming available when needed for God-given vision
- Timing that could not have been manufactured or manipulated

However, circumstances alone are an insufficient guide. Sometimes the path God has for us requires pushing through obstacles rather than interpreting them as closed doors. Sometimes material success or ease can lead us away from God's best rather than toward it.

Circumstances should generally be viewed as confirmation of guidance received through Scripture, the Spirit, and community—not as the primary source of direction.

Practical Steps for Seeking Guidance

Now that we understand the foundational elements of divine guidance, let's get practical. Here's how to develop a lifestyle of seeking and recognizing God's direction:

1. Build the Daily Habit of Listening

Guidance isn't primarily about big moments of decision; it's about the daily practice of listening to God that makes those big decisions clearer. As Jesus said in Luke 16:10, "One who is faithful in a very little is also faithful in much."

Practical steps for daily listening:

Scripture Immersion: Spend time daily reading the Bible with an attitude of receptivity, not just information gathering. Ask, "God, what are you saying to me through this passage?" Read slowly enough to allow for reflection.

Intentional Prayer: Include listening time in your prayers, not just talking. Try writing your prayers in a journal, then sitting quietly with pen in hand, ready to write any impressions or thoughts that come. This isn't about mystical experiences; it's about creating space to hear.

Media Fast: Regularly disconnect from the noise that drowns out God's voice. Silence your phone, turn off the TV, and step away from social media. This isn't punishment; it's creating bandwidth to hear the still, small voice that's often drowned out by constant input.

Regular Review: At the end of each day, reflect on where you sensed God's presence or direction. Where did you feel peace? What insights came to mind? What Scripture seemed particularly relevant? This trains your ability to recognize divine guidance in real-time.

2. Bring Everything to God, Not Just the "Big Stuff"

Many Christians only seek guidance for major life decisions while handling everything else autonomously. This creates a disconnected relationship where you're essentially a stranger to God most of the time, then suddenly expect intimate communication in moments of crisis.

Practical steps for comprehensive guidance-seeking:

Morning Direction: Start each day by inviting God into all aspects of your day. "Lord, guide my conversations, my work decisions, my responses to challenges."

Decision Triggers: Create a habit of pausing for a brief prayer before meetings, phone calls, shopping, or other routine activities. Simply ask, "God, how do you want me to approach this?"

Gratitude Prompts: Set reminders to thank God throughout the day, focusing attention on His ongoing presence and provision. Gratitude creates awareness of God's activity in your life.

Purpose Alignment: Regularly ask, "How does this activity/choice/priority align with God's purposes for my life?" This keeps even small decisions connected to bigger spiritual realities.

3. Learn to Recognize God's Voice

Developing the ability to distinguish God's voice from other voices requires intentional practice. As Henri Nouwen wisely noted, "The question is not 'Does God speak?' but 'Do we hear?'"

Practical steps for voice recognition:

Study the Character of God: The better you know who God is through Scripture, the easier it is to recognize communication that aligns with His character. Could the God revealed in Jesus say this thing you think you're hearing?

Test Impressions: When you sense guidance, apply these filters: Does it align with Scripture? Would mature believers confirm it? Does it produce the fruit of the Spirit? Does it glorify Christ rather than self?

Start Small: Practice listening for God's guidance in low-stakes situations before expecting crystal clarity on life-altering decisions. Did God prompt you to call someone, speak an encouraging word, or show kindness in a specific way? Following through on these smaller promptings builds confidence in hearing correctly.

Record and Review: Keep a journal of what you believe God has spoken to you, then review it over time. This helps you identify patterns, recognize when you've misheard, and build confidence in genuine guidance.

4. Develop a Personal Board of Directors

No significant organization makes major decisions based solely on the CEO's intuition. They have boards of directors that provide wisdom, accountability, and diverse perspectives. You need the same for your spiritual life.

Practical steps for community guidance:

Identify Wise Counselors: Look for people who: a) love God deeply, b) know you well, c) aren't afraid to tell you hard truths, and d) have demonstrated wisdom in their own lives. These aren't just friends who will validate whatever you want to do.

Regular Connection: Meet consistently with these individuals, not just in times of crisis. Share your life openly—your struggles, questions, and areas where you're seeking direction.

Structured Discernment: For major decisions, create a intentional process with your spiritual advisors. Share what you believe God might be saying, ask for their honest input, and commit together to prayer over a specified timeframe.

Accountability Questions: Invite specific questions about your walk with God, areas of temptation, and follow-through on guidance already received. "Have I obeyed the last thing God clearly showed me?" is often more important than seeking new guidance.

5. Make Peace Your Referee

Colossians 3:15 offers a practical test for guidance: "Let the peace of Christ rule [literally: act as referee or umpire] in your hearts." While peace isn't the only factor in discernment, it's an important indicator.

Practical steps for peace-based discernment:

Distinguish Types of Discomfort: Learn to differentiate between the discomfort of growth-producing challenge (which may be from God) and the disquiet of moving against your spiritual grain (which often signals a wrong direction). The first feels scary but right; the second feels wrong at a deep level.

Create Decision Space: When facing important choices, create enough margin to move beyond the anxiety of decision-making to a place where you can assess your true peace level. This might mean taking a personal retreat day or committing to a week of focused prayer before deciding.

Peace Inventory: When considering options, physically write down your peace level with each possibility on a scale of 1-10. Return to this inventory over several days, noting whether peace increases or decreases with time and prayer.

Physical Awareness: Pay attention to how your body responds to different options. Tension, tightness, or nausea might indicate a lack of peace, while relaxation and a sense of "rightness" often accompany peace-filled directions.

How to Navigate Big Decisions

While seeking guidance should be a daily practice, certain life decisions naturally call for more intentional discernment. Here's a process for navigating major choices:

Step 1: Clarify the Real Question

Often, we ask the wrong questions, which leads to unhelpful answers. Before diving into discernment, make sure you're addressing the actual issue.

For example, instead of "Should I take this job?" the real question might be:
- "What work environment allows me to best use my gifts?"
- "What matters most in this season of life—stability or growth?"
- "Am I running toward opportunity or away from challenges?"

Or instead of "Should I marry this person?" the deeper questions might include:
- "Are we spiritually aligned in our core values and vision?"

- "Am I seeking companionship out of wholeness or fear of being alone?"
- "Does this relationship draw both of us closer to Christ?"

Taking time to identify the real issues at stake creates space for more meaningful guidance.

Step 2: Consult Scripture First

Before seeking subjective confirmation, establish the objective boundaries from God's Word. This eliminates options that might feel right but contradict biblical wisdom or commands.

Ask:
- Are there clear biblical principles that apply to this situation?
- Does Scripture address the underlying motivations of my choices?
- What biblical examples might provide insight into this decision?
- Have I considered the wisdom literature (Proverbs, Ecclesiastes, James) for practical guidance?

For instance, Scripture won't tell you which house to buy, but it will give principles about debt, stewardship, hospitality, and contentment that should shape your housing decisions.

Step 3: Pray Specifically and Persistently

Too often, our prayers about big decisions are vague and sporadic. Instead:

- Write out specific prayers about each aspect of the decision
- Commit to praying for a defined period before deciding (unless there's genuine urgency)
- Include thanksgiving for guidance already received and trust in God's faithfulness
- Involve others in praying with and for you about the decision
- Be honest about your desires while remaining open to correction

Jesus modeled this approach in Gethsemane, praying specifically about the cup before Him while ultimately surrendering to the Father's will (Matthew 26:39).

Step 4: Gather Wise Counsel Strategically

Not all counsel is created equal, and seeking too many opinions can create confusion rather than clarity. Be intentional about whose input you seek:

- Identify people with relevant experience or expertise
- Include those who know you well enough to speak to your specific blind spots

- Seek diversity of perspective while maintaining unity of spiritual values
- Ask specific questions rather than just sharing the situation generally
- Listen fully before defending or explaining your preferred outcome

Proverbs 15:22 affirms, "Without counsel plans fail, but with many advisers they succeed." The emphasis is on the quality of counsel, not just the quantity of opinions.

Step 5: Evaluate Circumstances with Discernment

Look at the practical realities surrounding your decision, remembering that open doors aren't automatically divine direction, and obstacles aren't necessarily stop signs.

Consider:
- Which options align best with the overall direction God has been leading in your life?
- What unique opportunities or limitations might be part of God's guidance?
- How might timing be a factor in this decision?
- Are resources available in ways that seem providential rather than merely convenient?
- What "coincidences" might actually be divine coordination?

Acts 16:6-10 shows Paul navigating a combination of closed doors (being "forbidden by the Holy Spirit to speak the word in Asia") and open opportunities (the vision of the Macedonian man) to discern his missionary direction.

Step 6: Make a Faith-Based Decision

At some point, you must move from seeking guidance to acting on it. After thorough discernment, commit to a direction with faith that God will continue to guide as you move forward.

Remember:
- Few decisions are irreversible; most can be adjusted as you gain new clarity
- Paralysis from fear of making the wrong choice is not spiritual wisdom
- God can work through imperfect decisions made with sincere hearts
- Moving forward in faith often creates clarity that couldn't come through endless deliberation
- Obedience to clear guidance already received often precedes new guidance for next steps

Joshua didn't receive detailed battle plans for the entire Promised Land conquest at once. He received direction for Jericho, acted on it, and then received guidance for the next challenge. Guidance often unfolds as we walk in obedience to what we already know.

Step 7: Remain Flexible and Attentive

After deciding, continue listening for potential course corrections. Guidance isn't a one-time event but an ongoing relationship.

This means:
- Regularly evaluating whether you're experiencing the fruit expected from this direction
- Remaining humble enough to admit if you misunderstood or need to adjust
- Continuing spiritual practices that keep you sensitive to God's leading
- Trusting God's ability to redirect even if your initial discernment was imperfect

The disciples' early ministry in Acts shows this flexibility—they had plans, but remained responsive to divine redirection through circumstances, visions, and the Spirit's prompting.

Common Guidance Myths and Mistakes

Let's address some pervasive misconceptions that derail many Christians' attempts to discern God's guidance:

Myth #1: "If It's God's Will, It Will Be Easy"

This dangerous assumption has no biblical basis. In fact, Scripture often shows the opposite—God's will frequently leads through difficulty rather than around it. Moses, David, Esther, Jesus, Paul, and countless others experienced tremendous challenges while directly in the center of God's will.

What matters isn't whether the path is easy or difficult, but whether it aligns with God's character and purposes. Sometimes the ease of a path actually indicates it's not God's direction, as it may be too comfortable to produce the growth or impact He intends.

Jesus was explicit: "In the world you will have tribulation" (John 16:33). Expecting ease as confirmation of guidance sets you up for either deception or disappointment.

Myth #2: "God Only Speaks Through Supernatural Signs"

While God certainly can use dramatic means to guide (dreams, visions, angelic visitations, etc.), these are the exception rather than the rule in Scripture. More commonly, God guides through ordinary means: Scripture study, wise counsel, prayer, and the inner witness of the Spirit.

When we fixate on spectacular signs, we often miss the consistent, quiet guidance happening all around us. We're like Naaman, who initially rejected the simple direction to wash in the Jordan because he expected something more dramatic (2 Kings 5:1-14).

Jesus himself warned against sign-seeking, saying an "evil and adulterous generation seeks for a sign" (Matthew 12:39). True maturity involves recognizing God's voice in both the whirlwind and the whisper—and often, as Elijah discovered, God speaks in the whisper (1 Kings 19:11-13).

Myth #3: "God Has One Perfect Plan, and One Wrong Move Ruins Everything"

This myth creates paralyzing fear. People become terrified of making the "wrong" choice about a job, spouse, or home, believing they'll derail God's entire plan for their life if they choose incorrectly.

But Scripture presents God as infinitely more sovereign and gracious than this. While there are certainly better and worse choices, God is able to work through our imperfect decisions. Romans 8:28 promises that God works all things together for good for those who love Him—which would be impossible if one wrong turn permanently ruined His plans.

Think of guidance less like walking a tightrope (one wrong step and you fall) and more like navigating within the banks of a river. Within those banks—the boundaries of God's moral will and wisdom—there's often legitimate freedom of choice, with multiple options that could honor God.

Myth #4: "God's Will Is Primarily About My Happiness and Success"

American Christianity often subtly promotes the idea that God's guidance is mainly about maximizing our personal fulfillment, comfort, and achievement. But this self-centered approach contradicts Jesus' own teaching that following Him involves dying to self, not exalting it (Luke 9:23-24).

God's will certainly includes our joy and flourishing, but defines these very differently than our culture does. His guidance often leads us to places of service, sacrifice, and suffering for the sake of His kingdom and others' good—which ultimately produces deeper joy than pursuing self-interest ever could.

When seeking guidance, the primary question isn't "What will make me happy?" but "What will glorify God and advance His purposes?" The former makes us the center; the latter puts God at the center where He belongs.

Myth #5: "I Don't Need to Seek Guidance Until I Face a Crisis"

Many Christians practice what could be called "emergency spirituality"—ignoring God's guidance for months or years, then frantically seeking direction when facing a major decision or crisis.

This approach misunderstands the nature of guidance as a relationship rather than a transaction. Imagine ignoring a friend completely until you urgently need their help, then expecting immediate, intimate communication. That's not how relationships work.

Daily walking with God, attending to His voice in Scripture and prayer, and practicing obedience in small matters creates the relational context for recognizing His guidance in significant moments. As Jesus taught, "If you abide in me, and my words abide in you, ask whatever you wish, and it will be done for you" (John 15:7). Notice the condition: abiding precedes asking and receiving.

Mistake #1: Seeking Confirmation Bias, Not Truth

One of the most common errors in discernment is selectively focusing on inputs that support what we already want to do, while dismissing contrary evidence. We find the one verse that seems to support our preference, seek counsel only from those likely to agree with us, and interpret circumstances to confirm our desired direction.

Honest guidance-seeking requires a genuine openness to hearing "no" or "wait" or "consider this alternative." Without this openness, we're not really seeking guidance; we're seeking permission or validation.

Jeremiah warned against this tendency when he wrote about prophets who "speak visions of their own minds, not from the mouth of the LORD" (Jeremiah 23:16). We must be vigilant against hearing only what we want to hear.

Mistake #2: Confusing Feelings with Leading

Emotional responses are part of being human, but they're unreliable guidance systems. Feelings fluctuate based on fatigue, hormones, past experiences, and countless other factors unrelated to divine direction.

While the peace of Christ can certainly involve emotional components, true spiritual guidance transcends momentary feelings. It harmonizes with Scripture, makes sense to mature believers, and maintains consistency despite emotional ups and downs.

Jeremiah 17:9 cautions, "The heart is deceitful above all things, and desperately sick; who can understand it?" This doesn't mean emotions are worthless in discernment, but they require interpretation and validation through more objective channels of guidance.

Mistake #3: Abdicating Personal Responsibility

Some Christians use "seeking God's will" as an excuse for avoiding responsibility or delaying necessary action. They wait for perfect clarity before taking any step, which allows them to remain comfortably passive rather than actively engaging with life's challenges.

But guidance typically comes in the context of movement, not stagnation. The Israelites had to step into the Jordan before the waters parted (Joshua 3:13-17). The disciples had to begin their journey before experiencing the wind of Pentecost (Acts 1-2). Guidance often unfolds as we move forward in faith based on what we already know.

God empowers and directs human agency; He doesn't eliminate it. As Philippians 2:12-13 balances, "Work out your own salvation with fear and trembling, for it is God who works in you, both to will and to work for his good pleasure." We work, even as God works in us.

Special Guidance Challenges

Some situations present unique challenges for discerning God's direction. Let's address a few common ones:

When God Seems Silent

Seasons of divine silence are normal in the spiritual journey, but they can be profoundly disorienting when facing important decisions. If you're experiencing God's silence:

1. **Continue spiritual practices faithfully.** Silence doesn't mean absence. Keep reading Scripture, praying, and fellowshipping with believers even when you don't feel immediate connection or clarity.

2. **Examine potential blockages.** While God's silence isn't always due to sin, unconfessed sin can

create static in the communication line. Ask, "Is there anything I need to confess or resolve that might be hindering my ability to hear God?"

3. **Act on the last clear direction.** Often, silence indicates we haven't fully obeyed the last clear guidance we received. Before seeking new direction, ensure you've followed through on what God already showed you.

4. **Use the guidance tools you have.** When specific revelation seems absent, rely more heavily on Scripture, wise counsel, and sanctified common sense. These remain valid guidance channels even in spiritually dry seasons.

5. **Trust God's character in the silence.** Remember that God's apparent silence doesn't mean abandonment or indifference. As with Jesus in the Garden of Gethsemane, sometimes the silence itself is part of the spiritual formation process.

The Psalms are filled with honest expressions of feeling God's silence, yet consistently end with renewed trust despite the lack of immediate answers. This pattern offers a template for our own journey through silent seasons.

When Options All Seem Equally Good (or Bad)

Sometimes the challenge isn't hearing God but choosing between seemingly equal options. When facing this dilemma:

1. **Consider your deeper motivations.** Often, options that appear equal on the surface differ significantly in the heart attitudes and values they represent or develop. Ask, "Which option best cultivates Christlike character in me?"

2. **Evaluate long-term kingdom impact.** Look beyond immediate outcomes to consider how each choice might position you for future service and influence. Which option best stewards your gifts for God's purposes?

3. **Seek counsel from those who can see what you can't.** Others often notice differences between options that we miss because of our internal biases or limited perspective.

4. **Remember the freedom principle.** Within the boundaries of God's moral will and wisdom, Christians often have legitimate freedom to choose based on personal preference. As Augustine said, "Love God and do what you want"—not as permission for license, but recognition that a heart aligned with God will naturally want what honors Him.

5. **Make a provisional choice and test it.** Sometimes clarity comes through action rather than endless deliberation. Make a provisional decision, begin moving in that direction, and see whether confirmation or redirection follows.

1 Corinthians 10:31 provides a helpful framework: "So, whether you eat or drink, or whatever you do, do all to the glory of God." When options seem equal, choose the one that, for you, in your specific situation, best enables you to glorify God.

When Guidance Leads Where You Don't Want to Go

Perhaps the greatest test of our commitment to divine guidance is what we do when God's direction contradicts our preferences or plans. When facing this challenge:

1. **Honestly acknowledge your resistance.** Don't spiritualize or deny your reluctance. Bring it honestly before God, as Jesus did in Gethsemane: "My Father, if it be possible, let this cup pass from me" (Matthew 26:39).

2. **Identify the root of your resistance.** Is it fear? Comfort? Pride? Identifying the specific barrier helps address it directly rather than allowing vague uneasiness to derail obedience.

3. **Seek God's perspective on the situation.** Ask for eyes to see the opportunity, growth, or purpose within the unwanted direction. What might God be doing that you can't currently see?

4. **Find examples of others who followed difficult guidance.** Scripture and church history are filled with stories of reluctant followers who experienced God's faithfulness in unexpected places. Their testimonies can strengthen your resolve.

5. **Remember the cross principle.** Jesus taught that the path of discipleship involves dying to self to find true life (Mark 8:34-35). Uncomfortable guidance often leads to the deepest growth and greatest fruit.

Jonah provides a cautionary tale of what happens when we run from unwanted guidance, while Jesus offers the perfect example of embracing the Father's will despite personal preference: "Nevertheless, not my will, but yours, be done" (Luke 22:42).

The Lifelong Guidance Journey

Developing skill in discerning God's guidance isn't a one-time achievement but a lifelong journey of growing sensitivity and responsiveness to the Spirit. Here's how to continue maturing in this area:

Cultivate a Guidance History

Keep a record of how God has directed you in the past—both the guidance received and the outcomes of following (or not following) that direction. This personal guidance history serves multiple purposes:

- It builds confidence in God's faithfulness through tangible examples
- It helps you identify patterns in how God typically communicates with you
- It provides perspective during difficult discernment seasons
- It creates a legacy of God's work that can encourage others

The Israelites built memorial stones to remember God's faithful guidance at crucial junctures (Joshua 4:4-7). Your guidance journal serves a similar purpose, creating concrete reminders of God's direction in your life.

Develop Guidance Community

While individual discernment is important, guidance often functions best in community. Intentionally build relationships with people who are also pursuing sensitive obedience to God's direction. Together you can:

- Share discernment practices that have proven helpful
- Provide outside perspective on each other's blind spots
- Pray together about important decisions
- Hold each other accountable for following through on received guidance
- Celebrate God's faithfulness in directing your paths

The early church modeled this communal discernment repeatedly, particularly in Acts 13:1-3 and Acts 15:1-35, where major directional decisions were made through collective seeking of the Spirit's guidance.

Embrace Course Corrections

Even with the best discernment practices, you'll sometimes misread God's guidance or only partially understand His direction. Maturity involves recognizing and responding to these course corrections with humility rather than defensive justification.

The apostle Paul demonstrated this flexibility when his carefully planned missionary journeys required unexpected adjustments based on new guidance (Acts 16:6-10). His willingness to change direction when the Spirit redirected him exemplifies mature responsiveness to ongoing guidance.

Remember that course corrections aren't necessarily indications of failure in discernment; often they're simply the unfolding of guidance that couldn't be fully revealed at the outset. God frequently leads one step at a time rather than providing the entire roadmap in advance.

Deepen Your Knowledge of God

The ultimate goal of guidance isn't just making correct decisions but knowing God more intimately. Each guidance experience—whether clear or confusing, easy or challenging—reveals something of God's character, priorities, and ways of working.

As you seek and follow God's direction over time, consciously reflect on what each experience teaches you about who God is. This transforms guidance from a utilitarian tool for decision-making into a pathway for deepening relationship.

Jesus emphasized this relational dimension when He said, "My sheep hear my voice, and I know them, and they follow me" (John 10:27). Note the centrality of mutual knowing—the sheep recognize the shepherd's voice because of relationship, not just information transfer.

The 30-Day Guidance Challenge

Ready to develop stronger guidance-seeking muscles? Try this 30-day challenge designed to build the daily habits that make divine direction more recognizable:

Days 1-5: Foundation Building

For the first five days, focus on establishing or strengthening the fundamental practices that support clear discernment:

Day 1: Scripture Immersion
- Read Psalm 119:97-105 slowly and reflectively
- Commit to daily Bible reading for the next 30 days
- Create a specific plan for when, where, and what you'll read
- Ask at the end of each reading: "What is God saying to me through this passage?"

Day 2: Prayer Realignment
- Evaluate your current prayer patterns honestly
- Create a daily prayer routine that includes more listening than talking
- Practice the prayer Jesus taught: "Your will be done on earth as it is in heaven"
- End each prayer with: "I'm listening, Lord. What are you saying?"

Day 3: Silence Training
- Spend 10 minutes in complete silence, focusing only on God's presence
- Notice how difficult this is and what distractions arise
- Increase this silent listening time by one minute each day
- Journal any impressions, thoughts, or scriptures that come to mind during silence

Day 4: Guidance Community
- Identify 2-3 people who could form your personal "guidance council"
- Reach out to ask if they'd be willing to serve in this role
- Share with them one decision or direction you're currently seeking clarity about
- Schedule regular check-ins for accountability and counsel

Day 5: Guidance History
- Create a "guidance timeline" noting significant moments when you clearly sensed God's direction
- Record what happened when you followed (or didn't follow) that guidance
- Identify patterns in how God has typically communicated with you
- Express gratitude for specific examples of God's faithful guidance

Days 6-15: Daily Guidance Practice

For the next ten days, focus on recognizing and responding to God's guidance in everyday situations:

Day 6: Morning Direction
- Before looking at your phone or starting your day, pray: "God, direct my steps today"
- Write down one specific area where you need guidance today
- Check in midday to evaluate whether you're remaining attentive to God's direction
- End the day by noting any guidance you recognized

Day 7: Decision Awareness
- Notice how many decisions you make without seeking God's input
- Practice pausing before each choice to ask, "God, what would honor you here?"
- At day's end, identify one decision that changed because you paused to seek guidance

Day 8: Counsel Seeking
- Identify one current question or challenge where you need perspective
- Reach out to someone in your guidance community for input
- Listen fully to their counsel without defensiveness
- Thank God for speaking through others, even when the message is challenging

Day 9: Scripture Application
- Choose a specific verse or passage that seems particularly relevant to your current situation
- Meditate on it throughout the day, asking how it applies to your circumstances
- Look for practical ways to align your choices with this Scripture
- Share with someone how God used His Word to guide you today

Day 10: Interruption Attention
- View every interruption today as a potential guidance opportunity
- When plans change unexpectedly, ask, "God, are you redirecting me?"
- Notice whether resistance to interruptions might be resistance to divine guidance
- Record any insights that came through "disruptions" to your agenda

Day 11: Body Awareness
- Pay attention to physical responses as potential guidance signals
- Notice when your body tenses (potential warning) or relaxes (potential confirmation)
- Distinguish between fear-based anxiety and genuine caution
- Practice the habit of checking physical peace levels when making decisions

Day 12: Desire Examination

- Identify something you strongly want right now
- Honestly examine this desire: Is it aligned with God's character and purposes?
- Surrender this desire completely to God, holding it with open hands
- Notice any shift in clarity that comes through this surrender

Day 13: Guidance Obstacles
- Identify your biggest barrier to hearing God clearly (busyness, pride, fear, etc.)
- Take one concrete step to address this obstacle
- Ask someone to pray specifically about this barrier
- Commit to ongoing awareness of this vulnerability in your discernment

Day 14: Creation Listening
- Spend time in nature, asking God to speak through His creation
- Notice analogies or object lessons that might apply to your situation
- Reflect on what creation reveals about the Creator's character and ways
- Thank God for general revelation that complements special revelation

Day 15: No-Decision Day
- Practice complete trust by making no proactive decisions today unless absolutely necessary
- Respond to what comes rather than initiating action

- Notice what this practice reveals about your control tendencies
- Reflect on how trust and guidance interrelate

Days 16-25: Guidance in Specific Life Areas

For the next ten days, focus on seeking God's direction in particular domains of life:

Day 16: Relationship Guidance
- Identify one relationship that needs divine direction
- Pray specifically about this relationship, asking what God wants to do in and through it
- Seek relevant scriptural principles that apply to this relationship
- Take one step of obedience regarding this relationship

Day 17: Work/Vocation Guidance
- Reflect on your current work situation in light of your gifts and God's kingdom
- Ask: "God, how can I better serve you through my daily work?"
- Look for one opportunity to bring kingdom values into your workplace
- Consider whether any adjustments to your vocational direction might be needed

Day 18: Financial Direction

- Review your spending patterns for alignment with biblical values
- Ask God to show you any areas of financial stewardship requiring adjustment
- Make one concrete change based on whatever guidance you receive
- Practice generosity as an act of trust in God's provision and direction

Day 19: Time Usage Guidance
- Examine how you're spending your time in light of eternal priorities
- Ask God: "Is there anything you want me to start, stop, or change about my time allocation?"
- Implement one schedule adjustment based on what you hear
- Consider what your calendar reveals about your true values versus stated values

Day 20: Health and Body Guidance
- Ask God for wisdom regarding your physical health and self-care
- Listen for specific guidance about sleep, nutrition, exercise, or other health matters
- Implement one health-related change as an act of stewardship
- Thank God for the gift of your body and its capabilities

Day 21: Thought Life Direction

- Pay attention to your thought patterns throughout the day
- When negative or destructive thoughts arise, actively seek God's perspective instead
- Practice "taking every thought captive to obey Christ" (2 Corinthians 10:5)
- Notice how thought choices influence your ability to discern guidance clearly

Day 22: Attitude Adjustment
- Identify any attitude that might be blocking God's guidance (entitlement, bitterness, etc.)
- Confess this attitude and ask for God's transforming work
- Choose gratitude and trust as foundational attitudes for receiving guidance
- Record any new clarity that emerges as attitudes shift

Day 23: Spiritual Growth Direction
- Ask God: "What's the next step in my spiritual development?"
- Listen for guidance about spiritual practices, community involvement, or character growth
- Commit to whatever direction emerges, even if it's challenging
- Share this direction with an accountability partner

Day 24: Mission Clarification
- Reflect on your unique contribution to God's kingdom work

- Ask: "Lord, how can I better participate in your redemptive purposes?"
- Look for alignment between your passions, abilities, and opportunities
- Take one step toward greater mission clarity or engagement

Day 25: Family/Home Direction
- Pray about your family relationships and home environment
- Ask God to show you one way to better reflect His love and truth in this domain
- Implement whatever guidance you receive, even if it requires difficult conversations
- Consider what spiritual legacy you're creating through family life

Days 26-30: Integrating Guidance into Life

For the final five days, focus on cementing guidance-seeking as a lifelong practice:

Day 26: Guidance Assessment
- Review your experiences from the past 25 days
- Identify what practices have been most helpful for you personally
- Notice which areas of life have gained the most clarity through this process
- Celebrate specific examples of God's guidance during this challenge

Day 27: Ongoing Plan
- Create a sustainable plan for continuing guidance practices beyond this 30-day challenge
- Be realistic about what rhythms will work in your actual life circumstances
- Include accountability measures to maintain consistency
- Share this plan with your guidance community

Day 28: Guidance Testimony
- Write out a specific story of God's guidance in your life
- Share this testimony with at least one other person
- Notice how articulating the experience strengthens your own faith
- Invite the other person to share their guidance experiences

Day 29: Course Correction Practice
- Identify something you previously felt sure about that may need adjustment
- Practice the humility of saying, "I might have misunderstood God's direction"
- Make whatever correction seems appropriate based on new understanding
- Thank God for ongoing guidance that includes redirection when needed

Day 30: Guidance Celebration

- Express gratitude for 30 days of intentional guidance practice
- Identify three specific ways you've grown in discerning God's voice
- Commit to continuing this journey of learning to recognize and follow divine direction
- Pray for increased sensitivity to guidance in the coming season

The Kick in the Pants: Stop Making Excuses and Start Listening

Let's cut to the chase: if you're not seeking guidance, don't whine when things fall apart.

Most of us spend more time researching which Netflix show to watch or which phone to buy than we do seeking God's direction for major life decisions. Then we have the audacity to ask, "God, why did you let this happen?" when those poorly-discerned choices lead to predictable disasters.

The harsh truth is that God is speaking—you're just not listening. You're too busy, too distracted, too convinced of your own brilliance, or too afraid of what He might say to create the conditions necessary for hearing His voice.

Stop looking for signs and start looking for Scripture. Stop waiting for burning bushes and start building daily habits of listening. Stop treating God like a cosmic Magic 8-Ball you shake when you're stuck and start developing the kind of intimate relationship where you recognize His voice because you hear it every day.

God isn't hiding His will from you—He's inviting you into a guided life that's infinitely better than your self-directed chaos. But that guidance comes through relationship, not shortcuts. Through daily walking together, not emergency consultations.

Here's the reality: You will follow someone's guidance. Either the culture's, your emotions', your friends', or God's. The question isn't whether you'll be led; it's who's doing the leading.

If you want God's guidance, you have to create space to hear it. You have to humble yourself enough to seek it. You have to value it enough to wait for it. And you have to love Him enough to follow it, even when it contradicts what you want to hear.

Don't be like the people Jeremiah described: "They have ears, but do not hear" (Jeremiah 5:21). Don't be the one who says "Lord, Lord" but doesn't actually do what He says (Luke 6:46).

Instead, be like Samuel, who positioned himself to hear by saying, "Speak, for your servant is listening" (1 Samuel 3:10). Be like Mary, who sat at Jesus' feet, prioritizing listening over the busyness that consumed her sister (Luke 10:38-42). Be like Jesus Himself, who consistently sought and followed the Father's guidance, saying, "I do nothing on my own authority, but speak just as the Father taught me" (John 8:28).

The life of guidance isn't about having all the answers or never making mistakes. It's about developing such a close relationship with God that you recognize His voice amid the clamor of competing voices. It's about trusting Him enough to follow where He leads, even when the path doesn't make sense by worldly standards.

This won't happen through occasional, crisis-driven prayer. It happens through daily disciplines of listening, obeying, reflecting, and adjusting. It happens as you build a guidance-seeking life, not just guidance-seeking moments.

So put down your phone. Turn off the noise. Open your Bible. Quiet your heart. Seek wise counsel. Pay attention to the Spirit's promptings. And for God's sake, actually do what He shows you, instead of nodding in agreement while continuing to do whatever you wanted to do anyway.

Because here's the promise: "I will instruct you and teach you in the way you should go; I will counsel you with my eye upon you" (Psalm 32:8). God wants to guide you more than you want to be guided. The question is whether you'll create the conditions necessary to hear and follow that guidance.

The choice is yours. Will you continue stumbling along your self-determined path, occasionally crying out for divine intervention when you hit a wall? Or will you commit to the daily discipline of seeking and following God's guidance in every area of life?

The quality of your future depends largely on how you answer that question.

Chapter 8:

Simplicity – Cutting Through the Clutter

Let's be honest: your life is a cluttered mess.

Your closet is stuffed with clothes you don't wear. Your garage is full of things you never use. Your calendar is packed with commitments you don't even care about. Your phone is buzzing with notifications from people you barely know. Your mind is racing with worries about stuff that probably won't happen. Your spiritual life is a hodgepodge of random practices you've collected from podcasts, books, and that one retreat you went to in 2017.

And in the middle of all this noise and accumulation, you're wondering why you can't hear God's voice or find any peace.

Here's a radical thought: What if the problem isn't that you need more—more Bible studies, more worship experiences, more prayer techniques, more spiritual disciplines—but that you need less? Less distraction. Less stuff. Less commitments. Less noise.

What if the path to a deeper spiritual life runs directly through simplicity?

Jesus put it plainly in Matthew 6:33: "But seek first the kingdom of God and his righteousness, and all these things will be added to you." Notice the language: seek FIRST. Not seek fifteenth, after your career, your social media presence, your fitness goals, your side hustle, your Netflix queue, and your home renovation projects. FIRST.

But how can anything be first when everything is screaming for your attention? When your life is so cluttered with physical stuff, digital noise, relational obligations, and mental chatter that you can barely hear yourself think, much less hear the still, small voice of God?

This is where the spiritual discipline of simplicity comes in. Not as another thing to add to your already overflowing plate, but as a deliberate subtraction—a clearing away of the nonessential to make room for what truly matters.

In Luke 10, Jesus visits the home of Mary and Martha. While Martha rushes around distracted by "much serving," Mary sits at Jesus' feet, focusing on the one thing that matters. When Martha complains, Jesus gently corrects her: "Martha, Martha, you are anxious and troubled about many things, but one thing is necessary. Mary has chosen the good portion, which will not be taken away from her" (Luke 10:41-42).

One thing is necessary. Not twenty things. Not a hundred things. One.

In this chapter, we're going to explore how simplicity can transform your spiritual life by creating space for that one necessary thing. But be warned: this isn't going to be about cute organizational hacks or Instagram-worthy minimalism. We're talking about a radical reorientation of your relationship with stuff, time, technology, and even your own thoughts.

It might get uncomfortable. It will definitely get countercultural. But it just might save your soul from drowning in the tsunami of too much.

The Problem: We're All Drowning in More

Before we talk about the solution, let's get painfully clear about the problem. We are living in the most complex, cluttered, distracted time in human history. Consider:

Physical Clutter

The average American home contains over 300,000 items. We're using credit cards to buy things we don't need, to impress people we don't like, to live in houses that are too big, which we fill with more stuff that requires maintenance, insurance, and eventual disposal—creating a cycle of acquisition and anxiety that never ends.

Meanwhile, Jesus had "nowhere to lay his head" (Matthew 8:20) and told his disciples, "Take nothing for your journey, no staff, nor bag, nor bread, nor money; and do not have two tunics" (Luke 9:3). The contrast between our cluttered lives and Jesus' example couldn't be starker.

Digital Overload

The average person checks their phone 96 times a day—that's once every 10 minutes. We consume five times more information daily than people did in 1986. Our brains are constantly processing texts, emails, social media feeds, news alerts, and endless entertainment options.

This digital deluge trains our brains for constant stimulation and fractured attention—the opposite of the focused presence needed for prayer, meditation on Scripture, or hearing God's voice. No wonder Psalm 46:10, "Be still, and know that I am God," feels increasingly impossible.

Schedule Saturation

Most of us live with calendars so packed that we have to schedule time to breathe. Between work demands, family obligations, church activities, social commitments, and the endless maintenance of modern life, we're chronically overbooked and perpetually behind.

Jesus regularly "withdrew to desolate places and prayed" (Luke 5:16), prioritizing time with the Father even at the height of demand for his ministry. When was the last time you had a completely unscheduled day—not to catch up on tasks, but to simply be available to God?

Mental Clutter

Our minds are filled with to-do lists, worries, plans, regrets, social comparisons, and information overload. This mental noise forms a constant backdrop that makes silence feel uncomfortable and focused thought nearly impossible.

Paul's instruction to "take every thought captive to obey Christ" (2 Corinthians 10:5) assumes a level of mental awareness and discipline that seems foreign to our distracted minds. How can we take thoughts captive when we can barely track them as they race through our heads?

Relational Complexity

We're connected to more people than ever before through social media and digital communication, yet studies show we're lonelier and more isolated. We maintain hundreds of shallow connections at the expense of the deep, meaningful relationships that actually nurture our souls.

Jesus had thousands of followers but invested deeply in twelve disciples, and even more intimately in three (Peter, James, and John). He understood that relational depth, not breadth, produces transformation.

Spiritual Accumulation

Many Christians have turned spiritual growth into another form of accumulation—collecting Bible studies, worship experiences, prayer techniques, and spiritual practices without the depth that comes from sustained focus. We're spiritual collectors rather than committed disciples.

Jesus simplified the entire law into two commands: love God and love your neighbor (Matthew 22:37-40).

Yet we often complicate our spiritual lives with a constant search for the next experience, insight, or technique that promises growth without the difficult work of simplicity and focus.

The Countercultural Nature of Simplicity

In a culture that equates more with better, choosing simplicity isn't just a practical decision—it's a radical act of resistance. It's swimming upstream against powerful currents pushing you toward accumulation, distraction, and complexity.

These currents aren't just external. They tap into deep internal drives and fears:

The Fear of Missing Out

We accumulate experiences, possessions, and connections out of a deep-seated fear that we'll miss something important. What if the next purchase, the next scroll, the next commitment is the one that will finally make us happy or successful?

Jesus directly confronted this fear in the parable of the rich fool (Luke 12:13-21), who kept acquiring and storing up treasure only to die before enjoying any of it. "So is the one who lays up treasure for himself and is not rich toward God," Jesus concluded—a stark warning about misplaced priorities.

The Allure of Identity Through Accumulation

In our culture, what you own and what you do largely define who you are. Simplicity threatens this identity structure by suggesting you might be valuable apart from your possessions, achievements, and affiliations.

This is why Jesus' words in Luke 12:15 are so confronting: "Take care, and be on your guard against all covetousness, for one's life does not consist in the abundance of his possessions." He's not just giving financial advice but challenging the fundamental way we construct identity.

The Addiction to Stimulation

Our brains have become accustomed to constant stimulation, making silence and simplicity feel not just boring but almost physically uncomfortable. We reach for our phones at the first hint of downtime, filling every moment with input and avoiding the discomfort of quiet reflection.

Yet it's in this very quiet that God often speaks. As Elijah discovered, God was not in the wind, earthquake, or fire, but in "a low whisper" (1 Kings 19:11-12). If we're constantly surrounded by noise, we'll miss the whisper entirely.

The Status Quo of Complexity

Our economic and social systems are designed to promote complexity and consumption. Advertising, social media, career tracks, and even some church cultures push us toward more rather than enough. Swimming against this tide requires deliberate, conscious effort.

This is the context in which Paul's words to the Romans take on fresh significance: "Do not be conformed to this world, but be transformed by the renewal of your mind" (Romans 12:2). Choosing simplicity is a tangible way of refusing to be conformed to the pattern of endless acquisition and distraction.

Understanding these powerful currents helps explain why simplicity feels so difficult—and why it's so necessary. We're not just reorganizing our closets; we're challenging deeply ingrained patterns of thinking and living that have shaped us more than we realize.

Biblical Foundations of Simplicity

Simplicity isn't a modern lifestyle trend; it's deeply rooted in Scripture. Let's examine some key biblical principles that form the foundation for this discipline:

1. God is our provider, not our possessions

The most fundamental principle of simplicity is trusting God rather than stuff for our security and satisfaction. Jesus highlighted this in Matthew 6:25-34 when he told his followers not to worry about food or clothing because the Father knows their needs and will provide.

This trust enables us to hold possessions loosely rather than clutching them tightly. It frees us from the anxious accumulation that comes from believing our survival depends entirely on our own efforts and resources.

2. The kingdom of God is our primary pursuit

In Matthew 6:33, Jesus establishes a clear priority: "Seek first the kingdom of God and his righteousness." This "first" implies that other concerns—while not unimportant—must take secondary positions in our attention and devotion.

Simplicity helps us maintain this priority by removing competing claims on our ultimate allegiance. It creates space for kingdom concerns to take their proper place at the center rather than the periphery of our lives.

3. Contentment is a learned state of sufficiency

Paul makes a remarkable statement in Philippians 4:11-12: "I have learned in whatever situation I am to be content. I know how to be brought low, and I know how to abound. In any and every circumstance, I have learned the secret of facing plenty and hunger, abundance and need."

Note that contentment is something Paul learned—it didn't come naturally. The secret he discovered was that true sufficiency comes not from having more but from needing less and trusting God more.

4. Generosity flows from simplicity

When we recognize that everything we have belongs to God and trust Him as our provider, generosity becomes a natural expression of that trust. Acts 2:44-45 describes the early church: "All who believed were together and had all things in common. And they were selling their possessions and belongings and distributing the proceeds to all, as any had need."

This radical generosity wasn't a commanded program but a natural outcome of their understanding that possessions were tools for service rather than sources of security or status.

5. Material wealth brings spiritual danger

Jesus repeatedly warned about the spiritual dangers of wealth and possessions. His statement that "it is easier for a camel to go through the eye of a needle than for a rich person to enter the kingdom of God" (Mark 10:25) wasn't meant as mathematical hyperbole but as a serious warning about how possessions can capture our hearts.

Simplicity helps guard against this danger by keeping possessions in their proper perspective—as useful tools rather than ultimate goods, as gifts to be received with gratitude and shared with generosity rather than treasures to be hoarded.

6. Jesus modeled a life of focused simplicity

Jesus lived what he taught. Although not an ascetic (he enjoyed feasts and was even accused of being a glutton), he lived simply, traveled light, and remained focused on his mission. He didn't own property, accumulate possessions, or pursue status through acquisition.

Most significantly, he maintained a clear focus on his purpose despite countless demands and distractions. When crowds sought him for healing, he sometimes withdrew to pray (Luke 5:15-16). When his disciples invited him to return to a successful ministry location, he declined in order to move forward with his mission (Mark 1:35-38). His life demonstrated a compelling simplicity of purpose that cut through the complexity of competing demands.

Simplicity in Four Dimensions

Simplicity isn't just about owning fewer things, though that's part of it. It's a multidimensional discipline that touches every aspect of life. Let's explore four key dimensions:

1. Material Simplicity: Owning Less, Wanting Less

The most obvious dimension of simplicity involves our relationship with physical stuff. This isn't about asceticism (denying yourself any pleasure or comfort) but about intentionality—owning what serves your values and purpose rather than being owned by your possessions.

Practical steps toward material simplicity include:

- **Conducting a possession audit**: Evaluate everything you own against the question "Does this help me fulfill my purpose and values, or does it distract from them?"

- **Practicing the one-in, one-out rule**: For every new item that enters your home, remove one item—preventing gradual accumulation.

- **Asking deeper questions before purchases**: Instead of "Can I afford this?" ask "Does this align with my values? Will it require maintenance that disrupts my priorities? Could this money better serve God's kingdom elsewhere?"

- **Creating breathing room**: Aim for space in your home—empty shelves, clear surfaces, room to move and think without visual clutter constantly demanding attention.

- **Breaking the upgrade cycle**: Resist cultural pressure to constantly upgrade to newer versions of things that still function perfectly well.

Jesus warned in Luke 12:15, "Take care, and be on your guard against all covetousness, for one's life does not consist in the abundance of his possessions." Material simplicity is a practical application of this truth—a tangible reminder that life's meaning and purpose come from something far deeper than what we own.

2. Calendar Simplicity: Doing Less, Being More

Our time reflects our true priorities more accurately than our words. Calendar simplicity involves intentionally creating margin in your schedule for rest, relationships, and responsiveness to God's leading.

Practical steps toward calendar simplicity include:

- **Identifying your top priorities**: Name the 3-5 roles or responsibilities that matter most in this season of life. These become your filters for evaluating commitments.

- **Learning to say no**: Establish that "no" is a complete sentence. You don't need elaborate explanations for declining commitments that don't align with your core priorities.

- **Scheduling margin**: Block "nothing" time in your calendar—not for catching up on tasks, but for true availability to God and others.

- **Batching similar activities**: Group similar tasks (emails, phone calls, errands) to reduce the mental cost of constant context-switching.

- **Embracing regular rhythms**: Create sustainable patterns of work and rest rather than lurching between frantic activity and exhausted collapse.

Jesus modeled this calendar simplicity perfectly. Despite healing the sick, teaching thousands, and training disciples for world-changing ministry, he never appeared hurried or overwhelmed. He knew when to engage and when to withdraw, maintaining a rhythm that kept him connected to the Father's purposes.

3. Digital Simplicity: Connecting Deeper, Scrolling Less

Perhaps no area needs simplicity more urgently than our digital lives. The average American spends over 7 hours daily on screens—essentially a full-time job of consumption and distraction.

Practical steps toward digital simplicity include:

- **Conducting an app audit**: Delete apps that don't serve your values or that consistently leave you feeling worse after using them.

- **Creating tech boundaries**: Establish phone-free zones (bedroom, dinner table) and times (first hour after waking, last hour before bed).

- **Practicing digital sabbaths**: Set aside regular periods—whether hours or full days—completely disconnected from digital devices.

- **Disabling notifications**: Turn off all non-essential notifications to reduce the constant pull on your attention.

- **Curating information intake**: Be intentional about what voices you allow into your mental space through social media, news, and entertainment.

While Scripture doesn't specifically address digital technology, Paul's principle in 1 Corinthians 6:12 applies perfectly: "'All things are lawful for me,' but not all things are helpful. 'All things are lawful for me,' but I will not be dominated by anything." Digital simplicity is about refusing to be dominated by the constant demands of technology.

4. Mental Simplicity: Thinking Clearly, Worrying Less

Perhaps the most challenging dimension of simplicity involves our internal world—our thoughts, worries, and mental patterns. A physically uncluttered life still feels chaotic if our minds are racing with anxiety, rumination, and scattered attention.

Practical steps toward mental simplicity include:

- **Brain dumping**: Regularly transfer swirling thoughts from your mind to paper, reducing the mental load of trying to remember everything.

- **Single-tasking**: Focus on one activity at a time, giving it your full attention rather than dividing focus between multiple tasks.

- **Practicing thought capture**: As Paul suggests in 2 Corinthians 10:5, take thoughts captive by noticing unhelpful patterns and redirecting them toward truth.

- **Creating worry boundaries**: Designate specific times to address legitimate concerns rather than letting worry infiltrate every moment.

- **Developing present-moment awareness**: Train yourself to fully engage with what's happening now rather than constantly rehashing the past or rehearsing the future.

Jesus addressed mental simplicity directly in Matthew 6:34: "Therefore do not be anxious about tomorrow, for tomorrow will be anxious for itself. Sufficient for the day is its own trouble." This isn't dismissing legitimate concerns but recognizing that carrying tomorrow's potential problems into today only multiplies our mental burden.

The Unexpected Benefits of Simplicity

While simplicity might initially sound like deprivation or loss, those who practice it consistently report significant benefits that far outweigh whatever they've given up:

1. Increased capacity to hear God

When the background noise of possessions, activities, and digital distraction diminishes, God's voice becomes more discernible. Many Christians report that simplicity creates the quiet space in which spiritual discernment can flourish.

This aligns with God's invitation in Psalm 46:10: "Be still, and know that I am God." The stillness that simplicity creates becomes fertile ground for knowing God more intimately.

2. Greater clarity about purpose

In a complex life filled with competing demands, our sense of purpose often gets buried under an avalanche of activity. Simplicity strips away the nonessential, bringing our core calling back into focus.

Paul demonstrated this singular focus in Philippians 3:13-14: "One thing I do: forgetting what lies behind and straining forward to what lies ahead, I press on toward the goal for the prize of the upward call of God in Christ Jesus." Simplicity helps us identify and pursue our own "one thing."

3. Deeper, more authentic relationships

When we're no longer rushing from commitment to commitment or half-present due to digital distraction, we can offer the gift of true presence to the people in our lives. Relationships move from transaction to connection, from superficial to meaningful.

Jesus consistently gave people his full attention, whether speaking to crowds or engaging individuals like the Samaritan woman at the well (John 4). Simplicity creates space for this kind of focused presence with others.

4. Increased generosity

As our grip on possessions loosens and our trust in God's provision grows, generosity flows more naturally. We become more willing to share our resources—not just money, but also time, attention, and skills—because we're no longer frantically trying to secure our own future.

The early church exemplified this connection between simplicity and generosity. Acts 4:32-34 describes, "No one said that any of the things that belonged to him was his own, but they had everything in common... There was not a needy person among them."

5. Freedom from comparison and status anxiety

Simplicity liberates us from the exhausting treadmill of keeping up with cultural expectations about what we should own, achieve, or experience. It allows us to define success by internal values rather than external standards.

Jesus challenged these external measures in Luke 16:15: "What is exalted among men is an abomination in the sight of God." Simplicity helps us care less about impressing others and more about living faithfully.

6. Increased resilience during difficult times

Those who practice simplicity often find themselves better equipped to weather crises. With fewer possessions to lose, less attachment to status, and stronger trust in God's provision, they're less devastated by the losses and changes that inevitably come.

This resilience reflects Paul's experience in Philippians 4:12-13: "I know how to be brought low, and I know how to abound... I can do all things through him who strengthens me." Simplicity trains us for this kind of spiritual adaptability.

Practical Steps Toward a Simpler Life

Simplicity isn't achieved in a weekend decluttering spree. It's developed through consistent, intentional choices that gradually reshape your relationship with possessions, time, technology, and mental habits. Here are practical ways to begin:

Step 1: Identify Your Current Complexity Costs

Before diving into simplification tactics, take time to honestly assess how complexity is affecting your life right now:

- How is physical clutter impacting your mental state and spiritual focus?
- What relationships are suffering from your overcrowded schedule?
- How is digital distraction affecting your ability to be present with God and others?
- What does your spending reveal about what you truly value?
- Where do you feel most overwhelmed, scattered, or stretched thin?

This assessment creates motivation by connecting simplicity to the real pain points in your life rather than treating it as an abstract ideal.

Step 2: Clarify Your Core Priorities

Simplicity requires knowing what matters most so you can eliminate what doesn't. Take time to thoughtfully identify:

- Your primary calling in this season of life
- The 3-5 relationships that deserve your best time and attention
- The activities that genuinely restore and strengthen you
- The values you want your life to demonstrate
- The legacy you hope to leave

These priorities become your filters for evaluating every possession, commitment, and habit. Without this clarity, simplification becomes random downsizing rather than purposeful focusing.

Step 3: Start with Quick Wins

Build momentum by beginning with simplification moves that offer immediate relief with minimal resistance:

In your physical environment:
- Clear all flat surfaces in your main living areas
- Remove items from your car that don't belong there
- Delete unused apps from your phone's home screen
- Clean out your refrigerator of expired or unwanted items
- Unsubscribe from 5-10 email lists that clutter your inbox

In your schedule:
- Block one evening next week as completely commitment-free
- Identify one recurring obligation you can honorably exit
- Cancel or reschedule any non-essential appointments in the next two weeks
- Create a "not-to-do" list of activities that drain your energy without serving your purpose

In your digital life:
- Turn off all non-essential notifications on your phone
- Remove social media apps from your phone (access via browser instead)
- Unfollow accounts that consistently leave you feeling inadequate or agitated
- Set a specific time for checking email rather than responding to each notification

In your mental space:
- Start a worry journal to capture anxious thoughts rather than mentally cycling through them
- Create a "done list" at day's end to recognize accomplishments rather than fixating on what's unfinished
- Establish a simple end-of-day ritual that signals "work thoughts stop here"

These quick wins create breathing room and demonstrate the immediate benefits of simplicity, motivating deeper changes.

Step 4: Tackle One Life Area at a Time

While simplicity eventually touches every dimension of life, trying to simplify everything simultaneously leads to overwhelm. Instead, focus on one area for 2-4 weeks before moving to the next:

Month 1: Physical Environment
- Conduct a possession audit of one room each week
- Establish "homes" for frequently used items
- Create systems for managing incoming physical items (mail, gifts, purchases)
- Remove items that don't support your values or serve your purpose
- Organize remaining possessions for easy access and maintenance

Month 2: Schedule and Commitments
- Track how you actually spend time for one week
- Align your calendar with your stated priorities
- Establish boundaries around work hours
- Create regular rhythms for rest, connection, and renewal
- Practice saying no to requests that don't align with your core purposes

Month 3: Digital Life
- Establish tech-free zones and times in your home
- Curate information sources that nourish rather than drain
- Create intentional practices for social media use
- Organize digital files and information systems
- Develop healthy habits for email, messaging, and phone use

Month 4: Mental and Emotional Life
- Identify thought patterns that create unnecessary complexity

- Establish practices for mental offloading (journaling, lists, etc.)
- Create strategies for managing worry and rumination
- Develop routines that support mental clarity
- Practice presence and single-tasking

This sequential approach prevents the overwhelm that comes from trying to change everything at once.

Step 5: Build Accountability and Support

Simplicity is countercultural, which makes it difficult to maintain without support. Create structures that reinforce your commitment:

- Find a simplicity partner who shares your values and can provide encouragement
- Join (or start) a group focused on intentional living
- Share your simplicity goals with family members and close friends
- Regularly revisit your "why" for pursuing simplicity
- Celebrate progress and learn from setbacks rather than allowing perfectionism to derail you

Remember Ecclesiastes 4:9-10: "Two are better than one, because they have a good reward for their toil. For if they fall, one will lift up his fellow." This applies to the work of simplification as much as to any other endeavor.

Common Obstacles to Simplicity (And How to Overcome Them)

The path to simplicity isn't always smooth. Here are common obstacles you'll likely encounter, along with strategies for overcoming them:

Obstacle 1: Scarcity Thinking

Many people resist simplification because of an underlying fear that there won't be enough—enough money, time, opportunity, or security. This scarcity mindset keeps us clutching possessions and commitments even when they no longer serve us.

Overcoming Strategies:
- Practice gratitude daily to shift from scarcity to abundance thinking
- Create "enough" metrics for different areas of life (income, possessions, activities)
- Experiment with temporary limitations to prove sufficient doesn't mean deprived
- Meditate on promises like Philippians 4:19: "My God will supply every need of yours according to his riches in glory in Christ Jesus"

Obstacle 2: Identity Attachment

We often resist simplifying because we've attached our identity to what we own, what we achieve, or how busy we appear. Letting go feels threatening when possessions or activities have become extensions of who we believe ourselves to be.

Overcoming Strategies:
- Explore your core identity in Christ apart from possessions or achievements
- Notice how identity-based resistance manifests ("But I'm a person who...")
- Practice the discipline of obscurity—doing good things without recognition
- Reflect on Jesus' teaching: "For what will it profit a man if he gains the whole world and forfeits his soul?" (Matthew 16:26)

Obstacle 3: Social Pressure

Our social circles often unintentionally reinforce complexity through expectations about lifestyle, parenting, career advancement, or community involvement. Going against these expectations can trigger insecurity or even direct criticism.

Overcoming Strategies:
- Find examples of people who've chosen countercultural simplicity

- Prepare simple explanations for your choices without defensiveness
- Connect with others who share your simplicity values
- Remember Jesus' caution about living for human approval: "How can you believe, when you receive glory from one another and do not seek the glory that comes from the only God?" (John 5:44)

Obstacle 4: The Complexity Creep

Even with the best intentions, complexity gradually returns as new possessions, commitments, and digital distractions enter your life. Without regular attention, simplicity erodes through the accumulation of small compromises.

Overcoming Strategies:
- Schedule regular simplicity reviews (monthly or quarterly)
- Create "friction" for adding complexity (waiting periods for purchases, 24-hour holds on new commitments)
- Establish clear one-in-one-out policies for possessions
- Practice regular digital detoxes to reset baseline expectations
- Remember Jesus' warning about what happens when initial cleaning isn't maintained (Matthew 12:43-45)

Obstacle 5: All-or-Nothing Thinking

Perfectionism sabotages simplicity by suggesting that if you can't do it perfectly, you shouldn't do it at all. This leads to either dramatic but unsustainable purges or paralysis in the face of overwhelming complexity.

Overcoming Strategies:
- Focus on progress not perfection
- Celebrate small, sustainable changes
- Remember that simplicity is a lifelong practice, not a one-time achievement
- Take inspiration from Paul's perspective: "Not that I have already obtained this or am already perfect, but I press on..." (Philippians 3:12)

Simplicity in Different Life Seasons

Simplicity looks different depending on your life stage and circumstances. What's "simple" for a college student differs from what's simple for a parent of young children or a retiree. Here's how to adapt simplicity principles to different seasons:

Young Adults / Single Season

Young adulthood offers unique opportunities for establishing simple foundations before accumulating the responsibilities and possessions that come with later life stages.

Simplicity Focus Areas:
- Resist lifestyle inflation as income increases
- Establish strong digital boundaries before habits solidify
- Create intentional community rather than scattered social obligations
- Develop financial practices that prioritize generosity and freedom over acquisition
- Use geographic mobility thoughtfully rather than accumulating possessions that limit flexibility

Marriage / Partnership Season

Combining lives with another person introduces complexity as you navigate different habits, expectations, and priorities.

Simplicity Focus Areas:
- Create shared understanding of "enough" in various life dimensions
- Establish household systems that serve both people's values
- Build traditions and rituals that center your relationship without excessive consumption

- Navigate family and social expectations as a unified team
- Make intentional decisions about housing that prioritize connection over impression

Parenting Season

Raising children is inherently complex, but thoughtful simplicity can create the space and presence that nurtures flourishing family life.

Simplicity Focus Areas:
- Resist cultural pressure for overscheduled children
- Create simple family rhythms that everyone can rely on
- Be intentional about toy and activity accumulation
- Establish technology boundaries that support presence and connection
- Focus on relationship-building experiences over possession-centered experiences

Mid-Life / Career-Focused Season

Middle adulthood often brings peak responsibility in career, family, and community, making simplicity both more challenging and more essential.

Simplicity Focus Areas:
- Establish firm boundaries between work and rest

- Resist status-driven accumulation as career advances
- Create systems for managing complex responsibilities without mental overload
- Regularly evaluate commitments against core values
- Practice Sabbath disciplines amid high-demand seasons

Later Life / Retirement Season

Later adulthood offers opportunities to release accumulated possessions and responsibilities while focusing on legacy and meaningful contribution.

Simplicity Focus Areas:
- Downsize physical possessions before crisis points make it necessary
- Transition from achievement-based identity to relationship and wisdom-based value
- Create intentional inheritance plans that reflect your values
- Share accumulated resources generously rather than continuing to accumulate
- Focus time and energy on what matters most in light of life's finitude

Throughout all these seasons, Jesus' question remains relevant: "For what does it profit a man to gain the whole world and forfeit his soul?" (Mark 8:36). Simplicity helps ensure we don't sacrifice what matters most on the altar of what matters least, regardless of our life stage.

The 30-Day Simplicity Challenge

Ready to experience the transformative power of simplicity? Try this 30-day challenge designed to introduce key simplicity practices across all dimensions of life. Each week builds on the previous one, creating a gradual but significant shift toward a simpler, more focused life:

Week 1: Physical Simplicity

Day 1: Remove 10 unnecessary items from your main living space.

Day 2: Clear all flat surfaces in your home of everything except 1-3 intentional items.

Day 3: Delete 5 unused apps from your phone.

Day 4: Clean out your car completely.

Day 5: Unsubscribe from 10 email lists.

Day 6: Choose one drawer or small cabinet to completely empty, clean, and thoughtfully refill with only what belongs.

Day 7: Wear only your 10 favorite clothing items this week (work requirements excepted). Notice what you actually miss and what you don't.

Week 2: Calendar Simplicity

Day 8: Review your calendar for the next month. Cancel or reschedule at least one non-essential commitment.

Day 9: Block one evening this week as completely unscheduled. Protect it at all costs.

Day 10: Practice single-tasking all day. Focus completely on one activity at a time.

Day 11: Create a "not-to-do" list of activities that drain energy without serving your purpose.

Day 12: Batch similar tasks (emails, phone calls, errands) into specific time blocks rather than letting them fragment your day.

Day 13: Say no to one new request or invitation that doesn't align with your core priorities.

Day 14: Plan a minimalist Sabbath—a day of rest with maximum connection and minimum consumption.

Week 3: Digital Simplicity

Day 15: Turn off all notifications on your phone except calls and texts from key people.

Day 16: Unfollow/unfriend at least 20 accounts on social media that don't genuinely enrich your life.

Day 17: Establish a tech-free zone in your home (bedroom, dining area, or living room).

Day 18: Set specific times for checking email, social media, and news rather than allowing random access throughout the day.

Day 19: Delete one social media app from your phone (you can still access it via browser if needed).

Day 20: Practice a complete digital sabbath—24 hours without screens of any kind.

Day 21: Curate your information diet by identifying 3-5 trustworthy sources for news and information, and commit to those instead of random browsing.

Week 4: Mental Simplicity

Day 22: Start a worry journal. When anxious thoughts arise, write them down rather than mentally cycling through them.

Day 23: Practice "brain dumping" at the end of the day—transfer all swirling thoughts to paper so your mind can rest.

Day 24: Choose one small area of decision fatigue (breakfast, work clothes, etc.) and create a simple system to eliminate daily deliberation.

Day 25: Practice thought capture by noticing negative thought patterns and deliberately replacing them with truth.

Day 26: Identify your top 3 priorities for this season of life. Write them somewhere visible and use them as filters for decisions.

Day 27: Create a simple end-of-day ritual that helps you transition from productivity to rest.

Day 28: Practice present-moment awareness through a common daily activity (showering, washing dishes, walking). Focus completely on the experience rather than letting your mind wander.

Week 5: Integration

Day 29: Reflect on the past 28 days. What changes have had the most positive impact? What has been most challenging? What do you want to continue?

Day 30: Create a sustainable simplicity plan for moving forward. Include specific practices from each dimension (physical, calendar, digital, mental) that you commit to maintaining.

Throughout this challenge, keep a brief journal noting:
- Changes in your mental state and spiritual awareness
- Resistance that arises and where it comes from
- Benefits you experience from each simplification
- Insights about what actually matters in your life

This documentation helps reinforce the connection between simplicity choices and their positive outcomes, increasing motivation to maintain these practices beyond the 30-day challenge.

How Simplicity Transforms Your Relationship with God

While the practical benefits of simplicity are significant, its deepest value lies in how it transforms your spiritual life. Here's how simplicity creates space for a more vibrant relationship with God:

1. From distracted to present

In a cluttered, complex life, our attention is constantly fragmented. We try to pray while mentally reviewing our to-do list. We read Scripture while our phones buzz with notifications. We attempt to listen for God's voice while surrounded by literal and mental noise.

Simplicity creates the space and silence in which real presence with God becomes possible. As we remove distractions, we discover a quality of attention that allows for deeper communion rather than superficial religious activity.

This presence is what God invited when He said, "Be still, and know that I am God" (Psalm 46:10). Not "do more religious things and know that I am God" but "be still." Simplicity creates the conditions for this stillness.

2. From performance to trust

Complex lives often reflect an underlying belief that everything depends on our effort, planning, and control. We accumulate possessions as security, pack our schedules with achievements, and exhaust ourselves trying to manage all the variables.

Simplicity invites us to transfer trust from our own resources and efforts to God's provision and purpose. As Jesus taught in Matthew 6:25-34, true security comes not from stockpiling goods or frantically striving, but from recognizing that the Father knows what we need and will provide.

This shift from self-reliance to God-reliance transforms our spiritual life from religious performance to genuine relationship built on trust.

3. From acquisition to gratitude

Our consumer culture trains us for perpetual dissatisfaction—always wanting the next thing, the better experience, the newer model. This acquisitive mindset infiltrates our spiritual lives, creating a restless pursuit of more knowledge, more experiences, more spiritual accomplishments.

Simplicity cultivates contentment and gratitude by helping us recognize the abundance we already have rather than fixating on what's lacking. It shifts our attention from what we want to what we've received, from scarcity to sufficiency.

Paul reflected this gratitude-centered perspective when he wrote, "I have learned in whatever situation I am to be content" (Philippians 4:11). This contentment isn't passive resignation but active appreciation for God's provision in every circumstance.

4. From scattered to focused

When our lives are overflowing with possessions, commitments, and digital noise, our spiritual attention becomes equally scattered. We dabble in various practices, bounce between teachers, and flit from one spiritual experience to another without the depth that comes from sustained focus.

Simplicity helps us identify and commit to the specific spiritual practices, community relationships, and service opportunities that best nurture our unique relationship with God. Rather than trying to do everything, we focus on doing a few things well and consistently.

This focused approach reflects Jesus' commendation of Mary, who chose the "one thing necessary" (Luke 10:42) rather than being "anxious and troubled about many things" like her sister Martha.

5. From drivenness to receptivity

Complex, busy lives create a mentality of constant doing—even in our spiritual practices. We approach prayer as another task to complete, Bible reading as information to acquire, and worship as an experience to generate.

Simplicity creates space for receptivity—the capacity to receive from God rather than always producing for Him. It allows us to shift from spiritual drivenness to spiritual responsiveness, from exhausting effort to restful engagement.

Jesus modeled this receptivity when he said, "The Son can do nothing of his own accord, but only what he sees the Father doing" (John 5:19). His activity flowed from receptivity, not autonomous initiative.

The Kick in the Pants: Your Soul Wasn't Built for This Much Noise

Let's get brutally honest: your soul is suffocating under the weight of too much stuff, too many commitments, too much information, and too many distractions. You weren't designed to carry this load, and it's killing your spiritual life.

Your packed schedule has crowded out space for meaningful prayer. Your cluttered home has become a visual metaphor for your cluttered mind. Your attachment to possessions has made you a custodian of stuff rather than a conduit of love. Your phone addiction has decimated your attention span to the point where sitting in God's presence for more than five minutes feels impossible.

And then you wonder why God seems distant? Why Scripture doesn't come alive? Why prayer feels like talking to the ceiling? Why your spiritual life has all the depth of a kiddie pool?

Here's the uncomfortable truth: If your life is too full for God, then your life is too full—period.

Jesus didn't die to give you a more impressive life. He died to give you actual life—one characterized by peace, purpose, joy, and deep connection, not endless acquisition and achievement. He explicitly warned that "the cares of the world and the deceitfulness of riches and the desires for other things enter in and choke the word, making it unfruitful" (Mark 4:19).

Look around. Is that not precisely what's happened? Your spiritual life is being choked out by the very things our culture tells you to pursue.

This isn't about becoming some ultra-minimalist monk who owns three items and lives in silent contemplation. It's about creating enough space in your life that you can actually hear God's voice, focus on what matters, and live with purpose rather than perpetual distraction.

Jesus lived simply. He traveled light. He regularly withdrew from the noise. He wasn't controlled by others' expectations or his culture's definition of success. And he accomplished the most important mission in human history without the benefit of a smartphone, a full calendar, or a closet of options.

Maybe you don't need more—more Bible studies, more worship experiences, more spiritual disciplines, more religious activities. Maybe you need less. Maybe you need to clear away the accumulated clutter of possessions, commitments, digital distractions, and mental noise that's drowning out the still, small voice of God.

Because here's what's at stake: your soul. Not just your comfort or convenience, but your very capacity to know God, to live meaningfully, to love deeply. As Jesus asked, "For what does it profit a man to gain the whole world and forfeit his soul?" (Mark 8:36).

You get to choose. You can continue accumulating stuff you don't need, chasing affirmation on social media, packing your schedule with commitments that don't matter, and wondering why you feel spiritually empty. Or you can embrace the countercultural path of simplicity—owning less, wanting less, doing less—and discover the spaciousness in which God's presence becomes not just a theological concept but a lived reality.

Your soul wasn't built for this much noise. It was built for communion with its Creator. And that communion happens most profoundly not in the whirlwind of endless activity and acquisition, but in the quiet space of enough.

So what will it be? The cluttered life our culture sells as normal, or the focused simplicity that Jesus modeled and your soul desperately needs?

The choice is yours. But your spiritual life depends on it.

Chapter 9:

Silence – The Power of Shut Up

Let's face it: most of us suck at shutting up.

I'm not just talking about our mouths, though God knows we could use some help there too. I'm talking about the constant noise we surround ourselves with, the endless stream of content we consume, the reflexive way we reach for our phones the moment silence threatens to invade our space.

We wake up to alarm apps, fall asleep to Netflix, and fill every moment in between with podcasts, playlists, YouTube videos, audiobooks, news updates, and an endless scroll of hot takes from people we've never met. Even our "quiet time" with God often involves us talking nonstop, reading devotional after devotional, or listening to worship music at full blast.

The result? We've created lives so saturated with noise that we can't hear the thing we claim to want most: God's voice.

Here's the uncomfortable truth: God doesn't always shout. In fact, He rarely does. More often, He speaks in what 1 Kings 19:12 describes as "a low whisper"—a gentle voice easily drowned out by the cacophony of our noisy lives. And if you're never quiet, you'll miss it completely.

Think about it: when was the last time you sat in complete silence for more than five minutes? No music. No podcast. No TV in the background. No scrolling. Just... nothing. If you can't remember, you're not alone. But you're also missing out on one of the most powerful spiritual disciplines available to you.

Silence isn't just the absence of noise; it's the presence of something deeper. It's the space where we finally stop drowning out our own thoughts with distraction. Where we cease the endless performance of our public selves and encounter who we really are. Where we discover what's actually going on in our hearts beneath the surface-level emotions we're so quick to identify. And most importantly, it's where we create the conditions to hear God's voice with clarity.

As Psalm 46:10 commands, "Be still, and know that I am God." Notice the connection: stillness precedes knowing. Not "know that I am God, and then maybe be still if you feel like it." The stillness comes first. The knowing follows.

In this chapter, we're going to explore why silence is so damn hard, why it's absolutely essential, and how to actually practice it without losing your mind in the process. Fair warning: this discipline will make you uncomfortable. It will expose things you've been avoiding. It will challenge your addiction to noise. But it might also transform your relationship with God more profoundly than anything else you do.

Why We're Terrified of Silence

Let's start by addressing the elephant in the room: silence is scary. Most of us avoid it like the plague, and for good reason. Here's why silence freaks us out:

1. Silence forces us to face ourselves

When the noise stops, we're left alone with our thoughts, feelings, and the realities we've been working so hard to avoid. The distractions fall away, and suddenly we're confronted with who we really are—not the carefully curated version we present to others.

This self-confrontation can be deeply uncomfortable. We might become aware of painful emotions we've been suppressing, questions we've been avoiding, or truths about ourselves we'd rather not acknowledge. As Blaise Pascal observed centuries ago, "All of humanity's problems stem from man's inability to sit quietly in a room alone."

The Bible acknowledges this reality. Psalm 139:23-24 is a brave prayer precisely because it invites this kind of self-examination: "Search me, O God, and know my heart! Try me and know my thoughts! And see if there be any grievous way in me, and lead me in the way everlasting!" The psalmist recognizes that we often hide from ourselves, and only God can help us see clearly.

2. Silence feels unproductive

We live in a culture that worships productivity, efficiency, and visible results. Silence doesn't produce anything tangible. You can't measure it, post it on Instagram, or add it to your resume. It feels, by the world's standards, like a waste of time.

This perceived unproductivity triggers our guilt and anxiety. We feel like we should be doing something—anything—rather than just sitting in silence. The very idea of "wasting" time this way can create physical discomfort for those of us who've built our identities around constant activity.

Jesus directly countered this mentality when he told the hyperactive Martha, "you are anxious and troubled about many things, but one thing is necessary. Mary has chosen the good portion, which will not be taken away from her" (Luke 10:41-42). Mary's choice to simply sit at Jesus' feet appeared unproductive by cultural standards, but Jesus identified it as "necessary" and "good."

3. Silence exposes our addictions

The moment we attempt silence, we discover how addicted we've become to constant stimulation. Our fingers twitch for our phones. Our minds race, seeking something—anything—to focus on besides the silence. We feel an almost physical craving for input, entertainment, or distraction.

This withdrawal response reveals how dependent we've become on external stimulation to regulate our internal states. We use noise to avoid boredom, discomfort, anxiety, and loneliness. When that coping mechanism is removed, the underlying discomfort emerges full force.

In John 8:34, Jesus observed that "everyone who practices sin is a slave to sin." While he wasn't specifically addressing our addiction to noise, the principle applies. We've become enslaved to constant stimulation, and freedom requires facing the withdrawal symptoms that come with silence.

4. Silence feels socially awkward

Even in our interpersonal interactions, silence has become almost taboo. Think about the last time a conversation hit a pocket of silence. How quickly did someone rush to fill it? How uncomfortable did that moment feel?

We've been conditioned to equate silence with awkwardness, rejection, or social failure. A "successful" interaction keeps the noise flowing continuously. This social training follows us into our solitude and even into our relationship with God, where we feel compelled to fill every moment with words.

James addressed this tendency directly: "Let every person be quick to hear, slow to speak, slow to anger" (James 1:19). Being "slow to speak" requires comfort with silence—the ability to pause, reflect, and truly listen before jumping in with our own thoughts.

5. Silence opens us to hearing God

This might seem like a positive, not a fear—but stay with me. If we're truly honest, many of us are afraid of what God might say if we actually created space to hear Him. We fear He might challenge our comfortable theological assumptions, call us to something difficult, or address sin we've been conveniently ignoring.

It's often easier to keep talking at God, telling Him our plans and asking for His blessing, than to sit quietly and let Him direct the conversation. Our monologue prayers and noise-filled devotional times can become a way of controlling the relationship—keeping God at a safe, manageable distance.

When God asked Samuel to deliver a difficult message to Eli, Samuel was "afraid to tell the vision to Eli" (1 Samuel 3:15). Similarly, we're often afraid of what God might say if we truly listened, so we avoid creating the conditions where His voice becomes clear.

Understanding these fears is the first step toward overcoming them. Silence is difficult precisely because it's powerful—it creates space for truth, transformation, and authentic encounter with both ourselves and God. The discomfort it produces isn't a sign that something's wrong; it's evidence that something important is happening.

The Biblical Case for Shutting Up

The practice of silence isn't some New Age innovation or Eastern import—it's deeply rooted in Scripture. Let's explore some key biblical foundations for this discipline:

Elijah and the Sound of Low Whisper

Perhaps the most profound biblical illustration of silence comes in 1 Kings 19, when Elijah flees to Mount Horeb after his dramatic showdown with the prophets of Baal. Despite winning that public confrontation, Elijah feels defeated and alone. He needs to hear from God.

What happens next is fascinating:

"And behold, the LORD passed by, and a great and strong wind tore the mountains and broke in pieces the rocks before the LORD, but the LORD was not in the wind. And after the wind an earthquake, but the LORD was not in the earthquake. And after the earthquake a fire, but the LORD was not in the fire. And after the fire the sound of a low whisper. And when Elijah heard it, he wrapped his face in his cloak and went out and stood at the entrance of the cave." (1 Kings 19:11-13)

This story contains several crucial insights about silence:

1. **God often chooses not to speak through the obvious, dramatic channels.** The wind, earthquake, and fire were all impressive displays of power, but God wasn't in them. He chose instead to speak through "a low whisper" (sometimes translated as "a still, small voice").

2. **Hearing God's whisper requires attentive listening.** If Elijah had been distracted, ranting about his problems, or mentally rehearsing his next moves, he would have missed God's voice completely. The whisper demanded his full attention.

3. **God's quiet voice can be more transformative than dramatic displays.** What God said in that whisper changed the course of Elijah's ministry and Israel's history. The whisper wasn't weak; it was precise and powerful.

This story should shake us up. How many times have we missed God's whispered guidance because we were waiting for the dramatic wind, earthquake, or fire? How often have we failed to create the quiet conditions where His low whisper could be heard?

Jesus and His Rhythm of Withdrawal

Jesus—who had the most important mission in history and constant demands on His time—modeled a consistent practice of silence and solitude. Look at these examples:

- "And rising very early in the morning, while it was still dark, he departed and went out to a desolate place, and there he prayed." (Mark 1:35)

- "But he would withdraw to desolate places and pray." (Luke 5:16)

- "After he had dismissed the crowds, he went up on the mountain by himself to pray. When evening came, he was there alone." (Matthew 14:23)

These weren't occasional, random withdrawals. They formed a consistent rhythm in Jesus' life and ministry. He regularly disengaged from activity and noise to be alone with the Father in quiet places.

What's particularly striking is that Jesus often withdrew precisely when demand for Him was highest. In Mark 1, the whole town was gathering at His door with needs. In Matthew 14, He had just fed the 5,000 and the crowds wanted to make Him king. Rather than being driven by these external pressures, Jesus withdrew to reorient Himself to the Father's voice.

If Jesus—who was in perfect communion with the Father at all times—needed these periods of silence away from the noise, how much more do we need them?

The Psalmists and the Practice of Waiting Silently

The Psalms repeatedly emphasize silent waiting before God:

- "For God alone my soul waits in silence; from him comes my salvation." (Psalm 62:1)

- "Be still before the LORD and wait patiently for him." (Psalm 37:7)

- "I have calmed and quieted my soul, like a weaned child with its mother; like a weaned child is my soul within me." (Psalm 131:2)

This waiting isn't passive or empty. It's an active posture of receptivity—creating space for God to speak and move rather than filling every moment with our own agenda and noise.

The image in Psalm 131 is especially powerful. A weaned child sitting with its mother isn't frantically demanding milk or attention. It has learned to simply be present, content in the relationship rather than constantly seeking the next thing. This is the soul posture that silence cultivates.

Ecclesiastes and the Discipline of Fewer Words

The wisdom literature of the Bible explicitly connects silence with wisdom:

- "Be not rash with your mouth, nor let your heart be hasty to utter a word before God, for God is in heaven and you are on earth. Therefore let your words be few." (Ecclesiastes 5:2)

- "When words are many, transgression is not lacking, but whoever restrains his lips is prudent." (Proverbs 10:19)

These passages suggest that our tendency toward constant noise—whether literal speech or the metaphorical "noise" of our busy lives—often leads to folly, sin, and missing God's wisdom. Restraint in words and creating space for silence are marks of wisdom.

The command to "let your words be few" before God challenges our prayer practices. How many of us approach God with nonstop talking, as if we need to fill every moment with words? What might change if we approached prayer with more listening than speaking?

These biblical examples establish silence not as an optional add-on for the super-spiritual but as a core practice modeled by Jesus, the prophets, and the wisdom teachers of Scripture. Far from being unbiblical, silence is woven into the fabric of authentic biblical spirituality.

The Transformative Power of Shut Up

Silence isn't just biblically grounded; it's practically transformative. Here are some of the powerful things that happen when we incorporate regular silence into our spiritual lives:

1. Silence reveals what's really going on inside us

Most of us move through life with only a vague awareness of our actual emotional and spiritual condition. We identify surface feelings like stress, happiness, or frustration, but rarely touch the deeper currents moving beneath.

Silence changes that. When external noise stops, our internal world becomes louder. We start to notice the anxieties, longings, resentments, and questions we've been avoiding. Silence acts as an MRI for the soul, revealing what's actually happening beneath our busyness.

Psalm 139:23-24 is a prayer for precisely this kind of revelation: "Search me, O God, and know my heart! Try me and know my thoughts! And see if there be any grievous way in me, and lead me in the way everlasting!" Silence creates the conditions for this searching to occur.

This self-knowledge is essential for spiritual growth. We can't address what we don't acknowledge. We can't submit to God what we refuse to see. Silence brings our true condition into the light where it can be healed and transformed.

2. Silence trains our spiritual attention span

Our digital lives have decimated our attention spans. Studies show the average human now has an attention span shorter than a goldfish—about 8 seconds. This attention deficit doesn't just affect our work and relationships; it fundamentally impacts our ability to connect with God.

Silence works like spiritual attention training. When we sit in silence—resisting for even a few minutes the urge to reach for our phones or turn on music—we're strengthening our capacity to stay present. We're developing the muscle of sustained attention that real prayer requires.

Jesus highlighted the importance of this undivided attention when he taught, "The eye is the lamp of the body. So, if your eye is healthy, your whole body will be full of light" (Matthew 6:22). The "eye" here refers to our focus—what we give our attention to. Silence helps us develop the ability to fix our spiritual eyes on God rather than constantly darting between distractions.

3. Silence creates space for discernment

In our noisy lives, we often make decisions reflexively, based on surface-level analysis or immediate emotional responses. Silence creates the space needed for true discernment—the deeper wisdom that emerges when we stop reacting and start listening.

This is particularly important for distinguishing between God's voice and our own thoughts or cultural conditioning. When we're constantly surrounded by noise—whether external media or our own internal chatter—we easily mistake our preferences, fears, and conditioned responses for divine guidance.

Paul points to this deeper discernment in Romans 12:2: "Do not be conformed to this world, but be transformed by the renewal of your mind, that by testing you may discern what is the will of God, what is good and acceptable and perfect." This testing and discernment requires mental space that silence provides.

4. Silence helps process grief and pain

Our culture has few healthy mechanisms for processing grief, trauma, and deep emotional pain. Instead, we're encouraged to distract ourselves, "stay positive," and move on as quickly as possible. The constant noise in our lives often serves to numb and avoid these difficult emotions.

Silence removes these avoidance mechanisms, creating space for necessary emotional processing. The grief, loss, or pain we've pushed down has room to surface, be acknowledged, and begin healing. This isn't pleasant—which is why we avoid it—but it's essential for wholeness.

The book of Lamentations models this unflinching confrontation with pain, giving voice to grief rather than avoiding it. Jesus himself didn't avoid emotional suffering but entered fully into it, even expressing to the Father, "My soul is very sorrowful, even to death" (Matthew 26:38). Silence gives us space to follow this example, facing our pain in God's presence rather than running from it.

5. Silence deepens our awareness of God's presence

Perhaps the most significant benefit of silence is the way it attunes us to God's presence—not just intellectually, but experientially. When we silence the constant input that maintains our self-focused world, we create space to recognize the reality that has been there all along: God with us.

This isn't about manufacturing spiritual experiences. It's about removing the barriers to perceiving what's already true. As Jacob realized at Bethel, "Surely the LORD is in this place, and I did not know it" (Genesis 28:16). Silence helps us wake up to God's constant presence that our noise and busyness so often obscure.

Brother Lawrence, the 17th-century monk known for practicing God's presence in everyday tasks, found that regular silence was essential for maintaining awareness of God throughout active work. The quiet moments trained his perception, allowing him to carry that awareness even into busy activity.

6. Silence transforms how we speak

Finally, silence doesn't just change the quality of our quiet moments; it transforms how we engage when we're not silent. When we regularly practice silence, our words become more measured, thoughtful, and impactful.

James addresses this connection directly: "Let every person be quick to hear, slow to speak, slow to anger" (James 1:19). Being "slow to speak" isn't about talking less for its own sake, but about speaking from a place of deep listening—to others, to ourselves, and to God.

In a world of reactive hot takes, constant commentary, and words emptied of meaning through overuse, silence gives our speech a rare quality: weight. The person who knows how to be silent also knows how to speak words that matter.

Silence in a World That Never Shuts Up: Practical Steps

Understanding the importance of silence is one thing; actually practicing it in our noisy world is another challenge entirely. Here are practical approaches to incorporating silence into your life, starting with the most basic and moving toward deeper practices:

Beginner Level: Getting Comfortable with Basic Silence

If the thought of extended silence terrifies you, start with these simple practices to build your silence muscles:

1. The Daily Five

Begin with just five minutes of intentional silence each day. Find a quiet spot, turn off all devices, and simply sit. You don't need to "accomplish" anything—just experience the silence. When your mind starts racing (and it will), gently bring your attention back to the present moment.

Some helpful focuses during this time:
- Your breathing (simply notice the inhale and exhale)
- A simple prayer word or phrase (like "Jesus" or "be still")
- The sensations in your body (without trying to change them)

Do this daily for two weeks before trying to extend the time. Think of it like building any other muscle—start with manageable weight before adding more.

2. Silent Transitions

Most of us fill every transition in our day with noise—podcasts during commutes, music while exercising, videos while eating. Challenge yourself to keep one daily transition completely silent for a week.

Good candidates for silent transitions:
- Your morning routine before work
- Your commute (or part of it)
- The first 10 minutes after arriving home
- Your pre-bedtime routine

These transition silences create natural boundaries in your day and prevent the constant bleeding of activity and noise from one context to another.

3. The Phone Box

Our phones are silence-killing machines, designed to capture attention and fill every potential moment of quiet. Create physical and temporal boundaries for your device:

- Designate phone-free zones in your home (bedroom, dining area)
- Establish phone-free times (first hour after waking, meal times, hour before bed)
- Create a "phone box" where your device goes during these times

This practice isn't about demonizing technology but about reclaiming your attention from its constant pull.

4. Silent Walking

Walking in silence—without headphones, phone calls, or companions—is a gentle way to experience silence while moving. The physical activity helps manage the restlessness that can make sitting silence challenging for beginners.

Start with just 10-15 minutes of silent walking. Pay attention to:
- The sounds around you (birds, wind, distant voices)
- Physical sensations (feet on ground, air on skin, muscles moving)
- Your breathing and heartbeat

This practice helps break the association between silence and inactivity, showing how awareness can be maintained even in movement.

Intermediate Level: Deepening into Reflective Silence

Once basic silence becomes less intimidating, explore these practices that introduce more intentional reflection within silence:

1. The Silent Start and End

Bookend your day with silence. Begin with 10-15 minutes of silence before engaging with devices, news, or others' voices. End with a similar period before sleep.

During these bookends:
- Notice your mental and emotional state without judgment
- Become aware of what you're carrying into or out of the day
- Identify one quality you want to bear into the day or release before sleep

This practice creates a container around your day, preventing the world's noise from being the first and last thing shaping your consciousness.

2. The Awareness Examen

Adapted from Ignatius of Loyola's spiritual practice, this silent reflection helps you notice God's presence throughout your day. Spend 15 minutes in silence asking:

- For what moment today am I most grateful?
- For what moment today am I least grateful?
- Where did I sense God's presence today?
- Where did I resist God today?
- What is one thing I'm being invited to notice, change, or accept?

This practice trains you to see beyond surface events to the spiritual currents moving in your ordinary life.

3. Silent Reading

Most of us read in a utilitarian way—extracting information quickly before moving on. Silent reading as a spiritual practice involves reading small portions of Scripture or spiritual texts very slowly, with long pauses of silence.

Try reading just 3-5 verses or a short paragraph, then sitting in complete silence for several minutes, allowing the words to sink deeper than intellectual understanding. This practice, sometimes called Lectio Divina, treats reading as a doorway to presence rather than merely information acquisition.

4. Sabbath Silence

Set aside a portion of your Sabbath (or create a Sabbath if you don't observe one) for extended silence. This might be an hour or several hours where you disconnect from media, conversation, and productive activity to simply be present with God.

Unlike shorter silences that focus on a particular reflection, Sabbath silence creates space for God to bring to your attention whatever He wishes. It's an exercise in receptivity and trust.

Advanced Level: Extended and Communal Silence

For those ready to go deeper, these practices involve more substantial commitments to silence:

1. The Silent Retreat Day

Once per quarter, schedule a full day of intentional silence. This doesn't require going to a monastery—it can be done at home (if you can ensure no interruptions) or in a natural setting like a park, beach, or forest.

Structure for a retreat day:
- Begin with a simple intention for the day
- Alternate periods of silent sitting, walking, and gentle activity
- Bring Scripture or a spiritual book for occasional brief reading
- Include physical movement to manage restlessness
- End with reflection on what emerged during the silence

A full day of silence often allows deeper things to surface that shorter periods might not reach.

2. Silent Meals

Eating in silence—truly focusing on the food, the experience of eating, and gratitude—is a powerful practice in our distracted culture. Try one meal per week in complete silence, whether alone or with others who share the practice.

During silent meals:
- Notice the appearance, texture, smell, and taste of the food
- Become aware of hunger and fullness signals
- Reflect on the journey of the food from source to plate
- Express gratitude for each element of the meal

This practice transforms a daily necessity into a contemplative experience.

3. Technology Silence

Graduate from limited phone boundaries to periodic extended technology fasts. Once per month, try 24-48 hours completely disconnected from all optional technology (phones, computers, television, radio).

During these fasts:
- Notice withdrawal symptoms as they arise
- Become aware of habitual reaching for devices
- Observe how time perception changes
- Pay attention to the quality of your attention to others

These longer disconnections reveal technology dependencies that shorter boundaries might not expose.

4. Silent Community

Find or create opportunities for shared silence. This might be through:
- A contemplative service at a church
- A meditation group
- A silent retreat with others
- Regular "silent sits" with friends or family

Communal silence has a different quality than solitary silence. The presence of others creating space together often deepens the experience and provides accountability for maintaining the practice.

When Silence Gets Real: Navigating the Challenges

As you incorporate more silence into your life, you'll inevitably encounter challenges. Here's how to navigate some common difficulties:

Challenge 1: The Restless Mind

The moment you try to be silent, your mind seems to kick into overdrive. To-do lists, worries, creative ideas, and random memories flood in, making "mental silence" seem impossible.

How to Navigate It:

1. **Recognize this is normal.** A busy mind in silence doesn't mean you're failing; it means you're human. The goal isn't to empty your mind but to shift from being controlled by thoughts to observing them.

2. **Use a focus anchor.** Give your attention a home base to return to when thoughts pull you away. This might be your breathing, a prayer word, or physical sensations. When you notice your mind wandering, gently return to this anchor.

3. **Try the "leaves on a stream" approach.** Imagine your thoughts are leaves floating on a stream. You don't need to stop them or follow them—just watch them appear and float away.

4. **Consider journaling before silence.** Sometimes a "brain dump" on paper before silence helps clear mental clutter, making silence more accessible.

Jesus acknowledged the challenge of a wandering mind when he asked his disciples, "Why are you thinking these things in your hearts?" (Luke 5:22). He knew that human minds naturally fill with thoughts, some helpful and others distracting.

Challenge 2: Uncomfortable Emotions

Silence often brings to the surface emotions we've been avoiding through busyness and distraction. Unexpected sadness, anxiety, anger, or grief may emerge, making silence feel threatening.

How to Navigate It:
1. **Welcome emotions as messengers.** Difficult feelings aren't enemies to be vanquished but signals providing important information about your inner state.

2. **Practice being with emotions without acting on them.** Notice where you feel them in your body, what thoughts accompany them, and how they shift over time.

3. **Use the RAIN approach:**
    - Recognize the emotion
    - Allow it to be present without resistance
    - Investigate it with kind curiosity
    - Nurture yourself with compassion

4. **Know when to seek support.** If emotions feel overwhelming or traumatic memories emerge, consider working with a therapist or spiritual director who can provide guidance for processing difficult material.

The Psalms model this honest emotional expression before God. Feelings of abandonment, fear, grief, and even anger are brought directly to God rather than suppressed or avoided. As Psalm 62:8 encourages, "pour out your heart before him."

Challenge 3: The Resistance of Others

As you prioritize silence, you may face resistance from others who don't understand or feel threatened by this practice. Family members may interpret your need for silence as rejection, or friends might pressure you to stay constantly connected.

How to Navigate It:
1. **Explain the purpose.** Help others understand that silence isn't about avoiding them but about being more fully present when you are with them.

2. **Invite rather than impose.** Instead of demanding silence, invite others to experience smaller tastes of it with you—perhaps a silent meal or a brief period of quiet before an important conversation.

3. **Negotiate boundaries respectfully.** Work together to find times and spaces for silence that honor both your needs and important relationships.

4. **Model the fruits.** Let others see how silence changes you—creating more patience, presence, and peace—which often becomes the most compelling argument for its value.

Jesus faced this resistance regularly, with crowds and even disciples seeking constant access to him. His response was both firm in maintaining boundaries and compassionate toward those seeking him. Mark 1:35-39 shows how he balanced withdrawal for prayer with responsive engagement.

Challenge 4: Spiritual Dryness

Sometimes silence seems spiritually empty. Instead of profound connection with God, you experience boredom, doubt, or a sense of divine absence. These "desert" experiences can be deeply discouraging.

How to Navigate It:
1. **Recognize this as part of the journey.** Every major spiritual figure in Scripture and church history experienced periods of seeming divine absence. These seasons aren't failures but important parts of spiritual maturation.

2. **Continue the practice without demanding feelings.** Don't mistake emotional experiences for God's presence. Sometimes the deepest work happens in the apparent void.

3. **Explore what the dryness might be teaching.** Are you seeking God or spiritual experiences? Is there an invitation to deeper faith beyond feelings?

4. **Remember that training isn't always enjoyable.** Like physical exercise, spiritual disciplines aren't measured by how they feel in the moment but by how they shape you over time.

The Psalms honestly express these experiences. "My God, my God, why have you forsaken me?" begins Psalm 22—the very words Jesus quoted on the cross. Yet the same psalm ends with renewed trust despite the feeling of abandonment.

Silence in Different Life Contexts

The practice of silence doesn't look identical in every life situation. Here's how to adapt silence for different contexts:

For Parents of Young Children

Finding silence with young children in the house can seem impossible. Their needs are constant, and their natural volume level is "full." Yet silence remains vital for parental spiritual health.

Practical approaches:
- Use natural sleep rhythms (naps, earlier bedtimes) to create small pockets of silence

- Trade "silence shifts" with a partner or friend—each covering for the other for 30 minutes
- Teach even young children simple silence practices (1-2 minutes of "listening time")
- Use silent activities where children focus on drawing or building while you practice presence
- Redefine success—even 3-5 minutes of intentional silence is valuable in this season

Jesus demonstrated special care for parents, healing children and welcoming them when disciples tried to send them away. He understands the unique challenges of parenting and meets you in the stolen moments of silence you can find.

For Those in High-Pressure Careers

High-demand jobs with constant connectivity expectations present particular challenges for silence. The working world rarely values or protects quiet space.

Practical approaches:
- Schedule silence like any other important meeting—literally block it on your calendar
- Create transition silence between work and home (10 minutes in the car before entering the house)
- Use lunch breaks occasionally for silent walking or sitting

- Establish firm work/device boundaries (no email after 8pm, work-free Sabbath)
- Find a quiet space near work for brief midday silence retreats

Daniel maintained his prayer practices three times daily despite holding high office in Babylon. His commitment to spiritual disciplines actually enhanced his effectiveness rather than diminishing it (Daniel 6:3-10).

For Those in Communal Living Situations

Roommates, dorms, or multi-generational households can make physical silence hard to find. Shared spaces mean others' noise is often beyond your control.

Practical approaches:
- Use headphones with white noise or noise-canceling capabilities to create auditory space
- Find "third spaces" for silence (libraries, parks, places of worship open for prayer)
- Establish shared quiet hours that all household members respect
- Create a designated "quiet corner" in the home, even if it's small
- Invite housemates into occasional shared silence practices

The early church navigated communal living while maintaining spiritual practices. Acts 2:42-47 shows how they balanced shared life with devoted prayer.

For Those in Caregiver Roles

Caring for elderly parents, chronically ill family members, or others with high dependency needs creates unique silence challenges. The responsibility can be constant and mentally consuming even in quiet moments.

Practical approaches:
- Use respite care or family relief not just for errands but for silence
- Practice micro-silences (2-3 minutes) during natural breaks in care routines
- Find silence in parallel activities (sitting quietly while the person naps or watches a show)
- Join online silent prayer groups for support and accountability
- Remember that service itself can become a form of prayer and presence

Jesus regularly withdrew for prayer despite constant demands for healing and teaching. His example reminds caregivers that taking time for spiritual renewal isn't selfish but essential for sustainable service.

The 30-Day Silence Challenge

Ready to experience the transformative power of silence? This 30-day challenge gradually introduces silence practices, building from beginner to more advanced levels. Each week increases the depth and duration of silence, allowing you to develop comfort and skill with this discipline.

Week 1: Establishing the Foundation

Day 1: Find a quiet place and sit in complete silence for 5 minutes. No music, no phone, no media. Just you, being still. Notice what arises without judgment.

Day 2: Practice "transition silence" by turning off all media during your commute or another daily transition time. Notice how different the familiar experience becomes.

Day 3: Create a "silent start" by spending the first 5 minutes after waking in silence, before checking devices or beginning activities.

Day 4: Take a 10-minute silent walk. Leave your phone behind or put it on airplane mode. Pay attention to your surroundings with all your senses.

Day 5: Practice "presence pauses" throughout the day—3 moments where you stop for 60 seconds, take three deep breaths, and notice what's happening within and around you.

Day 6: Eat one meal in complete silence. Focus entirely on the experience of eating—the tastes, textures, and the act of nourishment.

Day 7: Reflect on the first week. What was challenging? What was surprisingly helpful? Write down your observations.

Week 2: Deepening the Practice

Day 8: Extend your silence practice to 10 minutes. Open your time with: "Here I am, Lord" and simply remain in God's presence.

Day 9: Create a "digital sunset"—a time each evening (start with 30 minutes before bed) when all screens are turned off, creating space for quiet reflection.

Day 10: Practice "thresholds of silence"—pause for 10 seconds of silence before entering new spaces or beginning new activities, resetting your attention.

Day 11: Try 10 minutes of silent scripture reading. Read a short passage very slowly, with long pauses between verses, allowing the words to sink in.

Day 12: Practice the awareness examen in silence: Spend 10 minutes reflecting on when you felt closest to and furthest from God today.

Day 13: Create a "silent space" in your home—a corner or area dedicated to quiet prayer and reflection, free from distractions.

Day 14: Take a "sound sabbath"—a 2-hour period without intentional noise (music, TV, radio, podcasts). Notice how this changes your perception.

Week 3: Building Endurance

Day 15: Extend your daily silence practice to 15 minutes. Use the breath prayer—breathing in with "Lord Jesus Christ" and out with "have mercy on me."

Day 16: Practice "silent listening" in conversation. Focus entirely on what the other person is saying without planning your response or interrupting.

Day 17: Engage in a creative activity in silence (drawing, gardening, cooking, etc.). Notice how the absence of background noise affects your creativity.

Day 18: Try "centering prayer"—15 minutes of silence using a sacred word (like "Jesus," "Peace," or "Love") to gently return your attention when it wanders.

Day 19: Practice "silence before speaking"—pause for 3 seconds before responding in conversations today, creating space to respond rather than react.

Day 20: Take a 30-minute silent nature walk. Pay attention to the sounds, sights, and sensations of the natural world.

Day 21: Plan a "mini-retreat"—90 minutes of intentional silence that includes sitting, walking, and reflection. Notice what emerges in this extended quiet.

Week 4: Integrating Silence into Life

Day 22: Extend your daily silence practice to 20 minutes. Begin with "Be still and know that I am

God," then gradually reduce the phrase: "Be still and know that I am," "Be still and know," "Be still," "Be."

Day 23: Practice a "complaint fast"—go 24 hours without complaining, criticizing, or speaking negatively, creating space for gratitude and constructive speech.

Day 24: Create a "silent morning"—spend the first hour after waking without media, conversation, or noise, allowing your day to begin from a centered place.

Day 25: Try "intercessory silence"—spend 20 minutes holding others in silent prayer, without words, simply bringing them into God's presence with love.

Day 26: Practice "work silence"—find ways to incorporate periods of silence into your workday (silent lunch, 5 minutes between meetings, quiet focus time).

Day 27: Experiment with "communal silence" by inviting a friend or family member to share 10 minutes of silence with you, then briefly discuss the experience.

Day 28: Take a "technology sabbath"—24 hours completely disconnected from optional technology (phones, computers, TV) to experience digital silence.

Day 29: Create a personalized silence practice plan for moving forward, based on what you've learned about yourself and what practices have been most meaningful.

Day 30: Reflect on the entire 30-day journey. How has silence changed your awareness of yourself, others, and God? What will you carry forward?

Throughout this challenge, keep a simple journal noting:
- Physical sensations during silence
- Emotional states that arise
- Insights or awareness that emerge
- Resistance or difficulties encountered
- Effects of silence on your relationships and daily activities

This documentation helps you recognize patterns and growth that might otherwise go unnoticed in the silence journey.

Why Most People Won't Do This

Let's be real: despite everything we've discussed about the biblical foundations and transformative benefits of silence, most people reading this chapter won't actually implement these practices. Here's why—and why you might want to be the exception:

1. Silence reveals what we're avoiding

Many of us maintain busy, noisy lives precisely because we're avoiding something: unprocessed grief, difficult decisions, uncomfortable questions about our identity or purpose, awareness of emptiness or disconnection. Silence threatens to bring these issues to the surface where we'd have to deal with them.

But here's the truth: what you're avoiding isn't going away. It's shaping your life from the shadows, influencing decisions and relationships in ways you don't recognize. Silence brings these hidden influences into the light where they can be acknowledged, addressed, and healed.

As Jesus said, "Nothing is hidden that will not be made manifest, nor is anything secret that will not be known and come to light" (Luke 8:17). Silence simply accelerates this inevitable process of revelation.

2. Silence feels like a luxury we can't afford

In our productivity-obsessed culture, silence feels like an indulgence for those with abundant leisure time—not for normal people with jobs, families, and responsibilities. We convince ourselves we'll practice silence "someday" when life is less demanding (which, of course, never happens).

But consider this: Jesus had the most important mission in human history—literally saving the world—and still prioritized silence and solitude. If silence was essential for Jesus, not optional, how can we possibly consider it a luxury rather than a necessity?

Mark 1:35-39 shows Jesus withdrawing for prayer even when crowds were searching for him and needs were overwhelming. His effectiveness flowed from these times of connection with the Father, not despite them.

3. Silence requires swimming upstream

Our entire culture is designed to eliminate silence. Restaurants have background music, waiting rooms have TVs, retail stores have carefully curated playlists, and our devices ensure we never have to experience a moment without stimulation. Choosing silence means deliberately countering these powerful cultural currents.

This countercultural stance isn't easy or comfortable. It might mean appearing strange to others, setting boundaries that aren't commonly understood, or missing out on some forms of cultural connection.

But as Romans 12:2 challenges us, "Do not be conformed to this world, but be transformed by the renewal of your mind." This transformation requires creating space that the world constantly tries to fill with noise and distraction.

4. Silence demands patience in an instant world

We live in an age of immediate results. We can get same-day delivery, stream any movie instantly, and become outraged if websites take more than a few seconds to load. Silence doesn't play by these rules.

The benefits of silence compound slowly over time. The first few attempts often feel uncomfortable, unproductive, or even like failures. Real transformation might take months of consistent practice before becoming noticeable.

Jesus used agricultural metaphors precisely because spiritual growth resembles farming more than manufacturing—it requires patience through seasons of apparent dormancy before harvest becomes visible. As James 5:7 advises, "Be patient, therefore, brothers, until the coming of the Lord. See how the farmer waits for the precious fruit of the earth, being patient about it, until it receives the early and the late rains."

Despite these challenges, the minority who do embrace silence discover something remarkable: beneath the initial discomfort lies a wellspring of clarity, peace, and connection that the noisy majority never experience. Which group will you choose to join?

Signs of Growth in the Silence Journey

How do you know if your silence practice is "working"? While the effects are often subtle and cumulative rather than dramatic, here are some indicators of growth:

1. Increased awareness of internal states

As silence becomes more familiar, you'll notice greater awareness of your thoughts, emotions, and bodily sensations. You'll catch yourself reacting earlier in the process, before reactions become automatic behaviors. This self-awareness creates space for choice rather than compulsion.

Paul points to this progression in Romans 7:15-8:2, moving from being controlled by impulses he doesn't understand to experiencing "the law of the Spirit of life" that brings freedom. Silence helps accelerate this movement toward conscious living.

2. More comfortable gaps in conversation

You'll find yourself less anxious about conversational silence and less compelled to fill every pause with words. This comfort with interpersonal silence creates space for more meaningful connection and more thoughtful responses rather than reactive word-filling.

Jesus demonstrated this comfort with silence during his trial, when "he gave him no answer, not even to a single charge, so that the governor was greatly amazed" (Matthew 27:14). This wasn't passive non-response but powerful restraint that came from deep centeredness.

3. Reduced reactivity to triggers

Regular silence practice creates a gap between stimulus and response. Things that previously triggered immediate emotional reactions—a critical comment, a disappointment, a change of plans—now pass through a space of awareness before you respond.

This gap is what allows the wisdom of James 1:19 to become practical: "Let every person be quick to hear, slow to speak, slow to anger." Without internal space cultivated through silence, being "slow to speak" and "slow to anger" remains a nice but impossible ideal.

4. Greater discernment of inner voices

Most of us have multiple internal "voices" competing for attention—the inner critic, the people-pleaser, the fearful child, the loving adult. Silence helps you distinguish between these voices rather than automatically identifying with whichever is loudest in the moment.

Most importantly, silence helps you recognize God's voice amid this internal committee. As Jesus said, "My sheep hear my voice, and I know them, and they follow me" (John 10:27). Regular silence develops this voice recognition that allows for clearer guidance.

5. Increased capacity to be present

Perhaps the most noticeable growth sign is an enhanced ability to be fully present—with others, with tasks, and with God. Rather than constantly being pulled to the next thing, rehashing the past, or anxiously anticipating the future, you find yourself more able to engage with what's actually happening now.

Jesus modeled this remarkable quality of presence. Whether with crowds, individuals, or his Father in prayer, he was fully there. His invitation to "abide in me" (John 15:4) is essentially a call to this kind of sustained presence—dwelling with him rather than just visiting occasionally.

None of these growth indicators typically happen overnight or in dramatic fashion. Like physical fitness, the benefits of silence compound through consistent practice rather than occasional intense efforts. Be patient with the process, celebrating small shifts that signal deeper transformation underway.

The Kick in the Pants: You Won't Hear God if You Never Shut Up

Let's get brutally honest: you say you want to hear from God, but you've structured your entire life to make that nearly impossible.

You wake up and immediately check your phone, bombarding your brain with other people's thoughts before you've even had a single one of your own. You fill every commute with podcasts or calls. You work with multiple screens open and notifications constantly pinging for your attention. You exercise with earbuds firmly inserted. You fall asleep to Netflix. Even your "quiet time" is probably filled with worship music, devotional reading, and your own nonstop talking to God.

And then you wonder why God feels distant? Why His voice seems muffled or nonexistent? Why your spiritual life feels shallow and unsatisfying?

Here's the uncomfortable truth: God is speaking. You're just too loud to hear Him.

Remember Elijah? He had just experienced the ultimate spiritual high—calling down fire from heaven, defeating hundreds of false prophets, ending a devastating drought. Talk about a mountaintop experience! But when threats sent him running into the wilderness, God didn't speak to him through more dramatic displays of power.

Instead, there came "a low whisper" (1 Kings 19:12). A divine murmur. A sacred hush. And had Elijah been distracted, ranting, or hitting refresh on his Twitter feed, he would have missed it completely.

That whisper contained the direction that would shape the rest of his ministry and the future of Israel.

The quietest divine communication carried the most significant content.

The same is true for you. God's most important guidance, His most profound comfort, His most personal affirmation often comes not in spiritual spectaculars but in the hushed moments when you're finally quiet enough to hear the whisper.

"But I'm too busy for silence," you protest. Really? You're busier than Jesus? He had three years to save the world, crowds constantly demanding His attention, and disciples who needed intensive training—yet He consistently withdrew to desolate places to pray. If Jesus couldn't fulfill His mission without regular silence, what makes you think you can?

"But silence is uncomfortable," you argue. Of course it is! Anything worth doing usually starts with discomfort. The first time you exercise, it hurts. The first time you try to pray in silence, your mind races and your body fidgets. But just as physical training eventually produces strength and endurance, silence practice gradually creates spiritual capacity you currently lack.

Look, God isn't going to shout over your Spotify playlist. He's not going to force His way through your Netflix binge. He's not going to compete with your social media scroll or your news addiction. He's offered something better: His presence, His guidance, His love—available in the silence you refuse to create.

As the psalmist discovered, "For God alone my soul waits in silence; from him comes my salvation" (Psalm 62:1). Not from more information, more activities, more noise—but from silence before God alone.

So here's your choice: you can continue drowning in the noise, spiritually malnourished while complaining that God doesn't speak to you. Or you can do the uncomfortable, countercultural work of creating silence—and discover the God who has been trying to reach you all along.

If Elijah had missed that whisper, he would have missed the next phase of his calling. What might you be missing because you can't shut up and listen?

The answer is waiting in the silence.

Chapter 10:

Evangelism – Sharing Your Truth Without Being a Jerk

Let's start with the uncomfortable truth: most Christians would rather get a root canal than talk about Jesus with a non-Christian friend.

We've turned "evangelism" into a terrifying ordeal—something that requires special training, perfect theology, and the argumentative skills of a seasoned debate champion. Or worse, we've reduced it to awkward conversations where we try to steer every chat about the weather into an opportunity to ask, "If you died tonight, do you know where you'd spend eternity?"

No wonder people avoid us at parties.

Here's another uncomfortable truth: a lot of non-Christians have evangelism trauma. They've been cornered by well-meaning but socially clueless believers who treated them like projects instead of people. They've been hit with manipulative tactics, guilt trips, or high-pressure spiritual sales pitches. They've watched Christians argue contradictions in their behavior by day and preach about Jesus by night.

And yet—despite our fear and despite our frequent screw-ups—Jesus still gave us a pretty clear directive in Matthew 28:19-20: "Go therefore and make disciples of all nations, baptizing them in the name of the Father and of the Son and of the Holy Spirit, teaching them to observe all that I have commanded you."

He didn't say, "Go therefore, and make sure everyone believes exactly the right theological positions before they die." He didn't say, "Go therefore, and win arguments on the internet." He certainly didn't say, "Go therefore, and be so obnoxious about your faith that people cross the street when they see you coming."

He said to make disciples—people who follow Him, learn from Him, and live like Him.

So how do we do that without being jerks? How do we share the most important truth we know without manipulating, pressuring, or annoying the people we care about? How do we talk about Jesus in a way that actually sounds like good news rather than a threat or an ultimatum?

That's what this chapter is about. Not street-preaching techniques or memorized gospel presentations, but how to authentically share your faith in a way that honors both the message and the human being receiving it. Because evangelism doesn't have to suck for you or the person you're talking to. In fact, when done right, it's one of the most life-giving things you can do.

The Evangelism Problem: Where We Went Wrong

Before we talk about how to share your faith effectively, let's address some of the problematic approaches that have given evangelism such a bad reputation:

The Sales Pitch Approach

Many of us were taught evangelism methods that feel more like selling timeshares than sharing good news. We memorize scripts, anticipate objections, and try to "close the deal" with a prayer. We reduce complex spiritual journeys to a single moment of decision, and we measure success by how many conversions we can count.

This approach treats people as targets rather than individuals with unique stories, questions, and perspectives. It prioritizes getting someone to say a prayer over building a genuine relationship where discipleship can happen organically.

Jesus never used this approach. He tailored His conversations to each person's specific situation. With Nicodemus, an educated religious leader, Jesus had a deep theological discussion about being born again (John 3). With the Samaritan woman, He started with a conversation about water before addressing her relationship history (John 4). He never used one-size-fits-all scripts.

The Information Dump Approach

Some Christians believe evangelism means transferring the maximum amount of theological information in the minimum amount of time. They overwhelm people with doctrinal details, Bible verses, and apologetic arguments—often before establishing any trust or understanding the person's actual questions.

This approach assumes that non-belief is primarily an information problem rather than a heart, will, or experiential issue. It focuses on convincing the intellect while potentially neglecting the whole person.

Paul recognized the limitation of mere information when he wrote to the Corinthians: "And I, when I came to you, brothers, did not come proclaiming to you the testimony of God with lofty speech or wisdom... my speech and my message were not in plausible words of wisdom, but in demonstration of the Spirit and of power" (1 Corinthians 2:1, 4). He understood that transformed lives speak more powerfully than clever arguments.

The Fear-Based Approach

Perhaps the most damaging approach uses fear as the primary motivator—painting vivid pictures of hell, judgment, and eternal torture to scare people into the kingdom. This method might produce short-term decisions, but it rarely creates mature disciples who understand God's love.

It presents God primarily as an angry judge ready to punish rather than a loving Father seeking reconciliation. It emphasizes escaping consequences rather than entering into relationship.

While Jesus certainly spoke about judgment, He more frequently emphasized the positive invitation of the kingdom. His central message wasn't "Flee from hell!" but "The kingdom of God is at hand; repent and believe in the gospel" (Mark 1:15). He called people toward something beautiful, not just away from something terrible.

The Argument-Winning Approach

Some Christians approach evangelism like a debate competition where the goal is to outargue the other person and emerge victorious. They focus on having the perfect response to every objection, proving the other person wrong, and winning intellectual battles.

This approach often produces more heat than light. Even if you win the argument, you might lose the person. It creates a competitive dynamic that can build walls rather than bridges.

Peter cautioned against this combative stance when he instructed believers to share their faith "with gentleness and respect" (1 Peter 3:15). The goal isn't to defeat people in verbal sparring but to lovingly guide them toward truth.

The Cultural Warrior Approach

Another problematic approach conflates evangelism with fighting cultural battles. It focuses more on opposing certain political positions, condemning specific behaviors, or winning back society than on introducing people to Jesus.

This approach often alienates the very people we're trying to reach before they even hear the gospel. It creates the impression that becoming a Christian means adopting a particular political stance or cultural identity rather than following Jesus.

Jesus consistently separated His kingdom message from the political agendas of His day. When people tried to make Him take sides in cultural power struggles, He repeatedly redirected the conversation to spiritual matters and individual transformation. His approach was revolutionary without being merely political.

A Better Way: Biblical Foundations for Effective Evangelism

Now that we've identified some unhelpful approaches, let's explore what Scripture actually teaches about sharing the good news effectively:

1. It Starts with Relationship

The gospel is fundamentally about a restored relationship with God, and it's most effectively shared in the context of genuine human relationships. Jesus invested deeply in people's lives before calling them to follow Him.

Consider the pattern in Luke 5:1-11. Jesus didn't begin by preaching at Peter. He entered Peter's world (his boat), helped with his work (fishing), demonstrated His power (miraculous catch), and only then called Peter to follow Him. The interaction was relational, not transactional.

This doesn't mean you need years of friendship before ever mentioning Jesus. But it does mean approaching evangelism as an ongoing conversation within authentic relationship, not a one-time information transfer between strangers.

2. It Requires Authentic Living

Our lives either amplify or contradict our message. Effective evangelism flows from a life visibly transformed by the gospel, not just from correct words about the gospel.

Jesus highlighted this connection when He told His followers, "By this all people will know that you are my disciples, if you have love for one another" (John

13:35). The way believers treat each other and others speaks volumes about the reality of their message.

Peter emphasized the same principle: "Keep your conduct among the Gentiles honorable, so that when they speak against you as evildoers, they may see your good deeds and glorify God" (1 Peter 2:12). Authentic Christian living creates credibility for verbal witness.

3. It Involves Actually Opening Your Mouth

While our lives should support our message, evangelism ultimately requires words. People need to hear the specific content of the gospel, not just observe its effects.

Paul makes this explicit in Romans 10:14: "How are they to believe in him of whom they have never heard? And how are they to hear without someone preaching?" Faith comes through hearing the message about Christ, not just by watching Christians live good lives.

Jesus commissioned His followers to be "witnesses" (Acts 1:8)—people who verbally testify to what they have seen and experienced. A witness in a courtroom would never silently point to their actions and expect others to understand their testimony. They speak up.

4. It's Empowered by the Holy Spirit

Effective evangelism isn't accomplished through human persuasion alone but through the work of the Holy Spirit. Our role is faithful witness; the Spirit's role is conviction and heart-change.

Jesus promised, "When the Holy Spirit has come upon you, you will be my witnesses" (Acts 1:8). The power for evangelism comes from God, not from our eloquence or strategic approaches.

John records Jesus explaining that the Spirit "will convict the world concerning sin and righteousness and judgment" (John 16:8). This takes significant pressure off us—we don't need to convict anyone. That's the Spirit's job. We simply need to share the truth in love and trust God with the results.

5. It Requires Listening, Not Just Speaking

Effective evangelism involves understanding the person you're talking to—their story, questions, and current spiritual perspective. This requires genuine listening, not just waiting for your turn to speak.

Jesus modeled this brilliantly. When the rich young ruler approached Him, Jesus didn't launch into a prepared speech but asked questions and carefully addressed the specific idolatry in the man's life (Mark

10:17-22). When Nicodemus came with questions, Jesus engaged directly with those questions rather than redirecting to unrelated topics (John 3:1-21).

James captures this priority: "Let every person be quick to hear, slow to speak" (James 1:19). This applies especially in evangelistic conversations, where understanding someone's actual spiritual condition matters more than delivering a generic message.

6. It's About Making Disciples, Not Just Converts

The Great Commission calls us to make disciples, not merely to record decisions. Effective evangelism is the beginning of a discipleship journey, not a one-time transaction.

Jesus emphasized this ongoing process: "Go therefore and make disciples of all nations, baptizing them...teaching them to observe all that I have commanded you" (Matthew 28:19-20). The goal is not just initial belief but lifelong following.

Paul modeled this disciple-making focus in his ministry: "Him we proclaim, warning everyone and teaching everyone with all wisdom, that we may present everyone mature in Christ" (Colossians 1:28). His goal wasn't just conversion but maturity.

7. It Respects Human Dignity and Freedom

Effective evangelism honors the image of God in each person by respecting their freedom to respond or not respond. It offers truth without manipulation, coercion, or disrespect.

Peter instructs believers to share their hope "with gentleness and respect" (1 Peter 3:15), recognizing that authentic faith cannot be forced or manipulated.

Jesus Himself demonstrated this respect for human freedom. When the rich young ruler walked away sad, Jesus let him go (Mark 10:22). He didn't chase him down, manipulate him emotionally, or pressure him to reconsider. Jesus offered truth in love but respected the man's freedom to respond.

Practical Steps: How to Share Your Faith Without Being a Jerk

With these biblical foundations in mind, let's explore practical ways to share your faith authentically and effectively:

1. Start with Your Own Story

Your personal testimony is uniquely powerful because it's yours—no one can argue with your experience. You don't need theological degrees or apologetics training to share how Jesus has changed your life.

Paul frequently used his own story as an evangelistic tool. In Acts 26, when speaking before King Agrippa, he shared his personal encounter with Jesus and its impact on his life. This approach is disarming because it's sharing experience, not just asserting doctrine.

Key elements of an effective testimony:
- Your life before Christ (without glamorizing sin)
- How you encountered Jesus
- The difference He's made in your life
- Specific examples of transformation

Keep it concise (2-3 minutes), authentic (no spiritual exaggeration), and relatable (avoid Christian jargon). Practice sharing it naturally, not as a memorized script.

2. Ask Good Questions and Actually Listen

Evangelism should be dialogical, not monological. Good questions demonstrate genuine interest in the other person and help you understand where they're coming from spiritually.

Jesus asked questions all the time—not because He needed information but because questions engage people in self-reflection. "Who do you say that I am?" (Matthew 16:15) remains one of the most important spiritual questions anyone can consider.

Helpful questions to ask:
- "What's your spiritual background?"
- "What's your impression of Jesus?"
- "What do you think happens after we die?"
- "If you could ask God one question, what would it be?"
- "What do you think is the biggest problem with the world?"

Listen to understand, not just to respond. Pay attention to both what's said and what's not said. Look for underlying assumptions, fears, and longings that might reveal spiritual openness.

3. Find Common Ground

Effective evangelism builds bridges, not walls. Look for shared values, experiences, or concerns that can serve as connection points for spiritual conversation.

Paul demonstrated this approach in Athens. Speaking to philosophers, he noted their religious interests and even quoted their own poets before introducing the gospel (Acts 17:22-34). He started with what they valued and built a bridge to Christ.

Potential common ground might include:
- Desire for purpose and meaning
- Concern about suffering and injustice
- Experience of broken relationships
- Questions about mortality
- Appreciation for certain moral values or virtues

Starting with shared concerns builds rapport and shows that you see the person as more than just a conversion target.

4. Address Actual Questions, Not Assumed Ones

Many evangelistic approaches answer questions no one is asking while ignoring the questions people actually have. Effective faith-sharing engages with real obstacles to belief, not just theoretical ones.

When the rich young ruler asked Jesus what he needed to do to inherit eternal life, Jesus directly addressed his specific obstacle—his attachment to wealth (Mark 10:17-22). Jesus didn't give him a generic gospel presentation but spoke to his particular spiritual condition.

Common questions people genuinely wrestle with include:

- How can a good God allow suffering?
- What happens to people who never hear about Jesus?
- Why are Christians often hypocritical?
- How is Christianity different from other religions?
- Doesn't science disprove faith?

Don't be afraid to say "I don't know" when appropriate. Honesty builds trust more than pretending to have all the answers.

5. Speak Their Language, Not Church-ese

Effective evangelism communicates in terms the listener can understand, avoiding insider religious jargon that creates barriers.

Paul recognized this principle: "To the Jews I became as a Jew, in order to win Jews... To those outside the law I became as one outside the law... I have become all things to all people, that by all means I might save some" (1 Corinthians 9:20-22). He adapted his communication style to his audience without changing his message.

Terms to explain or avoid:
- Saved/salvation (try "reconciled with God" or "forgiven")
- Sin (try "brokenness" or "falling short of what we were created for")

- Born again (try "spiritually transformed" or "starting a new life")
- Justified (try "made right with God" or "declared not guilty")
- Sanctification (try "becoming more like Jesus" or "spiritual growth")

Use stories and metaphors that connect with contemporary experience, just as Jesus used agricultural and fishing metaphors that resonated with His audience.

6. Prioritize Relationships Over Results

Effective evangelism values people as ends in themselves, not means to a conversion statistic. This means maintaining the relationship regardless of how they respond to your message.

Jesus maintained deep relationships with people who didn't immediately follow Him, like Nicodemus, who apparently became a believer much later. Jesus invested in people for their sake, not just to "close the deal."

This relational priority means:
- Continuing friendship even if they reject your message
- Respecting boundaries when they ask to change the subject

- Caring about their whole life, not just their spiritual status
- Being willing to serve with no strings attached
- Following their lead on the pace of spiritual conversations

People can tell when they're being valued versus being treated as projects. Love them regardless of outcome.

7. Live a Compelling Life

Your lifestyle either undermines or underscores your message. Effective evangelism flows from a life that makes others curious about its source.

Peter challenged believers to "live such good lives among the pagans that, though they accuse you of doing wrong, they may see your good deeds and glorify God" (1 Peter 2:12, NIV). The quality of your life creates credibility for your message.

Compelling Christian living includes:
- Integrity in work and relationships
- Genuine care for others, especially the vulnerable
- Distinctively different responses to hardship
- Generosity with time, resources, and forgiveness
- Non-anxious presence in a stressed-out culture

When your life visibly demonstrates the difference Jesus makes, your words about Jesus have far greater impact.

8. Embrace the Process

Effective evangelism recognizes that coming to faith is usually a process, not an event. Each conversation is part of a larger journey that may involve many people over time.

Paul acknowledged this reality: "I planted, Apollos watered, but God gave the growth" (1 Corinthians 3:6). Some Christians plant seeds, others water, but only God brings the harvest.

This process perspective means:
- Celebrating small steps toward Jesus, not just "decisions"
- Being content with your role, even if it's not the final one
- Taking a long-term view of spiritual influence
- Recognizing that people move toward faith at different paces
- Continuing to pray for people even when progress seems minimal

You might be the first Christian to show someone authentic faith, or you might be the twentieth person who helps them take the final step. Both roles matter equally in God's economy.

Navigating Difficult Evangelism Scenarios

Even with the best intentions and approaches, sharing your faith can present challenges. Here's how to handle some common difficult scenarios:

When They're Hostile to Christianity

Sometimes you'll encounter people with negative experiences or strong objections to Christianity. Their hostility isn't usually personal—it's often rooted in painful church experiences, unanswered questions, or misrepresentations of faith.

Effective approach:
- Acknowledge their concerns without defensiveness
- Apologize for ways Christians have failed to represent Christ well
- Distinguish between Jesus and flawed Christian expressions
- Ask permission before sharing your perspective
- Focus on understanding their story before defending your beliefs

Jesus showed remarkable patience with those who initially rejected Him. In Luke 9:51-56, when a Samaritan village refused to welcome Him, the disciples wanted to call down fire from heaven. Jesus rebuked this retaliatory attitude. Follow His example of patience with those who initially reject your message.

When They Ask Tough Questions You Can't Answer

You don't need perfect theological knowledge to share your faith effectively. When faced with questions beyond your understanding, honesty builds more trust than pretending to know.

Effective approach:
- Acknowledge the legitimacy of their question
- Admit when you don't know something: "That's a great question I don't have a complete answer for"
- Offer to research together: "Can I look into that and get back to you?"
- Share your personal perspective while acknowledging other viewpoints
- Remember that relationship matters more than having all the answers

The disciples themselves frequently asked Jesus questions they didn't understand, and He didn't reject them for their confusion. No one expects you to be an expert on everything except you.

When the Conversation Gets Derailed

Sometimes evangelistic conversations get sidetracked into political debates, arguments about church scandals, or discussions about peripheral issues that obscure the core message about Jesus.

Effective approach:
- Gently redirect to the central issue: "Those are important questions, but can we get back to Jesus himself for a moment?"
- Acknowledge complexity: "Christians have different views on that issue, but what unites us is..."
- Separate cultural Christianity from Jesus: "I understand why that bothers you. It bothers me too. But Jesus actually taught..."
- Ask if you can temporarily set aside the side issue: "Could we put that question on hold and come back to it later?"

Jesus regularly faced attempts to pull Him into divisive political and theological debates of His day (taxes to Caesar, divorce regulations, Sabbath observance). He consistently redirected to deeper spiritual matters without dismissing people's concerns.

When They Seem Completely Uninterested

Not everyone will be interested in spiritual conversations, and that's okay. Respect for their freedom means accepting when someone doesn't want to discuss faith.

Effective approach:
- Continue the relationship without pressure
- Live your faith visibly but without manipulation
- Pray for future opportunities
- Look for moments of openness during life transitions or difficulties
- Be ready to respond if they later show interest

The parable of the sower (Matthew 13:1-23) reminds us that not all soil is ready for seed at the same time. Your role is faithful sowing, not forcing growth in unwilling hearts.

When You Fear Damaging the Relationship

Many Christians avoid sharing faith because they fear losing friends or creating awkwardness. This concern is understandable but often overestimated.

Effective approach:
- Ask permission: "Would you mind if I shared something important to me?"

- Frame it as your experience rather than universal claims: "This is what I've found to be true in my life..."
- Invite rather than insist: "I'd love to hear your thoughts on this"
- Reassure them that your friendship isn't conditional on their response
- Follow their lead on when to continue or pause the conversation

Jesus valued honesty in relationships. In John 6:67-68, when many disciples turned away from His hard teachings, He asked the Twelve, "Do you want to go away as well?" He didn't manipulate or pressure them but honored their freedom while being truthful.

Digital Evangelism: Sharing Faith Online Without Being That Person

Social media and digital communication present unique opportunities and challenges for sharing faith. Here's how to navigate online evangelism effectively:

1. Be a Real Person, Not a Christian Bot

Effective online witness comes from being a genuine, multi-dimensional person, not someone who only posts Bible verses and religious content.

Share your actual life—your hobbies, interests, family moments, and everyday experiences, alongside occasional faith-related content. This authenticity makes your spiritual posts more credible because people see you as a real human being, not a propaganda account.

2. Ask Questions Rather Than Make Pronouncements

Social media tends toward declarative statements and pronouncements. Stand out by asking thoughtful questions that invite conversation rather than shutting it down.

Instead of "Abortion is murder, and here's why..." try "What factors do you think should guide our thinking about complex ethical issues like abortion?"

Instead of "Atheists have no basis for morality," try "I'm curious how those with a non-religious worldview think about the foundations of moral values."

Questions open dialogue; pronouncements typically end it.

3. Share Stories More Than Arguments

In the digital space, personal stories often have more impact than abstract arguments. Share specific ways faith has shaped your response to real-life situations.

For example, instead of posting about the theological concept of forgiveness, share how your faith helped you forgive someone who hurt you, what that process looked like, and how it changed you.

Stories are harder to argue with, easier to relate to, and more memorable than propositional statements.

4. Engage Privately with Public Disagreement

When someone challenges or questions your faith-related post, consider moving the conversation to private messages rather than having a public back-and-forth that often becomes performative.

Public theological debates on social media rarely change minds and often devolve into winner-takes-all arguments where saving face becomes more important than honest dialogue.

5. Share Content from Diverse Christian Voices

Instead of always creating original faith content, share thoughtful perspectives from diverse Christian voices—particularly those who might connect with your non-Christian friends in unexpected ways.

This demonstrates that Christianity isn't monolithic and exposes your network to thoughtful faith perspectives they might not otherwise encounter.

6. Be Quick to Listen, Slow to Post

The immediacy of social media tempts us to respond instantly to trending stories, cultural conflicts, or controversial statements. Resist this urge.

Take time to understand issues before commenting. Consider whether your post will generate more light than heat. Ask if your contribution is necessary or just adding to the noise.

James 1:19 applies perfectly to digital communication: "Let every person be quick to hear, slow to speak, slow to anger."

7. Remember Real People Are Reading

It's easy to forget that actual humans with complex lives, histories, and hurts are reading your posts.

Before sharing faith content, consider who might see it and how it might impact them.

A post condemning a particular sin might be read by someone struggling with that very issue, someone hurt by religious condemnation, or someone with loved ones directly affected. This doesn't mean never addressing difficult topics, but doing so with awareness of your unseen audience.

Evangelism Styles: Finding Your Authentic Approach

Not everyone shares faith the same way, and that's by design. Different personalities and gifts create different evangelistic styles, all of which can be effective in the right context. Identifying your natural style helps you evangelize authentically rather than trying to force yourself into someone else's approach.

The Relational Connector

You build deep, authentic relationships where faith conversations happen naturally over time. You're genuinely interested in people's lives and stories, which creates trust that makes spiritual discussions meaningful.

Biblical example: Matthew invited tax collectors and sinners to meet Jesus over dinner at his house (Luke 5:29).

Strengths:
- Creates lasting trust before spiritual conversations
- Demonstrates authentic faith through ongoing relationship
- Provides natural context for multiple faith conversations
- Allows you to tailor the message to their specific situation

Growth areas:
- Being intentional about eventually bringing up faith
- Not letting fear of damaging the relationship prevent spiritual conversations
- Recognizing when someone is spiritually ready to take a next step

The Intellectual Engager

You love addressing thoughtful questions, discussing ideas, and exploring the rational basis for faith. You're comfortable with philosophical and scientific discussions related to Christianity.

Biblical example: Paul reasoned in the marketplace and synagogue, engaging with philosophical ideas in Athens (Acts 17:16-34).

Strengths:
- Connecting with intellectually-oriented people
- Addressing substantive objections to faith
- Demonstrating that Christianity can be intellectually robust
- Creating space for honest questions and exploration

Growth areas:
- Remembering that conversion is more than intellectual agreement
- Not getting so caught in theoretical discussions that you miss heart issues
- Finding ways to move from abstract discussion to personal application

The Direct Communicator

You naturally share faith in clear, straightforward terms. You're comfortable initiating spiritual conversations and inviting direct responses to the gospel message.

Biblical example: Philip directly approached the Ethiopian eunuch and clearly explained the gospel (Acts 8:26-40).

Strengths:
- Clear communication of essential gospel truths
- Courage to initiate spiritual conversations

- Comfort with inviting specific response
- Ability to recognize and seize opportunities

Growth areas:
- Ensuring directness doesn't become pushiness
- Taking time to listen, not just speak
- Being patient with those who need a longer process
- Recognizing when directness might not be the best approach

The Service-Based Witness

You share faith primarily through practical service and meeting needs. Your actions open doors for explaining the hope behind your compassion.

Biblical example: Dorcas, whose practical care for widows created a powerful testimony (Acts 9:36-42).

Strengths:
- Demonstrating the tangible impact of faith
- Building credibility through consistent care
- Reaching people who might be skeptical of words alone
- Creating natural opportunities to explain your motivations

Growth areas:
- Finding ways to verbalize the faith behind your actions

- Recognizing when people are open to hearing more
- Not assuming service alone communicates the full gospel
- Integrating words and actions effectively

The Story-Telling Illustrator

You communicate faith through stories, metaphors, and illustrations that make spiritual truths accessible and memorable.

Biblical example: Jesus, who constantly used parables and everyday illustrations to communicate kingdom truths (Matthew 13).

Strengths:
- Making abstract concepts concrete and relatable
- Bypassing intellectual defenses through narrative
- Creating memorable explanations that stick
- Adapting complex truths to different audiences

Growth areas:
- Ensuring metaphors serve the message, not replace it
- Connecting stories to clear spiritual applications
- Developing a repertoire of illustrations for different contexts
- Being comfortable moving beyond storytelling to direct invitation when appropriate

The Invitational Host

You create environments and experiences where people can encounter faith communities and messages, inviting others into spaces where they can explore Christianity.

Biblical example: The Samaritan woman who invited her entire town to "Come, see a man who told me all that I ever did" (John 4:29).

Strengths:
- Removing initial barriers to faith exploration
- Creating low-pressure environments for spiritual exposure
- Connecting seekers with diverse Christian voices
- Facilitating natural community integration

Growth areas:
- Following up personally after corporate experiences
- Being prepared for one-on-one conversations that may result
- Not relying exclusively on others to communicate the message
- Recognizing when someone is ready to move beyond exploring

Understanding your natural evangelistic style doesn't exempt you from growth in other areas, but it helps you serve from strengths rather than constant frustration. The body of Christ needs all these styles working together—no single approach reaches everyone effectively.

The Long Game: Evangelism as a Lifestyle

Effective evangelism isn't primarily about individual conversations or techniques but about developing a lifestyle where sharing faith becomes natural and ongoing. Here are key elements of living evangelistically:

1. Pray Consistently for Non-Believing Friends

Prayer is the foundation of effective evangelism. Regularly pray for specific people in your life who don't know Jesus, asking God to work in their hearts and create opportunities for meaningful conversation.

Paul requested this kind of prayer support in Colossians 4:3-4: "Pray also for us, that God may open to us a door for the word, to declare the mystery of Christ... that I may make it clear, which is how I ought to speak."

Consider keeping a prayer list of people you're spiritually invested in, noting specific ways to pray for their unique journey toward faith.

2. Build Genuine Friendships with Non-Christians

Many Christians live in such a tight Christian bubble that they rarely have meaningful relationships with non-believers. Intentionally develop friendships with people outside the faith, not as projects but as genuine connections.

Jesus was known as a "friend of tax collectors and sinners" (Matthew 11:19), spending significant time with those far from God. Follow His example by entering spaces where you can naturally connect with people different from yourself.

This might mean joining community organizations, participating in neighborhood activities, pursuing hobbies in secular contexts, or being intentionally friendly with colleagues and neighbors.

3. Create a Hospitable Life

Hospitality creates natural contexts for spiritual influence. Opening your home and sharing meals provides relaxed settings for meaningful conversations that rarely happen in more formal environments.

In Romans 12:13, Paul instructs believers to "seek to show hospitality." This practice was central to early

Christian witness and remains a powerful evangelistic tool today.

Practical hospitality might include hosting dinners, organizing game nights, offering your home for neighborhood gatherings, or simply inviting someone for coffee. These settings create space for relationships to deepen beyond surface interactions.

4. Develop Your Story

Your personal testimony is a unique evangelistic asset. Take time to thoughtfully develop how you explain your faith journey in ways that connect with different audiences.

Different aspects of your story will resonate with different people. Someone struggling with addiction might connect with how God helped you overcome a particular habit. Someone questioning purpose might relate to how faith gave your life meaning.

Regularly reflect on how God is working in your current life, not just your conversion moment, so your testimony remains fresh and authentic.

5. Learn to Recognize Spiritual Openness

People show spiritual interest in various ways—often through questions, comments about meaning or purpose, expressions of struggle, or curiosity about your life choices. Develop sensitivity to these openness indicators.

Jesus was attentive to signs of spiritual hunger. With Nicodemus, He recognized the genuine question behind the surface inquiry (John 3). With the Samaritan woman, He saw past her evasion to her deeper spiritual thirst (John 4).

Common signs of spiritual openness include:
- Questions about your faith or church
- Expressions of life dissatisfaction or emptiness
- Interest in your perspective on current events
- Comments about meaning, purpose, or mortality
- Disclosing personal struggles or pain

When you notice these indicators, gently explore further rather than immediately launching into a full gospel presentation.

6. Respond to Current Events with Gospel Perspective

Cultural moments, tragedies, celebrations, and controversies provide natural opportunities to offer a distinctly Christian perspective that points to deeper spiritual realities.

The apostles regularly connected their message to current events and cultural contexts. Peter linked Pentecost to Joel's prophecy (Acts 2:14-21). Paul used the Athenians' unknown god as a starting point for introducing the true God (Acts 17:22-23).

When discussing current events, look for opportunities to move beyond political talking points to deeper kingdom values like reconciliation, justice, mercy, and hope in the face of suffering.

7. Live with Gospel Intentionality

An evangelistic lifestyle means making daily choices with gospel awareness—considering how your words, actions, social media presence, and time usage might create opportunities to reflect Christ.

This intentionality isn't mechanical or forced but flows from the question Paul asked in Colossians 4:5: "Walk in wisdom toward outsiders, making the best use of the time." Every interaction becomes a potential gospel moment, not through manipulation but through mindfulness.

Living with gospel intentionality might mean:
- Choosing where to eat lunch to build relationships with non-Christian colleagues

- Being transparent about struggles rather than projecting false perfection
- Mentioning your church involvement in natural conversation
- Offering to pray when someone shares a challenge
- Being noticeably different in how you handle conflict or disappointment

These daily choices create a lifestyle where evangelism happens naturally, not as an awkward addition to normal life.

The 7-Day Evangelism Challenge

Want to grow in sharing your faith? Try this week-long challenge designed to develop evangelistic attitudes and skills in practical ways:

Day 1: Prayer Foundation

Spend 15 minutes identifying five people in your life who don't know Jesus. Write their names down and pray specifically for:
- Their current life situations
- Any obstacles to faith you're aware of
- Opportunities for meaningful conversation
- Your relationship with them
- God to work in their hearts in ways you can't see

Throughout the day, set three prayer reminders on your phone to briefly pray for these five people again.

Day 2: Testimony Development

Take time today to write out your faith story in three different lengths:
1. A 30-second version (elevator pitch)
2. A 2-minute version (coffee conversation)
3. A 5-minute version (deeper discussion)

For each version, include:
- Your life before Christ (or key struggles if raised Christian)
- How you encountered Jesus
- The difference He's made
- Why this matters to others

Practice telling each version out loud, using natural language rather than religious jargon. Ask yourself: "Would this make sense to someone with no church background?"

Day 3: Question Cultivation

Today, focus on developing questions that invite spiritual conversation without being confrontational.

Write down 5-7 questions you could naturally ask in different contexts, such as:
- "What helps you get through difficult times?"
- "Do you have any spiritual beliefs that shape how you see the world?"
- "What do you think happens after we die?"
- "Have you ever had experiences you'd consider spiritual?"
- "What do you think is the biggest problem with the world?"

Find one opportunity today to ask someone one of these questions and practice active listening without immediately sharing your own perspective.

Day 4: Hospitality Action

Take a concrete step toward creating space for relationships that could lead to spiritual conversations:
- Invite someone for coffee or a meal
- Plan a future gathering at your home
- Reach out to a neighbor you don't know well
- Join a community group or activity where you'll meet new people

The goal today isn't necessarily having a spiritual conversation but creating the context where such conversations can naturally occur in the future.

Day 5: Gospel Clarity

Practice explaining the core gospel message in simple, clear terms that a 12-year-old could understand. Write out a 1-2 paragraph explanation that includes:
- The problem (separation from God)
- God's solution (Jesus' life, death, and resurrection)
- The response invited (trust and follow)
- The result (reconciliation with God and new life)

Avoid religious terminology that requires insider knowledge. Read your explanation to a trusted Christian friend and ask if it's clear, accurate, and accessible.

Day 6: Digital Witness Review

Examine your social media presence from the perspective of a non-Christian friend:
- What would they learn about your faith from your profiles and posts?
- Is your online persona authentic or performative?
- Does your digital presence create bridges or barriers to spiritual conversation?
- Where could you be more intentional about sharing your faith online without being pushy?

Make one specific change to your digital presence based on this review.

Day 7: Courageous Conversation

Today, take a step of faith by having one spiritual conversation with someone on your prayer list from Day 1. This might involve:
- Sharing part of your testimony
- Asking one of your spiritual questions
- Offering a Christian perspective on a current issue
- Inviting them to a church event or community
- Expressing how your faith helps you navigate a common challenge

Remember that success is defined by faithfulness, not results. Whether the conversation goes deep or stays surface-level, you're developing a crucial spiritual muscle.

Conclude the week by reflecting on what you learned about yourself, evangelism, and the people you're trying to reach. Identify one practice from this week that you want to continue regularly.

The Kick in the Pants: You've Got Good News—Stop Keeping It to Yourself

Look, I get it. Talking about Jesus feels awkward sometimes. You worry about being rejected, saying the wrong thing, or coming across like those cringe-worthy Christians who seem to ruin every family Thanksgiving with their ham-handed evangelism attempts.

But here's the uncomfortable truth: if you've experienced the life-changing power of the gospel and you're not sharing it with anyone, what does that say about either your experience or your compassion?

Think about it. If you found the cure for cancer, would you keep it to yourself because you're afraid of awkward conversations? If you discovered a path out of depression, addiction, or crushing debt, would you hide that knowledge from others struggling with those same issues?

Of course not. Because when you have genuinely good news, sharing it isn't an obligation—it's an overflow.

Paul put it this way: "For Christ's love compels us" (2 Corinthians 5:14, NIV). Not guilt. Not fear. Not religious obligation. Love. Christ's love for us and our resulting love for others naturally drives us to share the best news we know.

The problem might be that you've forgotten just how good the good news actually is. You've reduced it to religious concepts or moral improvement rather than the revolutionary message that the Creator God entered our broken world, took our brokenness upon Himself, defeated death, and offers reconciliation and new life to anyone who trusts Him. That's not just nice information—it's the hope of the world.

And speaking of the world—have you looked around lately? People are desperately searching for meaning, identity, purpose, and hope. They're trying to fill the God-shaped hole with career advancement, political causes, romantic relationships, chemical escapes, digital validation, and endless consumption. How's that working out for them?

Romans 10:14 asks the pointed question: "How are they to believe in him of whom they have never heard?" Your friends, family members, neighbors, and colleagues may never set foot in a church. They may never read the Bible or listen to a Christian podcast. For many of them, you might be their only connection to the gospel.

This doesn't mean you need to become a street preacher or walk around with a megaphone. But it does mean you need to care enough to have sometimes-uncomfortable conversations. It means prioritizing their eternal well-being over your temporary comfort. It means being willing to risk rejection for the sake of offering hope.

Yes, some people will dismiss you. Yes, some conversations will feel awkward. Yes, you'll sometimes say the wrong thing or not have the perfect answer. Join the club. The apostles themselves fumbled and misunderstood even with Jesus standing right in front of them, and God still used them to change the world.

The point isn't perfection. The point is love-driven faithfulness—caring enough to share the hope you have, even when it feels uncomfortable.

So stop waiting until you have perfect theological knowledge, a completely sanctified life, or magical conversation skills. Stop hiding behind the excuse that your life should be your only witness. Yes, your actions matter enormously—but as Romans 10:17 reminds us, "Faith comes from hearing, and hearing through the word of Christ."

At some point, you've got to open your mouth.

The world doesn't need more silent Christians who privatize their faith like it's something to be ashamed of. It needs believers who care enough to have real conversations about real hope in a really broken world.

You don't have to be loud—you just have to be honest. You don't have to be argumentative—you just have to be available. You don't have to have all the answers—you just have to point to the One who does.

Because at the end of the day, evangelism isn't about being right—it's about offering life. And if what you've found in Jesus is truly life-changing, keeping it to yourself isn't modesty—it's selfishness.

People need what you have. Will you care enough to share it?

Chapter 11:

Stewardship – Managing Your Sh*t

Let's be honest: most of us are terrible managers of our own lives.

We complain about not having enough money while dropping $7 on fancy coffee and maintaining six streaming subscriptions we barely use. We whine about being too busy while spending three hours a day scrolling through social media. We pray for God to use us while ignoring the talents He's already given us. We ask for better health while treating our bodies like garbage disposals on wheels.

And somehow, we've convinced ourselves this is everyone else's fault.

The economy. Our boss. Our upbringing. Our metabolism. Society. The church. That driver who cut us off and ruined our whole day. We're experts at playing the blame game while taking zero responsibility for the mess we've made of what God entrusted to us.

Here's the uncomfortable truth: Everything you have is on loan from God. Your money. Your time. Your energy. Your talents. Your relationships. Your physical body. None of it actually belongs to you. You're just the manager, not the owner.

As Paul bluntly puts it in 1 Corinthians 6:19-20, "You are not your own, for you were bought with a price. So glorify God in your body." That principle extends beyond just your physical self to everything in your life. It all belongs to God, and one day you'll give an account for how you managed it.

That's what stewardship is all about. Not just dropping a few bucks in the offering plate to ease your conscience, but recognizing that 100% of your life belongs to God and should be managed accordingly. It's about taking responsibility for your choices instead of blaming circumstances. It's about growing up and handling your business like the adult God created you to be.

In this chapter, we're going to get painfully practical about what it means to be a good steward of everything God has entrusted to you. Not so you can beat yourself up about past failures, but so you can start making choices that align with who God made you to be. Because the truth is, good stewardship isn't just about honoring God—it's about living a life that actually works.

The Owner vs. Manager Mindset

Before we dive into specific areas of stewardship, we need to address a fundamental mindset issue. Most of our problems with stewardship stem from one critical error: thinking we're the owners when we're actually just the managers.

The Owner Mentality

When you think you own your life and everything in it, you tend to:
- Feel entitled to use your resources however you want
- Get defensive when others (including God) suggest changes
- Make decisions based solely on personal preference
- View giving as optional generosity rather than returning what belongs to God
- Resent limitations on your freedom to do whatever you want

This ownership mindset isn't just spiritually problematic—it creates practical headaches too. When you think you own your life, every limitation feels like an infringement, every request feels like an imposition, and every setback feels like a personal attack on your sovereignty.

The Manager Mentality

When you recognize God as the true owner and yourself as the manager, everything changes. You start to:
- View resources as tools for fulfilling God's purposes, not just your desires
- Make decisions based on the owner's priorities, not just your preferences
- See limitations as helpful boundaries set by a wise owner
- Understand that you'll eventually give an account for your management
- Find freedom in knowing ultimate responsibility rests with the owner

Jesus consistently taught this manager (or "steward") mentality. In the Parable of the Talents (Matthew 25:14-30), the master entrusts his property to servants while he's away, then returns to settle accounts. The servants were never owners—just temporary managers expected to use the master's resources wisely until his return.

This isn't just abstract theology; it's a practical framework that transforms how you handle every aspect of your life. When you internalize the truth that "the earth is the LORD's and the fullness thereof, the world and those who dwell therein" (Psalm 24:1), it reshapes your entire approach to stewardship.

The Four Big Domains of Stewardship

While stewardship encompasses everything in your life, we're going to focus on four major domains where poor stewardship creates the most problems: time, money, body, and talents. Let's start with the resource everyone claims they don't have enough of:

1. Time: The Non-Renewable Resource

Time is the great equalizer. Whether you're Jeff Bezos or Joe Nobody, you get exactly 24 hours each day—no more, no less. The difference lies in how you steward those hours.

Jesus understood the precious nature of time. In John 9:4, he said, "We must work the works of him who sent me while it is day; night is coming, when no one can work." He recognized that time is limited and must be used intentionally.

The Time Stewardship Problem

Most of us suffer from chronological illiteracy—we're terrible at understanding where our time actually goes. We claim we're "too busy" for important things while unconsciously wasting hours each day on activities that add no value to our lives or God's kingdom.

The average American spends over three hours daily on their smartphone and another three hours watching TV. That's a quarter of your waking hours gone before you've done anything meaningful. And yet we insist with complete sincerity that we "just don't have time" for prayer, exercise, meaningful relationships, or serving others.

Our problem isn't lack of time. It's lack of honesty about how we're spending the time we have.

Biblical Time Management

The Bible offers several key principles for stewarding your time well:

1. Recognize time's finite nature

Psalm 90:12 urges, "Teach us to number our days that we may get a heart of wisdom." Good stewardship starts with the humbling acknowledgment that your days are numbered. When you truly internalize this truth, you become much more intentional about how you spend each hour.

This doesn't mean becoming anxiously hyperproductive. It means recognizing time's value and making conscious choices instead of drifting through your days on autopilot.

2. Establish proper priorities

Jesus provided the ultimate prioritization framework in Matthew 6:33: "But seek first the kingdom of God and his righteousness, and all these things will be added to you." Notice the word "first"—not second, fifth, or whenever you get around to it.

This doesn't mean you should only engage in overtly "spiritual" activities. It means filtering all your time decisions through the question: "Does this align with God's priorities for my life?" Sometimes the most spiritual use of your time is playing with your kids, doing excellent work at your job, or getting adequate rest.

3. Create purposeful rhythms

God established rhythms from the beginning of creation—work and rest, day and night, seasons and years. Ecclesiastes 3:1 reminds us that "there is a time for every matter under heaven." Good time stewardship means creating intentional rhythms that sustain you rather than drain you.

These rhythms should include:
- Daily time for spiritual renewal
- Weekly sabbath rest
- Regular periods of both productivity and recreation

- Seasons of greater intensity followed by seasons of recovery

When you fight against these natural rhythms, you end up exhausted, ineffective, and spiritually depleted.

Practical Time Stewardship Steps

Ready to stop complaining about your schedule and start managing it like a responsible adult? Try these practical steps:

1. Conduct a time audit

For one week, track how you actually spend your time in 30-minute increments. Be ruthlessly honest—no estimates, just facts. At week's end, categorize your activities and calculate the total hours spent in each category.

Most people are shocked by the results. That "quick check" of social media actually consumed 20+ hours. That Netflix show you "hardly watch" ate an entire workday. The "I don't have time to exercise" excuse evaporates when you realize you spent 14 hours watching sports.

Knowledge is power. You can't fix what you won't acknowledge.

2. Implement the "big rocks" principle

Imagine your life as a jar that you need to fill with rocks and sand. The big rocks represent your most important priorities—your relationship with God, family, health, key responsibilities. The sand represents the less important stuff—social media, entertainment, random activities.

If you put the sand in first, the big rocks won't fit. But if you put the big rocks in first, the sand can fill in around them. This is why successful people don't "find time" for important things; they schedule them first and let everything else fill in the gaps.

Practically, this means:
- Scheduling your most important activities before your calendar fills up
- Protecting those commitments as non-negotiable
- Saying no to good things that would crowd out the best things
- Being realistic about what actually fits in your jar

3. Create boundaries around technology

Your devices are designed by very smart people using behavioral psychology to maximize your screen time. Without intentional boundaries, they will steal your life one notification at a time.

Effective boundaries might include:
- Phone-free zones (bedroom, dinner table)
- Technology curfews (no screens after 9PM)
- Social media time limits (use app timers)
- Notification culling (turn off all non-essential alerts)
- Regular digital sabbaths (one day per week without optional technology)

These boundaries aren't legalistic restrictions; they're freedom-creating containers that protect your time for what actually matters.

4. Master the art of the strategic "no"

Every time you say yes to something, you're saying no to something else—whether you realize it or not. That yes to another committee means a no to family dinner. That yes to a Netflix binge means a no to adequate sleep.

Ephesians 5:15-16 advises, "Look carefully then how you walk, not as unwise but as wise, making the best use of the time, because the days are evil." Wise time stewardship requires saying no to good things so you can say yes to the best things.

This doesn't mean becoming a selfish jerk who never helps others. It means being thoughtful about your commitments rather than reflexively saying yes to every request.

2. Money: The Visible Value System

If you want to know what someone truly values, don't listen to their words—look at their bank statements. How you spend your money is perhaps the most honest reflection of your actual priorities, not your aspired ones.

Jesus understood this connection between money and values. That's why he said in Matthew 6:21, "For where your treasure is, there your heart will be also." Notice he didn't say "where your heart is, there your treasure will be." The relationship often works in reverse—your heart follows your money.

The Money Stewardship Problem

Most financial problems stem not from lack of knowledge but from lack of alignment between stated values and actual behavior. We claim to value financial security while accumulating consumer debt. We say we want to be generous while spending 99% of our income on ourselves. We complain about not having enough while wasting what we have on things that don't actually improve our lives.

Add to this the comparison trap amplified by social media, and you have a perfect storm of financial discontent and mismanagement. We're spending money we don't have to buy things we don't need to impress people we don't even like.

Biblical Money Management

The Bible contains more verses about money than almost any other topic, providing clear principles for financial stewardship:

1. Acknowledge God's ownership

Psalm 24:1 reminds us, "The earth is the LORD's and the fullness thereof." Every dollar in your account ultimately belongs to God. You're not the owner—just the manager of resources He's temporarily entrusted to you.

This perspective transforms spending from "What do I want to do with my money?" to "What does the Owner want done with His money?" It's a fundamental mindset shift that affects every financial decision.

2. Practice proportional giving

In the Old Testament, the starting point for financial stewardship was the tithe—giving the first 10% back to God. While the New Testament doesn't prescribe a specific percentage, the principle of generous, proportional giving remains.

Paul instructed the Corinthians in 2 Corinthians 9:7, "Each one must give as he has decided in his heart, not reluctantly or under compulsion, for God loves a cheerful giver." The amount matters less than the heart attitude and the recognition that giving is an act of worship, not charity.

3. Avoid the debt trap

Proverbs 22:7 observes, "The borrower is slave to the lender." Consumer debt creates financial bondage that limits your options, increases your stress, and often prevents you from being generous.

This doesn't mean all debt is sinful (mortgages and educational loans may be strategic tools), but it does mean approaching debt with extreme caution rather than casual acceptance.

4. Build margin through contentment

Financial freedom comes not from having more, but from wanting less. Paul wrote in Philippians 4:11-12, "I have learned in whatever situation I am to be content. I know how to be brought low, and I know how to abound."

Contentment creates margin between your income and expenses, allowing you to save for the future, respond to needs, and be generous without stress.

Without contentment, no amount of money will ever feel like "enough."

Practical Money Stewardship Steps

Ready to get your financial house in order? Try these practical steps:

1. Create a values-based budget

A budget isn't primarily a restriction tool; it's a values-alignment tool. Start by identifying what you truly value (security, generosity, experiences, etc.), then build a spending plan that reflects those values.

Effective budgeting involves:
- Tracking your current spending to establish a baseline
- Comparing that baseline to your stated values to identify misalignments
- Creating specific categories with purpose-driven allocations
- Building in accountability through regular review
- Using tools (apps, spreadsheets, etc.) that match your personality

The goal isn't perfection but progression—moving gradually toward greater alignment between your money and your values.

2. Implement the "give, save, live" sequence

The order of your financial operations matters enormously. Most people live first (spending on immediate wants), save if there's anything left, and give only from rare surpluses. This virtually guarantees financial stress and limited generosity.

The biblical pattern reverses this order:
- Give first (the "firstfruits" principle)
- Save second (creating security and future opportunity)
- Live on the remainder (adjusting lifestyle to what's left)

This sequence ensures that your highest financial values receive priority rather than leftovers.

3. Practice strategic generosity

Generous giving isn't just about supporting churches or charities; it's about intentionally using money to advance God's kingdom wherever you have influence.

Strategic generosity might include:
- Regular giving to your church community
- Supporting specific causes aligned with your values
- Maintaining an "opportunity fund" for unexpected needs
- Practicing hospitality in your home

- Investing in others' development and growth

The goal is moving from reactive, guilt-based giving to proactive, purpose-driven generosity that reflects God's character.

4. Build financial resilience

Good stewardship includes preparing for future uncertainties. Proverbs 21:20 observes, "Precious treasure and oil are in a wise man's dwelling, but a foolish man devours it." Saving isn't hoarding—it's responsible preparation.

Financial resilience includes:
- Building an emergency fund (3-6 months of expenses)
- Eliminating high-interest consumer debt
- Investing appropriately for long-term goals
- Maintaining proper insurance coverage
- Creating estate plans that reflect your values

These measures aren't about trusting money instead of God; they're about faithfully managing what He's entrusted to you.

3. Body: The Physical Temple

Your physical body is perhaps the most personal stewardship domain. It's literally the temple where

God's Spirit dwells, and how you care for it affects everything else in your life.

Paul makes this connection explicit in 1 Corinthians 6:19-20: "Do you not know that your body is a temple of the Holy Spirit within you, whom you have from God? You are not your own, for you were bought with a price. So glorify God in your body."

The Body Stewardship Problem

Many Christians have adopted a quasi-gnostic view that devalues the physical body while prioritizing the spiritual. We'll spend hours in Bible study but mock the idea of regular exercise. We'll carefully guard what media enters our minds while thoughtlessly stuffing our bodies with whatever is convenient or comforting.

This mind-body disconnect creates Christians who are spiritually passionate but physically depleted—running on caffeine, sugar, and sheer willpower while wondering why they're chronically tired, sick, and emotionally unstable.

Biblical Body Care

The Bible provides several principles for stewarding your physical body well:

1. Honor your body as God's dwelling place

Your body isn't just a temporary shell for your soul—it's the actual temple where God's Spirit resides. This gives physical stewardship a profound spiritual dimension. How you treat your body reflects how you value God's presence in your life.

2. Practice wisdom, not legalism

Biblical body stewardship isn't about achieving some ideal body type or following rigid rules. It's about making wise choices that honor God and enable you to fulfill your purpose.

Paul addressed this balance in 1 Corinthians 10:23: "'All things are lawful,' but not all things are helpful. 'All things are lawful,' but not all things build up." The question isn't "Is this allowed?" but "Is this helpful for the life God has called me to?"

3. Recognize the body-spirit connection

Scripture never compartmentalizes humans into separate physical and spiritual components. What affects your body affects your spirit, and vice versa. Elijah's spiritual despair in 1 Kings 19 was addressed first by physical rest and nourishment before the spiritual encounter with God.

This holistic perspective means caring for your physical health isn't separate from your spiritual life—it's an integral part of it.

Practical Body Stewardship Steps

Ready to start treating your body like the temple it is? Try these practical steps:

1. Prioritize adequate sleep

Sleep isn't a luxury or a sign of laziness—it's a biological necessity that affects every aspect of your health, including your spiritual clarity. Jesus himself prioritized rest, often withdrawing from ministry demands to recharge.

Practical sleep stewardship includes:
- Establishing consistent sleep-wake times
- Creating a screen-free wind-down routine
- Optimizing your sleep environment (dark, cool, quiet)
- Avoiding sleep disruptors (caffeine, alcohol, late meals)
- Building your schedule around sleep needs, not vice versa

If you wouldn't dream of missing church but regularly sacrifice sleep, you might need to reconsider your stewardship priorities.

2. Nourish, don't just feed

Food is more than fuel or entertainment—it's the raw material your body uses to create energy, repair cells, and maintain proper function. What you eat literally becomes you.

Nutritional stewardship doesn't require extreme diets or food obsession. It simply means:
- Emphasizing whole foods that support health
- Being mindful of portions and patterns
- Recognizing emotional eating triggers
- Viewing food as a gift to be enjoyed with gratitude
- Making conscious choices rather than defaulting to convenience

Daniel demonstrated this kind of food stewardship when he "resolved that he would not defile himself with the king's food" (Daniel 1:8), choosing simpler nourishment that aligned with his values.

3. Move regularly and intentionally

Your body was designed for movement, not prolonged sitting. Regular physical activity isn't just about appearance or longevity—it affects your energy, mood, cognitive function, and even spiritual receptivity.

Sustainable movement patterns include:

- Finding activities you genuinely enjoy
- Starting small and building gradually
- Incorporating movement throughout your day
- Balancing different types of exercise (strength, flexibility, endurance)
- Making movement social when possible

The goal isn't becoming an athlete unless that's your calling. It's simply honoring your body's design through regular, intentional movement.

4. Manage stress proactively

Chronic stress is one of the most destructive forces affecting your physical health, yet many Christians wear busyness and burnout as badges of honor. Jesus modeled a different approach, regularly withdrawing from demands to rest, pray, and recharge despite having the most important mission in history.

Practical stress management includes:
- Creating margin in your schedule
- Practicing regular sabbath rest
- Using breath work and prayer to calm your nervous system
- Setting appropriate boundaries on demands
- Addressing sources of chronic stress rather than just managing symptoms

These practices aren't self-indulgent; they're necessary maintenance for the temple God has entrusted to you.

4. Talents: The Gifted Investment

Beyond time, money, and your body, God has entrusted you with specific abilities, skills, gifts, and opportunities. These talents aren't meant to be buried or wasted but invested for kingdom impact.

Jesus addressed this directly in the Parable of the Talents (Matthew 25:14-30), where servants were judged not by how much they had received but by what they did with what they were given. It was the servant who buried his talent—playing it safe instead of putting it to use—who received the harshest judgment.

The Talent Stewardship Problem

Many Christians fail to steward their gifts effectively for several reasons:

- **False humility:** Downplaying abilities to appear humble while actually avoiding responsibility
- **Comparison paralysis:** Not using gifts because others are more talented
- **Misplaced priorities:** Using God-given abilities exclusively for personal advancement rather than kingdom purposes

- **Fear of failure:** Avoiding risk by never fully deploying gifts
- **Waiting for perfect conditions:** Delaying action until everything aligns perfectly

The result is a tragic waste of potential—abilities that could impact others and glorify God remain underutilized or misdirected.

Biblical Gift Stewardship

The Bible provides clear direction for how to steward your talents and abilities:

1. Recognize the source of your gifts

James 1:17 reminds us that "Every good gift and every perfect gift is from above, coming down from the Father of lights." Your abilities aren't self-created or accidental—they're intentional endowments from your Creator.

This perspective eliminates both pride ("Look what I can do!") and false humility ("I don't really have anything to offer"). Your talents are gifts to be gratefully acknowledged and faithfully deployed, not personal achievements to boast about or minimize.

2. Use gifts for their intended purpose

God doesn't distribute abilities randomly but purposefully. As Peter writes in 1 Peter 4:10, "As each has received a gift, use it to serve one another, as good stewards of God's varied grace."

Every gift has a purpose beyond personal benefit or recognition. Technical skills, creative abilities, interpersonal talents, intellectual capacity—all are meant to be used in ways that serve others and glorify God.

3. Develop what you've been given

Good stewardship requires not just using your gifts but growing them through intentional development. In 2 Timothy 1:6, Paul urges Timothy to "fan into flame the gift of God, which is in you." Gifts need to be cultivated, not just passively accepted.

This development mindset transforms how you approach learning, practice, feedback, and growth opportunities. You're not just enhancing personal skills but developing divine investments.

4. Deploy gifts courageously

Effective stewardship means using your abilities even when it feels risky or uncomfortable. The servants who doubled their talents in Jesus' parable had to engage with the world, take calculated risks, and act with confidence in their master's intentions.

This courage comes from recognizing that the ultimate results aren't your responsibility. You're accountable for faithful deployment, not perfect outcomes or universal acclaim.

Practical Talent Stewardship Steps

Ready to stop burying your talents and start investing them? Try these practical steps:

1. Conduct a personal gift inventory

Many people struggle with talent stewardship because they haven't clearly identified what they've been given. A thorough inventory includes:

- **Natural abilities:** What skills have always come easily to you?
- **Developed skills:** What capabilities have you acquired through education and experience?
- **Spiritual gifts:** What ministry-oriented gifts do you demonstrate?
- **Passion areas:** What issues or activities energize rather than drain you?
- **Opportunity contexts:** What unique contexts, relationships, or platforms do you have access to?

This inventory isn't about ego but about honest assessment of what God has entrusted to you. You can't steward what you won't acknowledge.

2. Seek confirmation through community

Individual assessment is important but incomplete. We often have blind spots regarding both our strengths and weaknesses. Ask trusted people who know you well:

- What abilities do you see in me that I might not recognize?
- Where have you seen me make the greatest impact?
- What gifts do you think I'm underutilizing?
- How could my abilities complement what God is doing in our community?

This feedback often reveals gifts you've overlooked or undervalued because they come so naturally to you that you assume everyone has them.

3. Create a development plan

Once you've identified your key gifts, create an intentional plan to develop them further. This might include:

- Formal education or training
- Mentorship from someone with similar gifts
- Regular practice and skill-building

- Feedback loops for ongoing improvement
- Resources (books, courses, tools) that enhance your effectiveness

Development isn't selfish when it's motivated by better stewardship. Jesus' parable shows that the master expected his servants to increase what they'd been given, not just maintain it.

4. Find your ministry sweet spot

The most effective gift stewardship happens at the intersection of:

- What you're good at (abilities)
- What you're passionate about (interests)
- What others need (opportunities)
- What God is blessing (fruit)

This sweet spot isn't always obvious at first. It often emerges through experimentation, prayer, and community confirmation. But when you find it, you experience both maximum impact and minimum burnout.

This doesn't mean service is always easy or comfortable. Sometimes faithfulness requires using your gifts in challenging contexts. But there's a difference between the healthy stretch of growth and the constant drain of misalignment.

5. Collaborate rather than compete

The most effective talent stewardship happens in community, not isolation. Paul uses the body metaphor in 1 Corinthians 12 to illustrate how diverse gifts are meant to function interdependently, not competitively.

Practical collaboration includes:
- Focusing on your core gifts while partnering with those who have complementary abilities
- Celebrating others' talents instead of feeling threatened by them
- Creating teams that maximize collective impact rather than individual recognition
- Sharing knowledge and opportunities rather than hoarding them
- Seeing yourself as part of a bigger story, not the whole story

This collaborative approach multiplies impact far beyond what isolated talent can achieve.

Common Stewardship Pitfalls

Even with the best intentions, we often fall into predictable traps that undermine our stewardship efforts. Recognizing these pitfalls is the first step to avoiding them:

1. The Compartmentalization Trap

Many Christians treat stewardship as a separate spiritual activity rather than an integrated lifestyle. We create artificial divisions—spiritual vs. secular, church vs. "real life"—that fragment our stewardship into disconnected compartments.

This fragmentation leads to inconsistent management: praying fervently on Sunday while making financial decisions with no reference to God on Monday, or carefully preparing Bible study lessons while neglecting physical health.

The antidote is holistic integration—recognizing that every domain of life falls under God's ownership and deserves thoughtful stewardship. Your exercise routine is as spiritually significant as your prayer routine. Your spending decisions are as morally important as your serving decisions.

2. The Tomorrow Fallacy

We often deceive ourselves with the illusion that we'll become better stewards "someday" when conditions improve: when we have more time, more money, better health, fewer responsibilities, or different circumstances.

This perpetual postponement ensures stewardship never moves from intention to action. Today's management decisions create tomorrow's reality, not vice versa.

The antidote is present-tense stewardship—faithfully managing whatever you have right now, however limited it seems. Like the servant with the smallest talent allocation, you're responsible for what you've actually received, not what you wish you had or hope to have someday.

3. The Comparison Disease

Social media has supercharged our tendency to measure our stewardship against others rather than against our personal calling. We compare our financial limitations to others' apparent abundance, our modest gifts to others' spectacular talents, or our ordinary impact to others' viral influence.

This comparison either produces discouragement ("Why bother when I have so little?") or pride ("I'm doing better than most people"), neither of which leads to faithful stewardship.

The antidote is personal accountability—recognizing that you'll give account for your stewardship, not someone else's. As Paul writes in Romans 14:12, "Each of us will give an account of himself to God"—not an account of how we measured up to our neighbor or the social media influencer we follow.

4. The Activity vs. Productivity Confusion

Many of us confuse busyness with effective stewardship. We fill our lives with constant activity—some of it even "Christian" activity—without evaluating whether these actions produce meaningful fruit or align with our specific calling.

This frantic motion creates the illusion of stewardship while actually wasting the resources God has entrusted to us. We exhaust ourselves doing good things while neglecting the best things.

The antidote is purposeful focus—regularly evaluating your activities against your calling and core responsibilities. Not everything worth doing is worth you doing, at least not in this season. Effective stewardship often means doing fewer things with greater excellence and intention.

5. The Ownership Reversion

Even when we intellectually affirm God's ownership, we easily slip back into practical ownership thinking. Financial pressure triggers scarcity mentality. Time demands awaken selfish protection. Health challenges prompt body resentment.

Under stress, our theoretical theology of stewardship often collapses into functional self-ownership with God as distant advisor at best.

The antidote is regular reorientation—deliberately renewing your manager mindset through consistent practices that reinforce God's ownership. This might include regular giving that loosens your grip on money, sabbath practices that release your control of time, or gratitude exercises that reframe your view of your body and abilities.

The Stewardship Development Path

Becoming a good steward doesn't happen overnight. Like any significant spiritual growth, it follows a developmental path with distinct stages. Understanding this progression helps you identify where you are and what next steps make sense:

Stage 1: Awakening to Ownership

The stewardship journey begins with the fundamental recognition that you don't actually own anything—it all belongs to God. This paradigm shift from owner to manager doesn't happen once and for all but requires ongoing renewal as your natural selfishness reasserts itself.

Signs you're at this stage:
- You're questioning assumptions about what belongs to you
- You feel both resistance to and freedom from the manager mindset
- You're noticing ownership thinking in your reactions and decisions
- You're beginning to filter choices through "Whose is this?" rather than just "What do I want?"

Growth practices for this stage:
- Regular meditation on Scriptures about God's ownership
- Daily acknowledgment of God as owner of specific resources in your life
- Creating visual reminders of your manager status
- Accountability relationships that challenge ownership thinking

Stage 2: Establishing Basic Management

Once you've begun to internalize the manager mindset, the next stage involves implementing basic stewardship practices in each domain. This is where you move from conceptual agreement to practical action.

Signs you're at this stage:
- You're creating initial systems for resource management
- You're developing rhythms of regular giving and sabbath rest
- You're making connections between stewardship domains (how sleep affects spiritual attention, etc.)
- You're experiencing both setbacks and small wins in implementation

Growth practices for this stage:
- Creating simple but consistent stewardship routines
- Learning basic management tools for each resource area
- Establishing accountability for follow-through
- Celebrating progress while honestly acknowledging struggles

Stage 3: Developing Strategic Stewardship

With basic practices in place, the third stage involves moving from reactive management to proactive strategy. Rather than just handling resources adequately, you begin deploying them purposefully for maximum kingdom impact.

Signs you're at this stage:
- You're thinking longer-term about resource development and deployment
- You're aligning stewardship practices more closely with your specific calling
- You're making intentional trade-offs based on kingdom priorities
- You're experiencing increased fruitfulness from more strategic management

Growth practices for this stage:
- Creating longer-term stewardship plans aligned with your calling
- Seeking wisdom from experienced stewards in specific domains
- Developing more sophisticated management systems
- Intentionally investing in others' stewardship growth

Stage 4: Multiplying Stewardship Impact

The mature stage of stewardship focuses on multiplication—using your well-managed resources to develop stewardship capacity in others and create sustainable impact beyond your direct involvement.

Signs you're at this stage:
- You're mentoring others in stewardship principles and practices
- You're creating stewardship systems that will outlast your direct management
- You're experiencing spontaneous fruit from earlier strategic investments
- You're holding resources with increasing openness and generosity

Growth practices for this stage:
- Creating intentional stewardship mentoring relationships
- Developing resources that help others grow as managers
- Building sustainable stewardship systems in communities and organizations
- Modeling radical generosity that inspires others

The 30-Day Stewardship Challenge

Ready to move from theoretical agreement to practical action? Try this 30-day stewardship challenge designed to help you develop concrete management habits across all four domains:

Week 1: Time Stewardship

Day 1: Conduct a complete time audit. Track every 30-minute block for 24 hours, noting exactly how you spend your time.

Day 2: Identify your top 3-5 priorities for this season of life. Create a "big rocks" list of what matters most given your current calling and responsibilities.

Day 3: Block your ideal week in a calendar, scheduling your big rocks first before other commitments fill the space.

Day 4: Create a morning routine that sets your day on a positive trajectory. Include elements that center you spiritually, physically, and mentally.

Day 5: Establish technology boundaries. Decide when and where you'll use devices, and create specific limits for potentially addictive applications.

Day 6: Practice saying "no" to one request or opportunity that doesn't align with your core priorities, however good it might seem.

Day 7: Review your week. What worked? What barriers emerged? What adjustments would make your time management more effective?

Week 2: Money Stewardship

Day 8: Track every expense for 24 hours, no matter how small. Note not just the amount but the purpose and value it provided.

Day 9: Review your recurring subscriptions and automatic payments. Cancel anything that doesn't clearly align with your values and priorities.

Day 10: Create a simple budget with three initial categories: Give, Save, Live. Determine percentages for each based on your current situation and values.

Day 11: Set up automated giving to your church or key ministries. Making giving your first financial transaction simplifies stewardship and ensures consistency.

Day 12: Create a debt reduction plan if needed. List all debts with amounts and interest rates, then establish a strategic payment approach.

Day 13: Identify one area of unnecessary spending to reduce, and one area of value-aligned spending to potentially increase.

Day 14: Review your week. What money management practices were most challenging? What insights emerged about your relationship with money?

Week 3: Body Stewardship

Day 15: Assess your current physical stewardship honestly. Rate your habits in key areas: sleep, nutrition, movement, and stress management.

Day 16: Create a sleep improvement plan. Establish consistent sleep-wake times and a screen-free bedtime routine to enhance rest quality.

Day 17: Conduct a kitchen audit. Remove or reduce items that undermine health, and stock up on nourishing alternatives that make healthy choices easier.

Day 18: Establish a sustainable movement routine. Find activities you genuinely enjoy and create a realistic plan for regular physical activity.

Day 19: Practice stress management through intentional breathing. Take three 5-minute breaks today for deep breathing and tension release.

Day 20: Create an environment that supports physical stewardship. Modify your home, workspace, or routine to make healthy choices the default.

Day 21: Review your week. Which physical stewardship practices made the biggest difference in how you felt? What obstacles arose, and how might you address them?

Week 4: Talent Stewardship

Day 22: Complete a comprehensive gift inventory. List your natural abilities, acquired skills, spiritual gifts, passionate interests, and unique opportunities.

Day 23: Ask 3-5 people who know you well what gifts they see in you and where they've noticed you making the greatest positive impact.

Day 24: Identify one key gift to develop further. Create a specific growth plan including learning resources, practice opportunities, and feedback mechanisms.

Day 25: Evaluate your current gift deployment. Where are your talents being used effectively? Where might they be underutilized or misdirected?

Day 26: Create a personal mission statement that captures how your specific gifts and calling shape your approach to stewardship across all domains.

Day 27: Identify one new way to use your gifts to serve others this week. Look for needs at the intersection of your abilities and others' challenges.

Day 28: Review your week. What insights emerged about your unique gifting? How might you more effectively steward your talents moving forward?

Integration Days

Day 29: Create a comprehensive stewardship plan that integrates all four domains. Look for connections and synergies between time, money, body, and talent management.

Day 30: Establish ongoing accountability for your stewardship journey. Share your plan with a trusted friend, mentor, or small group who can provide support and honest feedback.

Throughout this challenge, keep a journal noting:
- Insights about your current stewardship patterns
- Obstacles and resistance that emerge
- Practical adjustments that increase effectiveness
- Connections between different stewardship domains
- Evidence of God's presence and guidance in the process

This record will help you recognize patterns, celebrate progress, and identify next steps as you continue developing as a faithful manager of everything God has entrusted to you.

The Kick in the Pants: Stop Making Excuses and Start Managing Your Sh*t

Let's get brutally honest: Your life is a mess not because you lack resources but because you mismanage the ones you have.

You squander hours on mindless scrolling while complaining you don't have time to pray. You waste money on subscription services you barely use while claiming you can't afford to give. You neglect basic physical maintenance while wondering why you're always tired. You bury your talents in the backyard of excuses and then wonder why God isn't using you more significantly.

And somehow, none of this seems like your fault. It's the economy, your upbringing, your metabolism, your circumstances, your boss—anyone but you.

Here's the uncomfortable truth: You can't follow Jesus and remain perpetually irresponsible with what He's entrusted to you. At some point, spiritual maturity must produce practical responsibility.

Romans 14:12 puts it bluntly: "Each of us will give an account of himself to God." Not an explanation of why you couldn't manage things well, not a list of people to blame, but an account of what you did with what you were given.

Imagine standing before God and trying to explain why you never had enough time for spiritual growth while maintaining a detailed knowledge of every Netflix series. Or why you couldn't afford to support His work while funding an impressive collection of shoes, gadgets, or whatever your particular indulgence happens to be. Or why you were too exhausted for ministry while refusing to address basic health habits that drained your energy.

The excuses that seem so reasonable now will sound hollow in the presence of the One who entrusted those resources to you in the first place.

This isn't about perfection or performance. It's about honesty and responsibility. It's about acknowledging that everything you have—your time, your money, your body, your talents—belongs to God and should be managed accordingly. It's about growing up and handling your business like the adult God created you to be.

The good news is that becoming a better steward doesn't require superhuman discipline or dramatic lifestyle changes. It starts with small, consistent choices that gradually align your management with your values:

- Giving the first portion of your income, not the leftovers

- Scheduling your most important priorities before your calendar fills with lesser concerns
- Making basic health choices that honor your body as God's temple
- Using your gifts to serve others, not just impress them

These choices aren't about earning God's favor but expressing your gratitude for it. They're not about rigid rules but about living in alignment with reality—the reality that everything you have is a gift from the Creator to be managed for His purposes, not yours.

So stop with the excuses. Stop blaming your circumstances. Stop waiting for some magical future when stewardship will somehow become easier.

Start managing your sh*t like it actually belongs to God—because it does.

Your life is not your own. You were bought with a price. Start living like it.

Chapter 12:

Humility – Getting Over Yourself

Let's start with the uncomfortable truth: you think about yourself way too much.

Don't take it personally—we all do. We're walking, talking monuments to self-absorption. We analyze how every situation affects us, how we look to others, whether we're getting enough respect, if our Instagram post got enough likes, and if that slightly ambiguous text meant the sender secretly hates us.

We're the stars of our own mental movies, with everyone else relegated to supporting roles or extras. Even our "selfless" moments often come with a side of self-congratulation: "Look how humble I am! Notice my sacrifice! Appreciate my generosity!"

Then we wonder why we're anxious, insecure, easily offended, and constantly exhausted. We're carrying a burden we were never designed to bear: the crushing weight of our own self-importance.

This is where humility enters the chat—not as a downer that makes you feel bad about yourself, but as the liberation you desperately need. Because here's the paradox: the path to genuine confidence, inner peace, and spiritual growth runs straight through getting over yourself.

As C.S. Lewis famously noted, "Humility is not thinking less of yourself, it's thinking of yourself less." It's the freedom that comes when you stop making everything about you. It's the wisdom that emerges when you recognize your proper place in the universe—neither a worthless worm nor the center of all things, but a beloved creation with both dignity and limitations.

In a culture that worships self-promotion, self-expression, self-care, and self-actualization, humility feels counterintuitive, even dangerous. Won't I get trampled? Won't others take advantage of me? Won't I miss out on the recognition I deserve?

These fears reveal how deeply we've absorbed the lie that life is all about us. The gospel offers a radical alternative: life is about God and others, and you're actually most fulfilled when you stop orbiting around yourself.

As Jesus bluntly put it in Matthew 16:25, "For whoever would save his life will lose it, but whoever loses his life for my sake will find it." The divine paradox is that self-focus leads to misery, while self-forgetfulness leads to joy. Humility isn't self-destruction—it's self-discovery of who you were actually created to be.

In this chapter, we're going to expose the sneaky ways pride manifests in your life (spoiler: it's not just boasting), explore what biblical humility really looks like (hint: Jesus is the model), and outline practical ways to develop this foundational Christian virtue in your everyday life. Fair warning: this might be uncomfortable. Pride doesn't go down without a fight. But the freedom waiting on the other side is worth every bruise to your ego.

The Many Disguises of Pride

When most of us hear the word "pride," we picture an arrogant jerk bragging about their accomplishments, wealth, or status. That's certainly one manifestation, but pride is far more versatile and sneaky than that. It's like the master of disguise in the spiritual realm, shape-shifting to avoid detection while keeping you firmly at the center of your universe.

Let's unmask some of pride's favorite costumes:

1. Perfectionism: "I can't fail or show weakness"

Perfectionism often masquerades as excellence or high standards, but it's actually pride wearing a suit of armor. The perfectionist isn't just pursuing quality—they're desperately avoiding the perceived shame of imperfection. They've staked their identity on being flawless, and any mistake threatens their carefully constructed self-image.

The Bible addresses this directly in Proverbs 16:18: "Pride goes before destruction, and a haughty spirit before a fall." The perfectionistic need to maintain an unblemished façade inevitably leads to either spectacular failure (when you can't sustain the impossible standard) or spiritual stagnation (when you avoid risks to protect your perfect record).

True humility allows you to pursue excellence without needing perfection. It gives you the freedom to fail, learn, and grow without your identity crumbling. It enables you to say "I don't know" or "I need help" without experiencing existential crisis.

2. Chronic Comparison: "I need to be better than others"

The comparison trap is pride's favorite playground. Whether you're comparing upward (feeling inferior to those you perceive as "above" you) or downward (feeling superior to those you consider "beneath" you), you're still making everything about your relative position in some imaginary hierarchy.

Paul addressed this in Galatians 6:4-5: "But let each one test his own work, and then his reason to boast will be in himself alone and not in his neighbor. For each will have to bear his own load." In other words, your only meaningful comparison should be between who you are and who God is calling you to become—not between you and the person next to you.

Humility frees you from the exhausting hamster wheel of comparison. It allows you to celebrate others' successes without feeling threatened and to acknowledge others' struggles without feeling superior. It lets you be fully yourself without constantly checking how you measure up.

3. Attention-Seeking: "Notice me!"

The constant need for validation and visibility is pride wearing a spotlight. While healthy humans certainly need appropriate recognition, the attention-seeker has made others' affirmation their primary source of identity and worth.

Jesus called this out in Matthew 6:1: "Beware of practicing your righteousness before other people in order to be seen by them, for then you will have no reward from your Father who is in heaven." He wasn't condemning public good deeds—He was exposing the prideful motivation of doing things primarily for human applause.

Humble people can do good things publicly when necessary, but they don't need an audience to validate their worth. They find deep satisfaction in acts no one will ever see because they're living for an Audience of One rather than human applause.

4. Victimhood: "Everything happens TO me"

The professional victim might seem like the opposite of pride, but it's actually pride in disguise. By casting yourself as the perpetual victim, you make every situation about you and your suffering, positioning yourself at the center of a narrative where others exist primarily as either villains who hurt you or potential rescuers who should help you.

The apostle Peter, who knew something about genuine persecution, warned against this mindset in 1 Peter 4:19: "Therefore let those who suffer according to God's will entrust their souls to a faithful Creator while doing good." He acknowledged real suffering but discouraged wallowing in victimhood, instead pointing toward entrusting oneself to God and continuing to do good regardless of circumstances.

Humility allows you to acknowledge genuine wrongs without defining your entire identity by them. It helps you recognize that while some things do happen to you, not everything is about you. It creates space for both honest grieving and gracious moving forward.

5. Excessive Independence: "I don't need anyone"

The fierce independence our culture celebrates is often pride masquerading as strength. The person who "never needs help" and "handles everything themselves" isn't actually displaying admirable self-sufficiency—they're revealing a prideful inability to acknowledge their inherent limitations and interdependence.

Scripture consistently presents humans as created for community and mutual support. Ecclesiastes 4:9-10 observes, "Two are better than one, because they have a good reward for their toil. For if they fall, one will lift up his fellow. But woe to him who is alone when he falls and has not another to lift him up!" The refusal to ever need others isn't strength—it's prideful self-deception.

True humility acknowledges both your strengths and your limitations. It allows you to offer help without condescension and to receive help without shame. It recognizes that needing others isn't weakness—it's part of being human.

6. Defensive Pride: "I'm never wrong"

The person who can't handle criticism, immediately deflects blame, or launches into elaborate justifications whenever their mistakes are pointed out is displaying classic defensive pride. Their self-image is so fragile that any suggestion of imperfection feels like an existential threat.

Proverbs 12:1 addresses this directly: "Whoever loves discipline loves knowledge, but he who hates reproof is stupid." The bluntness of this proverb reveals how seriously Scripture takes our ability to receive correction. Defensiveness doesn't protect you—it prevents you from growing.

Humility gives you the security to hear hard truths without crumbling. It allows you to say those liberating words—"I was wrong"—without feeling like your entire identity is under attack. It enables you to separate your actions (which may need correction) from your worth (which remains intact regardless).

7. False Humility: "I'm just terrible at everything"

Perhaps the most insidious disguise pride wears is false humility—the performative self-deprecation that actually seeks reassurance and attention. The person who constantly puts themselves down isn't displaying humility but engaging in a manipulative form of pride that makes others responsible for building them up.

Paul warned against this in Colossians 2:18, speaking of those who delight in "false humility," using apparent self-abasement to actually draw attention to themselves. True humility isn't about performative self-flagellation but about honest self-assessment and appropriate self-forgetfulness.

Genuine humility allows you to acknowledge both your gifts and your limitations with equal honesty. It doesn't need to exaggerate either your strengths or your weaknesses. It simply sees you as you actually are—a complex, valuable, flawed human being who doesn't need to be either the best or the worst to matter.

The Biblical Vision of Humility

Now that we've exposed pride's favorite disguises, let's explore what genuine humility actually looks like according to Scripture. Far from the meek, mild, doormat caricature many envision, biblical humility is a powerful, transformative virtue grounded in reality rather than either grandiosity or false self-deprecation.

1. Humility Begins with God-Centered Reality

The foundation of biblical humility is a right understanding of who God is and who you are in relation to Him. It's not about artificial self-loathing but about accurate self-placement in the created order.

Isaiah had this perspective-altering encounter in Isaiah 6:1-5: "I saw the Lord sitting upon a throne, high and lifted up... And I said: 'Woe is me! For I am lost; for I am a man of unclean lips, and I dwell in the midst of a people of unclean lips; for my eyes have seen the King, the LORD of hosts!'" Isaiah's humility wasn't self-manufactured—it was the natural response to glimpsing God's majesty and holiness.

This God-centered reality check doesn't crush you; it correctly orients you. When you recognize the infinite gap between Creator and creation, you stop trying to be God in your own life (controlling everything, knowing everything, being the center of everything). This isn't degrading—it's liberating. You were never designed to bear the weight of being God, and humility frees you from that impossible burden.

2. Humility Acknowledges Both Dignity and Dependence

Biblical humility holds together two seemingly contradictory truths: humans have immense God-given dignity and worth, and humans are utterly dependent creatures who can do nothing apart from their Creator.

Genesis 1:27 establishes human dignity: "So God created man in his own image, in the image of God he created him; male and female he created them." This divine image-bearing gives every human inherent value that can't be earned or lost.

Yet John 15:5 establishes human dependence: "I am the vine; you are the branches. Whoever abides in me and I in him, he it is that bears much fruit, for apart from me you can do nothing." This dependent relationship means even our accomplishments ultimately flow from God's enabling grace.

True humility neither exaggerates your importance (pride) nor denies your value (false humility). It simply acknowledges the beautiful, balanced truth: you matter immensely while remaining utterly dependent on God for your next breath.

3. Humility Expresses Itself in Christlike Service

The clearest biblical picture of humility in action is Jesus washing His disciples' feet in John 13:3-5: "Jesus, knowing that the Father had given all things into his hands, and that he had come from God and was going back to God, rose from supper. He laid aside his outer garments, and taking a towel, tied it around his waist. Then he poured water into a basin and began to wash the disciples' feet and to wipe them with the towel that was wrapped around him."

Notice the stunning contrast: precisely because Jesus knew His divine identity and authority ("knowing that the Father had given all things into his hands"), He was free to serve in the most menial way without feeling diminished. His humility flowed from security, not insecurity. He didn't need to prove His importance because He knew exactly who He was.

This same pattern appears in Philippians 2:5-8, where Paul urges believers to "have this mind among yourselves, which is yours in Christ Jesus, who, though he was in the form of God... emptied himself, by taking the form of a servant... he humbled himself by becoming obedient to the point of death, even death on a cross."

Biblical humility isn't about thinking you're worthless; it's about being so secure in your God-given identity that you're free to serve others without needing recognition or status. It's the strength that comes from knowing your value isn't determined by human opinion or relative position.

4. Humility Creates Space for Others to Flourish

One of the most beautiful expressions of biblical humility is genuine delight in others' success and growth. Pride sees others as either competition or tools for personal advancement. Humility sees others as image-bearers whose flourishing matters regardless of how it affects you.

The apostle Paul modeled this in Philippians 2:3-4: "Do nothing from selfish ambition or conceit, but in humility count others more significant than yourselves. Let each of you look not only to his own interests, but also to the interests of others."

This doesn't mean pretending others are more talented or valuable than you in some objective sense. It means approaching interactions with a genuine interest in others' well-being and growth, not just your own advancement or recognition. It means creating space for others to shine rather than needing to be the star in every scene.

John the Baptist exemplified this when his disciples worried about Jesus' growing popularity. John responded with beautiful humility in John 3:30: "He must increase, but I must decrease." John understood that his role was not to build his own platform but to point to Jesus—and he found joy, not resentment, in fulfilling this purpose.

5. Humility Receives Grace Without Entitlement

The humble heart can receive gifts, help, and grace without either entitlement ("I deserve this") or self-degradation ("I'm not worthy"). It simply accepts with gratitude, acknowledging both the genuine need and the genuine gift.

James 4:6 highlights this connection between humility and grace: "God opposes the proud but gives grace to the humble." Pride creates a barrier to receiving grace because it either denies the need for it or demands it as a right. Humility opens the hands to receive what God freely gives.

Jesus illustrated this in the parable of the Pharisee and the tax collector (Luke 18:9-14). The Pharisee, though ostensibly thanking God, was actually celebrating his own righteousness. The tax collector simply acknowledged his need for mercy without excuse or pretense. Jesus said it was the tax collector—the one who humbly received grace—who "went down to his house justified."

This humble receptivity extends beyond spiritual grace to practical help from others. The humble person can say "thank you" without either dismissing the help ("Oh, it was nothing, I could have done it myself") or feeling diminished by needing assistance. They can receive compliments without either fishing for more or deflecting them entirely.

The Surprising Benefits of Humility

If pride is so natural to us, why should we fight it? What makes humility worth the uncomfortable work of getting over ourselves? Beyond simply avoiding the spiritual danger of pride ("God opposes the proud"), there are several powerful benefits that come from developing genuine humility:

1. Humility Accelerates Growth

Nothing stunts growth like thinking you've already arrived. Pride creates a defensive shell against feedback, criticism, and new perspectives—all essential ingredients for meaningful development.

The proud person is stuck at their current level of maturity because they can't bear to acknowledge they have room to grow.

Proverbs 9:8-9 observes this dynamic: "Do not reprove a scoffer, or he will hate you; reprove a wise man, and he will love you. Give instruction to a wise man, and he will be still wiser; teach a righteous man, and he will increase in learning." The humble person (the "wise man" in this proverb) can receive correction without defensiveness, which creates continuous learning and growth.

This growth advantage applies to every area of life—relationships, career, spiritual development, skills, emotional intelligence. The humble person progresses faster not because they're inherently more talented but because they're more teachable. They can say "I don't know" without shame, ask questions without embarrassment, and revise their views without identity crisis.

2. Humility Creates Authentic Connection

Pride creates distance in relationships. Whether through superiority, defensiveness, attention-seeking, or comparison, pride puts invisible barriers between you and others. Humility, by contrast, creates the conditions for genuine connection.

James 5:16 points to this vulnerability-based connection: "Therefore, confess your sins to one another and pray for one another, that you may be healed." The proud person maintains an exhausting façade of having it all together, preventing others from knowing the real person behind the performance. The humble person can acknowledge struggles, ask for help, and allow genuine reciprocal relationship.

This authenticity doesn't mean inappropriate oversharing or using vulnerability as attention-seeking. It means appropriate openness that allows others to know the real you, not just the carefully curated version. It means listening as much as speaking, showing interest in others' stories rather than making every conversation about your experiences.

The result is relationships with actual intimacy rather than superficial interaction. The humble person has fewer "followers" but more genuine friends. Their connections are deeper, more satisfying, and more enduring because they're built on mutual knowledge and care rather than impression management.

3. Humility Produces Inner Peace

Pride creates a state of constant anxiety. When your sense of worth depends on outperforming others, maintaining perfect appearances, or receiving constant validation, you live in perpetual insecurity. Every interaction becomes an opportunity for either validation or threat. Every accomplishment provides only temporary relief before you need the next hit of affirmation.

Jesus offered a different way in Matthew 11:28-29: "Come to me, all who labor and are heavy laden, and I will give you rest. Take my yoke upon you, and learn from me, for I am gentle and lowly in heart, and you will find rest for your souls." The humility of Christ ("lowly in heart") is directly connected to the rest He offers.

Humility produces peace because it liberates you from the exhausting work of maintaining appearances, comparing yourself to others, and needing constant validation. When you accept both your dignity and limitations, when you recognize your value doesn't depend on outperforming others, you can exhale. You can rest in who you actually are rather than frantically trying to be something you're not.

4. Humility Enables Resilience

Pride makes you brittle in the face of failure and criticism because your identity is staked on performance and perception. The proud person experiences setbacks not just as practical problems but as existential threats to their core self.

The humble person, by contrast, can weather failures and criticism without being devastated because their identity isn't built on perfect performance or universal approval. As Proverbs 11:2 observes, "When pride comes, then comes disgrace, but with the humble is wisdom." The humble person has the wisdom to distinguish between who they are and what they do, between their inherent value and their variable performance.

This resilience doesn't mean immunity to hurt feelings or disappointment. It means those negative experiences don't define you or determine your worth. You can acknowledge the pain of failure without it becoming an identity crisis. You can receive criticism without either dismissing it entirely or being crushed by it.

5. Humility Enhances Leadership

Counterintuitively, humility makes you more effective in positions of influence and leadership. The proud leader creates environments of fear, competition, and image management. The humble leader creates cultures of psychological safety, collaboration, and innovation.

Peter addresses this in 1 Peter 5:5-6: "Clothe yourselves, all of you, with humility toward one another, for 'God opposes the proud but gives grace to the humble.' Humble yourselves, therefore, under the mighty hand of God so that at the proper time he may exalt you." The paradox is clear: the path to true influence ("he may exalt you") runs through humility, not self-promotion.

Humble leaders demonstrate this through:
- Giving credit rather than taking it
- Admitting mistakes promptly rather than covering them up
- Seeking input rather than assuming they have all the answers
- Developing others rather than hoarding spotlight and opportunity
- Serving their teams rather than expecting to be served

The result is not diminished influence but enhanced impact. People follow humble leaders willingly rather than compliantly. They bring their best ideas, effort, and creativity because they know they'll be valued rather than exploited or overshadowed.

Practical Steps Toward Humility

Understanding humility conceptually is one thing; developing it practically is another challenge entirely. Pride is our default setting, and humility requires intentional cultivation. Here are practical steps to help you develop this countercultural virtue:

1. Start with a Reality Check

Humility begins with honest self-assessment—seeing yourself as you actually are, not as you wish to be seen. This requires courage to look at both strengths and weaknesses without either inflation or deflation.

Conduct a pride audit by asking yourself:
- In what areas am I most defensive when criticized?
- Where do I most need others to notice or praise me?
- When do I feel threatened by others' success?
- Where am I unwilling to admit ignorance or ask for help?
- In what relationships do I insist on being right?
- How do I react when my plans or preferences are overruled?

These questions reveal pride's hiding places in your life. The areas where you feel most defensive, competitive, or attention-seeking are precisely where pride has its strongest grip.

For deeper insight, ask a trusted friend, "Where do you see pride operating in my life?" Warning: only do this if you're prepared to receive the answer without defensiveness. Their outside perspective might reveal blind spots you can't see from the inside.

2. Practice Strategic Self-Forgetfulness

Humility isn't achieved by thinking about yourself less favorably; it's developed by thinking about yourself less frequently. The goal is healthy self-forgetfulness, not negative self-preoccupation.

Here's how to practice this self-forgetfulness:
- Set a phone timer to beep randomly throughout the day. When it sounds, note whether your thoughts were self-focused or externally focused. No judgment—just awareness.
- When entering a room or situation, mentally shift your question from "How do I look?" or "What will they think of me?" to "Who here might need encouragement?" or "How can I add value?"
- During conversations, count how many questions you ask versus statements you make about yourself. Aim to increase the ratio of questions to personal statements.
- After group activities, write down three things you noticed about others rather than evaluating your own performance first.
- When receiving compliments, practice simple gratitude ("Thank you") rather than either fishing for more praise or deflecting with self-deprecation.

The goal isn't to never think about yourself (which would actually be a bizarre form of self-obsession) but to develop the capacity to focus beyond yourself for increasingly longer periods.

3. Volunteer for Invisible Service

Nothing challenges pride like serving in ways no one will notice or praise. These hidden acts of service train you to find satisfaction in the act itself rather than the recognition it might bring.

Look for opportunities like:
- Cleaning a public space when no one is watching
- Anonymously meeting a need without revealing yourself as the giver
- Taking care of thankless tasks that others avoid
- Serving in roles that support others' visibility rather than creating your own
- Doing something kind for someone who will never be able to repay or even acknowledge it

Jesus directly addressed this in Matthew 6:3-4: "But when you give to the needy, do not let your left hand know what your right hand is doing, so that your giving may be in secret. And your Father who sees in secret will reward you." The principle extends beyond financial giving to all forms of service.

Start with small acts of invisible service and work up to larger commitments. Notice the freedom that comes from doing good without needing credit. Pay attention to how this shifts your motivation from external validation to internal integrity.

4. Cultivate Purposeful Gratitude

Pride thrives in entitlement and withers in gratitude. When you recognize that everything—from your talents to your opportunities to your very existence—is ultimately a gift, pride loses its foothold.

Develop gratitude through practices like:
- Keeping a daily gratitude journal where you record three specific gifts you didn't earn or create
- Verbalizing thanks to people whose contributions often go unnoticed (janitors, administrative staff, behind-the-scenes workers)
- Acknowledging the "shoulders you stand on"—people who helped you develop skills, access opportunities, or overcome obstacles
- Practicing gratitude for basic provisions that billions lack—clean water, shelter, education, healthcare
- Recognizing your dependence on God for your next breath, heartbeat, and moment of consciousness

Paul modeled this perspective in 1 Corinthians 4:7: "What do you have that you did not receive? If then you received it, why do you boast as if you did not receive it?" This question cuts to the heart of pride's self-sufficiency illusion. Everything you have and are ultimately comes from beyond yourself.

The goal isn't manufactured guilt for your blessings but genuine recognition of their source. This shifts your fundamental orientation from entitlement ("I deserve this") to grateful stewardship ("I've been entrusted with this").

5. Learn the Art of the Genuine Apology

Few things reveal pride more clearly than the inability to offer a clean, non-defensive apology when you're wrong. Learning to apologize well is both an expression of humility and a practice that develops it further.

Elements of a genuine apology include:
- Clear acknowledgment of the specific wrong (not vague "if you were hurt" language)
- Absence of justifications, explanations, or blame-shifting
- Recognition of the impact on the other person
- Concrete steps to prevent recurrence when applicable
- No expectation of immediate forgiveness or reciprocal apology

The goal isn't performative self-flagellation but honest ownership of your mistakes and their effects on others. A genuine apology doesn't diminish your worth; it demonstrates your maturity and integrity.

Start with small matters where apologizing feels less threatening, then work toward addressing larger wrongs as your humility muscles develop. Notice how honest apologies actually strengthen relationships rather than diminishing your standing within them.

6. Seek and Implement Feedback

Pride insulates you from growth-producing feedback. Humility intentionally seeks it out, not as self-torture but as a pathway to development and excellence.

Practical steps for feedback cultivation:
- Identify specific areas where you want to grow, and ask targeted questions rather than fishing for general affirmation
- Express genuine appreciation for constructive criticism, even when it stings
- Implement at least one suggestion from every feedback conversation to demonstrate you value the input
- Follow up with those who gave feedback to share how you used their insights

- Become equally comfortable with hearing both strengths and growth areas

This practice directly counters the defensive pride that rejects correction. As Proverbs 15:32 notes, "Whoever ignores instruction despises himself, but he who listens to reproof gains intelligence." The humble person recognizes that feedback isn't an attack on their worth but a gift for their growth.

Start with low-stakes feedback in areas where you feel relatively secure, and gradually expand to more sensitive domains as your humility develops. Pay attention to your internal reactions to criticism—the goal isn't absence of emotional response but constructive engagement despite the discomfort.

7. Practice the Ministry of Celebration

Pride makes others' success feel threatening. Humility allows you to genuinely celebrate when good things happen to others, even in areas where you also aspire to excel.

Develop this capacity through practices like:
- Keeping a "celebration journal" where you record others' wins and successes, especially in areas where you might naturally feel competitive
- Being the first to publicly acknowledge and praise others' achievements

- Sending specific, thoughtful congratulations when peers receive recognition
- Sharing others' content, ideas, and accomplishments without needing to add your perspective
- Finding joy in being the supporter rather than always needing to be the star

Romans 12:15 instructs believers to "Rejoice with those who rejoice." This isn't just about being polite; it's about developing the capacity to find genuine joy in others' flourishing regardless of how it compares to your own circumstances.

Start with celebrating people whose success feels least threatening to you, and gradually work toward genuine celebration of direct peers and competitors. Pay attention to how this practice frees you from the exhaustion of constant comparison and competition.

The Humility Journey: Stages of Development

Developing humility isn't an instant transformation but a gradual journey with distinct stages. Understanding these stages helps you recognize progress and persevere through challenges:

Stage 1: Awakening to Pride

The humility journey begins with the uncomfortable recognition of pride's pervasive presence in your life. This awareness often comes through painful experiences—relational conflict, leadership failure, spiritual dryness, or simply the exhaustion of maintaining a prideful façade.

Signs you're at this stage:
- Increasing awareness of your defensive reactions to criticism
- Recognition of competitive or jealous responses to others' success
- Noticing how often your thoughts revolve around yourself
- Feeling convicted about attention-seeking behaviors
- Seeing the connection between pride and relational difficulties

This awakening doesn't immediately change behavior, but it creates essential self-awareness. Without this recognition, pride remains invisible and therefore untouchable. The awakening stage is uncomfortable but necessary—the spiritual equivalent of turning on the lights in a room you thought was clean, only to discover it's actually quite messy.

Growth practices for this stage:

- Honest prayer acknowledging specific manifestations of pride
- Reading about humility to develop language for what you're experiencing
- Listening to feedback without immediate defensiveness
- Noting pride triggers in daily interactions
- Finding trusted friends who will speak truth about your blind spots

Stage 2: Intentional Counter-Practice

Once you recognize pride's operation in your life, the next stage involves deliberate practices that counter your prideful defaults. This stage requires intentional choices that often feel uncomfortable or even artificial at first.

Signs you're at this stage:
- Consciously choosing humble responses that don't come naturally
- Feeling the internal resistance of pride when practicing humility
- Catching yourself in prideful patterns and making mid-course corrections
- Experiencing both small victories and discouraging setbacks
- Developing new habits that support humility (listening better, apologizing more readily, seeking feedback)

This stage involves significant internal conflict as established pride patterns resist change. Think of it as reprogramming deeply ingrained software—the old code doesn't surrender without a fight. You'll experience both progress and regression, sometimes within the same day or even the same conversation.

Growth practices for this stage:
- Creating specific humility "triggers" for situations where pride typically emerges
- Finding accountability partners who can gently flag pride in action
- Celebrating small victories without perfectionism
- Learning from setbacks without self-condemnation
- Focusing on concrete behaviors rather than vague aspirations

Stage 3: Growing Authenticity

With consistent counter-practice, humility gradually becomes more natural and authentic rather than forced or performative. This transitional stage marks significant progress while still requiring conscious attention.

Signs you're at this stage:
- Finding genuine satisfaction in others' success
- Experiencing decreased defensiveness when criticized

- Noticing increased capacity to listen without self-reference
- Feeling less anxious about how you're perceived
- Developing intuitive responses that align with humility rather than pride

At this stage, the internal conflict between pride and humility hasn't disappeared, but the balance of power has shifted. Humble responses come more readily, require less conscious effort, and feel more aligned with your authentic self rather than imposed from outside.

Growth practices for this stage:
- Noticing the differences between performative and authentic humility
- Developing language to describe your evolving relationship with pride
- Finding contexts that especially challenge your growing humility
- Mentoring others earlier in their humility journey
- Integrating humility practices across more life domains

Stage 4: Habitual Humility

The mature stage of humility development is characterized by habitual other-centeredness and self-forgetfulness. Pride hasn't been completely eradicated, but humble responses have become your default setting rather than requiring constant vigilance.

Signs you're at this stage:
- Experiencing extended periods of genuine self-forgetfulness
- Finding joy in others' success without conscious effort
- Receiving criticism with curiosity rather than defensiveness
- Navigating both praise and criticism without identity disruption
- Using influence to elevate others rather than showcase yourself

This stage represents significant spiritual maturity but never complete arrival. Even at this stage, pride can reassert itself in moments of stress, new contexts, or areas of particular vulnerability. The difference is that you recognize and address pride more quickly, with less self-judgment and more practical wisdom.

Growth practices for this stage:
- Remaining vigilant in areas of particular pride vulnerability
- Developing others in their humility journey through mentoring and example
- Creating environments that cultivate humility in communities and organizations
- Maintaining practices that reinforce humble perspectives

- Remembering that humility is maintained through ongoing relationship with God, not achieved as a permanent state

Humility in Different Life Contexts

Humility expresses itself differently depending on your life circumstances and roles. Here's how humility might manifest in various contexts:

For Leaders and People with Influence

If you occupy a leadership position—whether in business, church, family, or community—humility takes particular forms:

- Soliciting and implementing feedback from those you lead
- Sharing credit generously while taking responsibility for failures
- Creating psychological safety where others can speak truth without fear
- Using your power to elevate others rather than advancing yourself
- Acknowledging your limitations and building complementary teams

Jesus modeled leadership humility when he washed his disciples' feet (John 13:3-5) and when he taught, "Whoever would be great among you must be your servant" (Mark 10:43). The humble leader sees position not as a platform for self-importance but as an opportunity for greater service.

For Those in Learning or Subordinate Positions

If you're in a season of learning, development, or working under authority, humility looks like:

- Being teachable without constant validation-seeking
- Respecting authority without either rebellion or unhealthy deference
- Offering ideas confidently while remaining open to guidance
- Embracing the learning journey without shame about not knowing everything
- Using your fresh perspective to add value while honoring established wisdom

As Proverbs 18:13 wisely notes, "If one gives an answer before he hears, it is his folly and shame." The humble learner listens thoroughly before speaking, asks questions before offering solutions, and approaches even disagreements with respect rather than arrogance.

For the Highly Successful

If you've achieved significant success or recognition, humility includes:

- Acknowledging the role of privilege, timing, and others' contributions
- Using your platform to address meaningful issues rather than self-promotion
- Remaining accessible and grounded despite status changes
- Continuing to seek growth rather than resting on achievements
- Creating opportunities for others rather than hoarding spotlight and resources

Joseph demonstrated this form of humility in Genesis 41:16. When Pharaoh praised his interpretive abilities, Joseph immediately redirected: "It is not in me; God will give Pharaoh a favorable answer." He acknowledged both his legitimate ability and its ultimate source.

For Those Facing Limitation or Setback

If you're in a season of limitation, failure, or setback, humility looks like:

- Accepting help without shame or excessive self-deprecation

- Acknowledging reality without either denial or identity collapse
- Learning from failures without being defined by them
- Allowing your limitations to create empathy rather than bitterness
- Finding ways to contribute value despite constraints

The apostle Paul modeled this in 2 Corinthians 12:9-10, embracing his limitations ("thorn in the flesh") while continuing his mission: "Therefore I will boast all the more gladly of my weaknesses, so that the power of Christ may rest upon me... For when I am weak, then I am strong."

For the Naturally Gifted

If you possess exceptional natural talents or abilities, humility includes:

- Recognizing your gifts as precisely that—gifts, not self-generated
- Using your abilities to serve rather than to impress
- Developing your talents with diligence rather than entitlement
- Creating space for others to contribute their different gifts
- Showing genuine interest in others' strengths rather than centering conversations on your own

Bezalel, the tabernacle craftsman described in Exodus 35:30-35, exemplifies this balance. Though extraordinarily gifted, he used his abilities in service to a larger purpose, worked collaboratively with others, and recognized his skills as divine endowments rather than personal achievements.

For Those Building Platforms or Public Personas

If you're developing a public presence—whether through social media, speaking, writing, or other visible platforms—humility looks like:

- Creating content that genuinely serves others, not just builds your brand
- Sharing failures and limitations alongside successes
- Highlighting others' voices, especially those with less access
- Engaging criticism thoughtfully rather than defensively
- Remembering that your platform exists for service, not status

John the Baptist modeled this when his disciples worried about Jesus gaining greater popularity. Rather than competing for audience, John stated with remarkable humility, "He must increase, but I must decrease" (John 3:30).

The 30-Day Humility Challenge

Ready to develop this foundational Christian virtue? Try this 30-day challenge designed to help you recognize pride and practice humility in everyday situations:

Week 1: Awareness Building

Day 1: Pride Inventory
Take 30 minutes to honestly assess where pride operates in your life. Answer questions like:
- When do I get most defensive?
- Where do I most need recognition or praise?
- In what situations do I find it hardest to admit mistakes?
- Where do I compare myself to others most frequently?

Write down your insights without self-judgment—just honest observation.

Day 2: Feedback Request
Ask one trusted person: "Where do you see pride or defensiveness in how I interact with others?" Listen without defending yourself, simply thanking them for their honesty. Journal what you learn.

Day 3: Self-Reference Tracking
For one full day, keep a tally of how often you:

- Turn conversations back to yourself
- Share your accomplishments or expertise
- Make statements starting with "I"
- Reference your own experiences when others share theirs

The goal isn't condemnation but awareness of your current baseline.

Day 4: Social Media Audit

Review your last 15 posts on your most-used social platform. Count how many:
- Seek validation or attention
- Highlight your accomplishments or qualities
- Position you as an expert or authority
- Compare your life favorably to others

Notice patterns without judgment, simply building awareness.

Day 5: Thought Monitoring

Set a timer to beep randomly 5 times throughout your day. Each time, notice:
- Were your thoughts self-focused or others-focused?
- Were you thinking about how you appear to others?
- Were you comparing yourself to someone else?
- Were you rehearsing your own importance or accomplishments?

Record your observations without self-criticism.

Day 6: Defensive Trigger Identification

Identify 3-5 specific situations that reliably trigger defensiveness in you. For each, note:

- What exactly makes you defensive
- How you typically respond
- What you're protecting or afraid of losing
- How the situation threatens your self-image

This awareness creates the foundation for changed responses.

Day 7: Reflection Day
Review your insights from the week. What surprised you? What patterns emerged? Where does pride seem most entrenched? Where did you notice potential for growth? Write a brief prayer acknowledging what you've discovered and asking for help in the journey ahead.

Week 2: Basic Pride Interruption

Day 8: The Three-Second Pause
Practice pausing for three seconds before responding to any correction, criticism, or challenging feedback. Don't use the pause to formulate defenses—use it to absorb what was said before reacting. Notice what this small space reveals about your automatic responses.

Day 9: The Clean Apology
Identify one situation where you were wrong or made a mistake, even in a small way. Offer a clean, non-defensive apology that:
- Clearly acknowledges what you did

- Doesn't include justifications or "but" statements
- Takes responsibility without blaming others
- Doesn't demand or expect immediate forgiveness

Note how it feels to apologize without qualifiers.

Day 10: The Credit Redirect

Today, look for at least one opportunity to redirect credit or recognition that comes your way. When praised or thanked, highlight others' contributions that made your work possible. Be specific about who helped and how they contributed.

Day 11: The Expert Fast

For one full day, practice not positioning yourself as the expert or authority on any topic. Instead:
- Ask questions rather than making authoritative statements
- Express curiosity rather than certainty
- Acknowledge the limits of your knowledge
- Learn something new from someone you wouldn't usually see as a teacher

Notice how this changes the quality of your interactions.

Day 12: The Invisible Service

Perform one act of service that no one will know you did. Clean a mess you didn't make, meet a need anonymously, or do something helpful that will never be traced back to you. Pay attention to how it feels to serve without recognition.

Day 13: The Last Place Practice
In at least three situations today, deliberately take the "last place" position:
- Let others go first (in line, in traffic, in conversations)
- Choose the least desirable seat or task
- Serve others before serving yourself
- Listen fully before sharing your perspective

Notice how this small practice of "going last" affects your internal attitude.

Day 14: Reflection Day
Review your experiences from Week 2. Which practices were most challenging? Which revealed the most about your default patterns? Where did you experience freedom or joy through humility? Write down one insight and one commitment for the coming week.

Week 3: Deeper Humility Development

Day 15: The Celebration Practice
Identify someone who has succeeded in an area where you also aspire to excel. Take concrete action to celebrate their success:
- Send a genuinely enthusiastic congratulatory message
- Share their achievement with others
- Write down three specific aspects of their success you admire

- Reflect on how their success might actually benefit rather than threaten you

Notice your internal resistance and practice celebrating anyway.

Day 16: The Learning Posture

Identify one area where you tend to present yourself as knowledgeable. Today, approach that topic with a deliberate learning posture:
- Acknowledge the limits of your understanding
- Ask questions that reveal your non-expert status
- Seek to learn from someone you'd normally try to impress
- Be open about something you've misunderstood or been wrong about

Note how this vulnerability affects both you and others.

Day 17: The Status Symbol Fast

For one day, abstain from mentioning or displaying status markers you typically use to establish credibility or importance:
- Professional titles or accomplishments
- Educational credentials
- Connections to influential people
- Material possessions that signal success
- Past achievements or experiences that elevate your status

Practice letting your words and presence stand on their own without status enhancement.

Day 18: The Feedback Request
Ask for specific feedback in an area where you're typically sensitive to criticism. Approach someone trustworthy and ask:
- "What's one way I could improve in this area?"
- "What do you see as my blind spot here?"
- "How could I be more effective in this role?"

Practice listening fully without defensiveness, asking clarifying questions, and expressing gratitude for the input regardless of how it feels.

Day 19: The Limitation Acknowledgment
Identify one personal limitation you typically hide or compensate for. Today, practice appropriate transparency about this limitation:
- Acknowledge it matter-of-factly when relevant
- Ask for help without shame or excessive apology
- Separate your limitation from your worth
- View it as an opportunity for collaboration rather than a personal defect

Notice how honest acknowledgment differs from both denial and self-flagellation.

Day 20: The Curiosity Conversation
Have one conversation today where your sole objective is learning about the other person. Practice:
- Asking open-ended questions about their experiences and perspectives
- Listening without planning your response
- Following up on what they say rather than redirecting to your experiences

- Expressing genuine interest in topics that wouldn't naturally engage you

Notice how this other-centered attention changes the conversation quality.

Day 21: Reflection Day
Review your experiences from Week 3. Which practices created the most internal resistance? Where did you experience unexpected freedom or connection? What's becoming easier as you practice humility more consistently? Write down one key insight and one commitment for the final week.

Week 4: Humility Integration

Day 22: The Recovery Practice
Notice when pride emerges today (defensiveness, attention-seeking, comparison, etc.). Instead of self-condemnation, practice quick recovery:
- Internally acknowledge the pride response
- Take a deep breath and reset your perspective
- Choose a humble alternative in the moment
- Move forward without dwelling on the lapse

The goal isn't perfection but developing the ability to course-correct quickly.

Day 23: The Gratitude Lens
Practice viewing your entire day through a gratitude lens that acknowledges dependence:

- Note specific gifts, opportunities, and strengths you didn't create or earn
- Identify at least 10 people who made your current situation possible
- Recognize "shoulders you stand on"—teachers, mentors, supporters
- Acknowledge seemingly "small" contributions from often-overlooked people

This practice directly counters pride's illusion of self-sufficiency.

Day 24: The Platform Share

If you have any form of platform (leadership role, social media following, speaking opportunity, decision-making authority), use it today to elevate someone else:
- Highlight their work or contribution
- Share their content or perspective
- Create an opportunity they wouldn't otherwise have
- Transfer some of your influence or access to benefit them

Notice how this differs from either hoarding your platform or using faux humility to actually increase your visibility.

Day 25: The Truth Reception

Create space to receive truth about yourself from three different sources:
- Scripture (spend time in passages that challenge your self-perception)

- Trusted relationships (invite specific feedback about your growth edges)
- Self-reflection (honestly assess areas where you need to mature)

The goal isn't self-criticism but accurate self-perception that allows for growth.

Day 26: The Delight-in-Others Day
Practice finding genuine delight in others' qualities and contributions:
- Notice specific strengths in people you encounter
- Express specific appreciation for others' gifts and perspectives
- Look for beauty and value in unexpected people and places
- Celebrate complementary strengths that differ from your own

This practice counters the competitive comparison that fuels pride.

Day 27: The Identity Reset
Take time to reconnect with your core identity beyond accomplishments, roles, or reputation:
- Write down who you are apart from what you do
- Reflect on your unchanging value as God's beloved creation
- Distinguish between your performance and your worth
- Release the need to prove your importance

This foundation of secure identity makes ongoing humility sustainable.

Day 28: The Integration Practice
Identify one key humility practice from the past four weeks that you want to continue long-term. Create a sustainable plan for integration:
- Set realistic frequency and parameters
- Establish reminders or triggers
- Create accountability with someone you trust
- Plan how you'll handle inevitable setbacks

Sustainable humility comes from consistent small practices, not occasional grand gestures.

Day 29: The Community Dimension
Explore how you might foster humility beyond your individual practice:
- Identify one relationship where you can create more space for the other person
- Consider how you might encourage humility in a group you're part of
- Look for systems or cultures that encourage pride, and consider how you might influence them
- Find ways to celebrate and elevate humble examples around you

Humility flourishes in community, not just in individual practice.

Day 30: Final Reflection
Take time to reflect on your entire 30-day journey:
- What surprised you most about your relationship with pride and humility?

- Where did you experience the greatest resistance to humility practices?
- What unexpected benefits or freedoms emerged as you practiced getting over yourself?
- How has your understanding of humility evolved beyond initial concepts?
- What will you carry forward from this month-long experiment?

Create a simple plan for continuing your humility development beyond the challenge, focusing on sustainability rather than intensity.

The Kick in the Pants: Your Life Is Not The You Show

Let's get painfully honest: You think you're the main character in a movie called "The Amazing Story of You." Everything and everyone else exists as supporting characters, plot devices, or background extras in your personal narrative.

And it's making you miserable.

This self-centered perspective isn't just spiritually problematic—it's exhausting. You're constantly maintaining your image, defending your reputation, pushing for recognition, and feeling threatened when others succeed. You're trapped in an endless cycle of comparison, either feeling superior (which makes you arrogant) or inferior (which makes you resentful). Your relationships are limited because you're too busy managing impressions to genuinely connect. Your growth is stunted because you're too defensive to receive correction.

And worst of all, this ego-centric lens distorts your relationship with God. When you're the main character, God becomes either a supporting actor who exists to fulfill your dreams or an antagonist who's not giving you what you deserve. Either way, you've got the story completely backward.

As Jesus bluntly put it in Luke 9:23, "If anyone would come after me, let him deny himself and take up his cross daily and follow me." Notice the first requirement of discipleship: deny yourself. Not hate yourself, not diminish your value, but deny the false self that demands to be the center of everything.

This self-denial isn't punishment—it's liberation. The more you cling to making life about you, the more miserable you become. The more you practice getting over yourself, the more freedom, joy, and connection you experience.

The hard truth is that God opposes the proud (James 4:6). Not because He's petty or easily offended, but because pride fundamentally distorts reality. It's like trying to navigate using a map where your house is drawn as the center of the universe—you'll get lost every time.

Humility reorients you to reality—a reality where God is the center, not you; where other people are equally valuable image-bearers, not supporting characters in your story; where your worth isn't based on outperforming others but on being loved by your Creator.

Think about Jesus. As Philippians 2:6-8 describes, He "did not count equality with God a thing to be grasped, but emptied himself, by taking the form of a servant... he humbled himself by becoming obedient to the point of death, even death on a cross."

If the Son of God didn't demand recognition, insist on His rights, or make everything about Himself, what's your excuse? If the only person who ever had the right to absolute centrality chose the path of humility and service, how ridiculous is your demand to be constantly acknowledged, approved, and applauded?

The invitation of the gospel isn't to build your platform, establish your brand, or become your best self. It's to die to yourself so you can truly live. It's to stop playing god in your own life so you can know the actual God who loves you more than you can imagine. It's to get over yourself so you can discover the freedom waiting on the other side of ego.

This journey isn't comfortable, but it's essential. Pride will rot your soul from the inside out. It will isolate you from others, disconnect you from reality, and erect barriers between you and God. Humility, by contrast, will heal your relationships, ground you in truth, and open channels for grace to flow freely into your life.

So here's your challenge: Stop making everything about you. Stop filtering every situation through "how does this affect me?" Stop measuring your worth by comparison to others. Stop expecting applause for basic decency. Stop defending your ego at the expense of truth and growth.

Instead, practice the freedom of self-forgetfulness. Find joy in others' success. Admit when you're wrong. Serve without recognition. Listen more than you speak. Give credit rather than taking it. Embrace your limitations as well as your gifts.

Because here's the beautiful paradox: When you stop trying to be the star of your life, you'll finally find the purpose you were created for. When you stop protecting your ego at all costs, you'll discover a security deeper than any self-made identity. When you stop demanding that life revolve around you, you'll find yourself caught up in a story far more meaningful than the one you were trying to write.

It's time to get over yourself. Not because you don't matter, but because you matter too much to stay trapped in the prison of pride. Your life was made for something bigger than the exhausting project of self-importance.

And that something begins with humility.

Chapter 13:

Perseverance – Sticking With It When It Sucks

Let's be honest: Sometimes following Jesus sucks.

I know, I know—that's not what the Christian bookstore bestsellers would have you believe. Not what your Instagram-perfect church friends post about. Definitely not what your pastor says in those upbeat sermons about "living your best life now."

But it's true. And if we can't admit that, we're setting people up to bail on their faith the moment it stops feeling good.

Because here's what actually happens: You have that powerful conversion moment. Or that incredible retreat experience. Or that worship night where God feels closer than your own breath. You're on fire. You're all in. You swear nothing will ever be the same.

Then life happens. The spiritual high fades. Bible reading starts to feel like a slog. Prayer feels like talking to the ceiling. Church becomes a routine. Doubt creeps in. Disappointment piles up. Your prayers seem to go unanswered. The Christians around you reveal themselves to be flawed, hypocritical humans. And suddenly, staying faithful to Jesus feels less like floating on clouds and more like trudging through mud.

This is the moment—not the mountaintop, but the valley—that separates the people who are actually following Jesus from those who were just enjoying a spiritual buzz. This is where perseverance comes in.

Hebrews 10:36 puts it bluntly: "For you have need of endurance, so that when you have done the will of God you may receive what is promised." Notice the writer doesn't say "for some of you" or "occasionally you might need." No—you HAVE NEED of endurance. It's not optional. It's essential.

Because faith isn't a sprint; it's a marathon. And not one of those pleasant, scenic marathons either. It's more like an ultra-marathon through challenging terrain, unexpected weather, and occasional stretches where you can't see the path at all. The difference between those who finish and those who don't isn't usually talent, emotions, or even strength. It's perseverance—the gritty willingness to keep going when every fiber of your being is screaming to stop.

In this final chapter, we're going to get real about what it takes to stick with faith for the long haul. Not because your salvation depends on white-knuckling your way through spiritual disciplines, but because the God who saved you is worth pursuing even when it's hard. Even when it doesn't feel good. Even when it flat-out sucks.

Because here's the truth: on the other side of perseverance is a depth and richness of relationship with God that the quitters never experience. As James 1:12 promises, "Blessed is the man who remains steadfast under trial, for when he has stood the test he will receive the crown of life, which God has promised to those who love him."

So let's talk about how to stay the course when everything in you wants to bail.

Why Faith Gets Hard: The Reality Check

Before we talk about how to persevere, let's acknowledge the very real reasons why faith gets difficult. These aren't just challenges for "weak Christians"—they're normal experiences that every sincere believer encounters:

1. The Emotion Fade

Spiritual experiences that feel amazing—powerful worship, transformative prayer, profound insights, intense community connections—are real and valuable. But they're not sustainable as constant states. The emotional high always fades, not because you're doing something wrong, but because that's how emotions work.

This emotional cycle is all over Scripture. Look at Elijah, who experienced the incredible victory against the prophets of Baal on Mount Carmel in 1 Kings 18, only to crash into depression and ask God to take his life in chapter 19. Or David, who wrote both exuberant psalms of praise and gut-wrenching laments questioning where God had gone.

The problem isn't the emotional fade—it's our culture's assumption that if you don't feel good, something must be wrong. We've bought the lie that authentic faith should always feel exciting, fulfilling, and emotionally validating. When it doesn't, many conclude they're doing it wrong or it isn't working at all.

2. Life Trauma and Disappointment

Faith doesn't exempt you from life's hardships—job loss, relationship breakdown, health crises, financial stress, grief, trauma, or injustice. In fact, Jesus explicitly promised trouble: "In this world you will have tribulation" (John 16:33).

When suffering hits, it naturally raises hard questions: Where is God in this? Why didn't He prevent it? Does prayer actually work? Is God good if He allows such pain? These aren't signs of weak faith—they're normal human responses to suffering.

Job, widely considered the most righteous man of his time, questioned God intensely during his suffering. David repeatedly asked "How long, O Lord?" in the psalms. Jesus Himself cried out, "My God, my God, why have you forsaken me?" from the cross (Matthew 27:46).

Disappointment and questioning aren't failures of faith—they're part of honest faith. But they do make continuing in faith much harder.

3. Unanswered Questions and Intellectual Doubts

As you grow in faith, you inevitably encounter questions that don't have easy answers: theological puzzles, apparent Bible contradictions, philosophical problems, scientific challenges. These intellectual hurdles can be deeply troubling, especially if you've been taught that "real Christians" don't question.

Thomas, who wanted physical evidence of Jesus' resurrection, isn't portrayed as faithless in Scripture but as honest. Jesus meets him in his doubts rather than condemning him for having questions (John 20:24-29).

The father who brought his demon-possessed son to Jesus honestly admitted, "I believe; help my unbelief!" (Mark 9:24)—and Jesus responded with compassion, not rejection. Faith has always existed alongside questions, not in their absence.

4. Community Disappointment

The church is made up of imperfect humans who sometimes hurt each other, fail to live up to their professed values, create toxic cultures, abuse power, or simply annoy the heck out of each other. When the very community that's supposed to represent Jesus lets you down—or actively wounds you—it can shatter faith.

Paul and Barnabas had such a sharp disagreement they parted ways (Acts 15:39). Paul had to confront Peter to his face over hypocrisy (Galatians 2:11-14). The early churches dealt with division, immorality, and false teaching. Christian community has never been perfect because it's always been human.

When church hurt happens (and it will), many find it easier to walk away from faith entirely rather than do the hard work of healing while maintaining faith.

5. The Daily Grind

Sometimes faith gets hard not because of dramatic crises but because of sheer routine. The daily discipline of prayer feels boring. Bible reading becomes a chore. Church attendance turns into going through the motions. The initial excitement of discovery gives way to the long work of implementation.

Even the Israelites, who saw God part the Red Sea and provide manna from heaven, quickly grew bored with God's miraculous provision. Numbers 11:6 records their complaint: "But now our strength is dried up, and there is nothing at all but this manna to look at." They had literal bread from heaven and still got bored with it!

Spiritual practices that once felt fresh and life-giving can become rote and lifeless—not because they've lost their value, but because the novelty has worn off and the real work of growth has begun.

6. Cultural Hostility

Depending on where you live, being a Christian might subject you to anything from mild social awkwardness to actual persecution. Standing for faith-informed values in an increasingly post-Christian culture can lead to being labeled intolerant, irrational, or even hateful.

Jesus warned, "If they persecuted me, they will also persecute you" (John 15:20) and "You will be hated by all for my name's sake" (Matthew 10:22). The earliest Christians faced execution for their faith. Today's challenges in Western countries are typically far milder, but the social cost of faith is still real and rising.

When faith starts costing you—relationships, career opportunities, social standing, or even physical safety—continuing requires a level of commitment that many find too demanding.

7. Spiritual Warfare

While some Christians overemphasize spiritual warfare, seeing demons behind every difficulty, Scripture does teach that we face spiritual opposition. Ephesians 6:12 reminds us that "we do not wrestle against flesh and blood, but against the rulers, against the authorities, against the cosmic powers over this present darkness."

This doesn't mean every challenge is a direct demonic attack, but it does suggest that forces beyond the physical realm can create resistance to spiritual growth and faithfulness. This opposition often intensifies precisely when you're making significant progress or taking steps of obedience.

Recognizing this dimension doesn't mean becoming obsessed with it, but it does help explain why persistence in faith sometimes feels like swimming upstream against a current that's actively working against you.

The Biblical Case for Hanging On

The Bible doesn't sugarcoat the reality that faith gets hard. Instead, it repeatedly emphasizes the critical importance of endurance, using various metaphors and examples to drive home the point:

The Race Metaphor

The New Testament frequently compares the Christian life to a long-distance race that requires endurance rather than just initial enthusiasm:

"Therefore, since we are surrounded by so great a cloud of witnesses, let us also lay aside every weight, and sin which clings so closely, and let us run with endurance the race that is set before us" (Hebrews 12:1).

"Do you not know that in a race all the runners run, but only one receives the prize? So run that you may obtain it" (1 Corinthians 9:24).

"I have fought the good fight, I have finished the race, I have kept the faith" (2 Timothy 4:7).

These passages emphasize completion, not just commencement. The prize comes from finishing, not just starting well. The writers knew that many begin with excitement but fail to endure when the race gets difficult.

The Farming Analogy

Scripture also uses agriculture to illustrate the patience required in spiritual growth:

"And let us not grow weary of doing good, for in due season we will reap, if we do not give up" (Galatians 6:9).

"Be patient, therefore, brothers, until the coming of the Lord. See how the farmer waits for the precious fruit of the earth, being patient about it, until it receives the early and the late rains" (James 5:7).

Farmers understand that harvest doesn't immediately follow planting. There's a long season of waiting, watering, weeding, and working before results appear. Giving up during this seemingly unproductive middle period guarantees no harvest.

The Refining Fire

The Bible often uses the metaphor of metal being refined by fire to describe how trials develop spiritual maturity:

"In this you rejoice, though now for a little while, if necessary, you have been grieved by various trials, so that the tested genuineness of your faith—more precious than gold that perishes though it is tested by fire—may be found to result in praise and glory and honor at the revelation of Jesus Christ" (1 Peter 1:6-7).

"Behold, I have refined you, but not as silver; I have tried you in the furnace of affliction" (Isaiah 48:10).

Metal becomes pure and strong through the intense heat that burns away impurities. Likewise, faith develops depth and authenticity through difficulties that reveal what's truly in our hearts.

The Examples of the Faithful

Throughout Scripture, those held up as examples of faith are not those who had perfect, trouble-free journeys but those who persevered through immense challenges:

Abraham waited decades for the promised son, even when the biological reality made it seem impossible.

Joseph endured slavery and imprisonment for years before seeing God's purpose fulfilled.

Moses led a grumbling, rebellious people through 40 years in the wilderness.

David waited years between being anointed king and actually taking the throne, spending much of that time as a fugitive.

Jesus Himself "endured the cross, despising the shame" (Hebrews 12:2), persevering through suffering to accomplish salvation.

Hebrews 11, often called the "faith hall of fame," emphasizes not just the initial faith of these spiritual heroes but their endurance through difficulty: "who through faith conquered kingdoms, enforced justice, obtained promises, stopped the mouths of lions, quenched the power of fire, escaped the edge of the sword, were made strong out of weakness" (Hebrews 11:33-34).

The Direct Commands

Beyond metaphors and examples, Scripture directly commands perseverance:

"Blessed is the man who remains steadfast under trial" (James 1:12).

"Be steadfast, immovable, always abounding in the work of the Lord" (1 Corinthians 15:58).

"You have need of endurance, so that when you have done the will of God you may receive what is promised" (Hebrews 10:36).

"The one who endures to the end will be saved" (Matthew 24:13).

These aren't suggestions but imperatives, indicating that perseverance isn't optional for those serious about following Jesus.

Why Most People Quit: The Perseverance Killers

Understanding why people typically abandon faith helps us identify and counter these perseverance-killing patterns. Here are the most common faith-quitters and how to avoid becoming one:

The Emotional Junkie

This person mistakenly equates faith with feelings. When the spiritual high fades and faith no longer provides the emotional rush it once did, they conclude, "It's not working anymore," and move on to the next experience that might deliver that feeling.

The emotional junkie hasn't grasped that spiritual maturity involves continuing in faith even when emotions fluctuate. They're like a person who only exercises when they "feel like it" and then wonders why they never get fit.

Antidote: Recognize that emotions are part of faith but not its foundation. Commit to spiritual practices regardless of your feelings about them. Understand that emotional dryness isn't failure but a normal season that can actually deepen faith if you persist through it.

The Expectations Manager

This quitter had specific expectations about how God would respond to their faith: healing their illness, resolving their financial problems, bringing them a spouse, or making them successful. When God doesn't fulfill these expectations on their timeline, they feel betrayed and walk away.

The expectations manager treats God more like a vending machine than a sovereign being with His own purposes and timeline. They've created a transactional relationship where their faith is contingent on God meeting their demands.

Antidote: Examine your unspoken expectations about what God "owes" you for your faith. Remember that Jesus promised tribulation in this world, not freedom from all suffering (John 16:33). Focus on who God is rather than what He gives, finding value in the relationship itself rather than just its benefits.

The Lone Ranger

This person tries to maintain faith in isolation, disconnected from Christian community. When challenges arise—doubts, temptations, or suffering—they have no support system to help them endure.

The lone ranger often has legitimate reasons for disconnection: they've been hurt by the church, can't find a community that feels right, or simply find relationships too messy and inconvenient. But isolated faith rarely survives long-term.

Antidote: Pursue authentic Christian community, even when it's difficult or disappointing. This doesn't mean attending every church event but having at least a few relationships where you can be honest about your faith struggles. Remember Ecclesiastes 4:9-10: "Two are better than one... For if they fall, one will lift up his fellow. But woe to him who is alone when he falls and has not another to lift him up!"

The Perfectionist Quitter

This person abandons faith when they repeatedly fail to live up to their spiritual ideals. After cycling through determination, failure, shame, and renewed determination enough times, they conclude they're simply not cut out for this Christian thing.

The perfectionist quitter doesn't understand that spiritual growth includes failure and that grace covers not just past sins but ongoing struggles. They've turned faith into a performance evaluation rather than a relationship based on grace.

Antidote: Embrace the gospel's message that your acceptance by God is based on Christ's perfection, not yours. Recognize that spiritual formation is a lifelong process of gradual transformation, not immediate perfection. As Philippians 1:6 promises, "He who began a good work in you will bring it to completion at the day of Jesus Christ"—it's His work, not just your effort.

The Minimum Viable Faith Person

This quitter never developed robust spiritual practices or deep biblical understanding, maintaining only a superficial connection to faith. When serious challenges arise, their shallow roots can't sustain them.

Jesus described this pattern in the Parable of the Sower: "As for what was sown on rocky ground, this is the one who hears the word and immediately receives it with joy, yet he has no root in himself, but endures for a while, and when tribulation or persecution arises on account of the word, immediately he falls away" (Matthew 13:20-21).

Antidote: Invest in developing depth—through regular Bible study, prayer, worship, service, and community—during relatively stable seasons so you'll have deep roots when storms come. Don't be content with a faith that's a mile wide but an inch deep.

The Unrepentant Compromiser

This person gradually abandons faith because they're unwilling to address sin patterns that contradict their professed beliefs. Rather than dealing with the growing cognitive dissonance between their beliefs and behavior, they find it easier to adjust their beliefs to match their chosen lifestyle.

They often don't make a dramatic exit from faith but slowly drift away as the gap between their actions and their stated beliefs becomes too uncomfortable to maintain.

Antidote: Deal honestly with areas where your life contradicts your faith. Seek accountability and practical strategies for life change rather than rationalizing sin or gradually abandoning the beliefs that convict you. Remember 1 John 1:9: "If we confess our sins, he is faithful and just to forgive us our sins and to cleanse us from all unrighteousness."

The One-Crisis Quitter

This person abandons faith in response to a single significant trauma or disappointment—a death, a divorce, a medical diagnosis, a job loss, or a church hurt. The pain is real and significant, but rather than wrestling with God through it, they walk away entirely.

The one-crisis quitter often feels that God has failed or abandoned them in their moment of greatest need. Their faith wasn't prepared to integrate suffering, so when serious suffering came, their faith collapsed.

Antidote: Develop a theology that includes suffering rather than promising exemption from it. Study biblical examples of faithful people who endured tremendous hardship without abandoning God. Find communities and resources that help you lament honestly while still holding onto faith. Remember that the biblical response to disappointment with God is not walking away but wrestling honestly, like Job, David, and Jesus Himself.

The Perseverance Toolkit: Practical Ways to Keep Going

When faith gets hard—and it will—these practical strategies can help you persevere rather than quit:

1. Develop Realistic Expectations

Many people quit faith because their expectations were unrealistic to begin with. They expected constant emotional connection, freedom from normal life problems, or rapid transformation into spiritual superstars.

Scripture presents a much more realistic picture: faith as a long journey with mountaintops and valleys, progress and setbacks, clarity and confusion. Embracing this biblical reality helps you navigate difficult seasons without assuming something is terribly wrong.

Practical steps:
- Study biblical examples of spiritual giants who experienced dry seasons and doubts
- Find honest Christian biographies that don't sanitize the struggles of the faith journey
- Identify and examine your unspoken expectations about how faith "should" feel or what God "should" do
- Reframe challenges as normal parts of faith rather than signs of failure

2. Build Sustainable Spiritual Rhythms

Just as physical endurance comes from consistent training, spiritual perseverance develops through sustainable practices maintained over time. The key word is "sustainable"—practices you can actually maintain through different life seasons.

Practical steps:
- Create a minimum viable daily practice (even just 5-10 minutes) that you can maintain even on your worst days
- Identify your strongest connection points with God (nature, music, scripture, silence, etc.) and intentionally incorporate them into regular rhythms
- Design different practice sets for different seasons—having a "normal mode," "survival mode," and "intensive mode" for varying life circumstances
- Focus on consistency over intensity, understanding that daily small acts of faithfulness matter more than occasional spiritual marathons

3. Leverage the Power of Micro-Commitments

When continuing feels overwhelming, reduce the commitment to the smallest possible unit. Don't think about maintaining faith for the rest of your life; focus on the next step.

Practical steps:
- When prayer feels impossible, commit to just one minute
- When Bible reading seems daunting, commit to just one verse
- When church attendance feels too hard, commit to just showing up, even if you sit in the back and leave early

- When doubts overwhelm, commit to holding just one truth that still makes sense to you

These micro-commitments maintain connection to spiritual practices during difficult seasons, preventing complete disconnection that makes return much harder.

4. Create Accountability Structures

External accountability dramatically increases perseverance in any difficult endeavor, including faith. When you know someone else is aware of your commitments and cares about your follow-through, you're much more likely to continue even when motivation wanes.

Practical steps:
- Find at least one person who will regularly ask about your spiritual practices
- Join a small group that provides natural accountability through relationships
- Use technology tools that track habits or send reminders
- Create consequences or rewards connected to maintaining key practices
- Schedule regular check-ins with a mentor, spiritual director, or trusted friend

5. Remember Your "Why"

Perseverance weakens when you lose sight of why you're doing something difficult. Reconnecting with your foundational reasons for following Jesus provides motivation when feelings fade.

Practical steps:
- Write out your faith story, highlighting moments where God's reality was clearest to you
- Create a personal mission statement that captures why your faith matters
- Keep a gratitude journal focused specifically on how faith has positively impacted your life
- Regularly revisit scriptures or books that originally ignited your passion for God
- Identify what's at stake if you abandon faith—what would actually be lost beyond social expectations

6. Find Your Perseverance Community

Trying to endure alone is unnecessarily difficult. Finding others who are committed to the long haul creates mutual support when individual motivation falters.

Practical steps:
- Seek relationships with Christians who have weathered significant faith challenges

- Join groups specifically designed for those navigating doubts or difficulties
- Read books by authors who honestly discuss faith struggles without easy answers
- Build friendships with people in different faith stages, both those ahead of and behind you
- Consider formal spiritual direction or counseling during particularly difficult seasons

7. Practice Strategic Remembering

The Israelites built memorial stones to remind themselves of God's faithfulness when future challenges made them doubt. Similarly, creating concrete reminders of God's work in your life helps sustain faith when His presence feels distant.

Practical steps:
- Keep a "faithfulness journal" documenting specific ways you've experienced God
- Create physical reminders of significant spiritual moments (photos, objects, artwork)
- Develop personal faith rituals that connect you to your broader faith history
- Regularly share your faith story with others, reinforcing your own memory in the process
- Establish anniversary practices to commemorate significant spiritual milestones

8. Embrace Lamenting as Faith, Not Failure

Many abandon faith because they think their anger, disappointment, or doubt disqualifies them. Learning to lament—to express honest pain to God without abandoning the relationship—creates a faith resilient enough to incorporate suffering.

Practical steps:
- Study biblical laments in Psalms, Lamentations, and Job
- Write your own honest prayers of lament, following the biblical pattern of complaint, request, and trust
- Find communities where authentic expression of spiritual struggle is welcomed, not shamed
- Create art, music, or other creative expressions of your faith questions and difficulties
- Practice praying your actual feelings, not the feelings you think you should have

9. Adjust Rather Than Abandon

When particular expressions of faith no longer work, many make the mistake of abandoning faith entirely rather than adjusting its expression. Perseverance sometimes means finding new ways to pursue the same God.

Practical steps:

- Experiment with different spiritual traditions and practices when your current ones feel dead
- Explore new ways of engaging Scripture when old methods become rote
- Consider whether you need a different church community, not no community
- Try different forms of prayer when your usual approach yields nothing but silence
- Distinguish between core faith commitments and particular expressions that can evolve

10. Remember It's Not All About Feelings

Perhaps the most important perseverance principle is recognizing that faith is about commitment more than emotion. Like marriage, its strength is measured not by constant passion but by persistent faithfulness through all emotional seasons.

Practical steps:
- Practice faith actions regardless of accompanying feelings
- Recognize emotional dryness as a normal season, not a crisis
- Study the concept of "the dark night of the soul" in Christian spiritual tradition
- Find language for different seasons of faith that normalizes periods of disconnection
- Focus more on your actions than your emotions as the measure of your faith

The Seven Seasons of Faith: Navigating Different Perseverance Challenges

Faith perseverance looks different depending on which season you're experiencing. Understanding these common seasons helps you respond appropriately rather than panicking when your faith journey changes:

1. The Honeymoon Season

Characteristics: High emotions, excitement, clear sense of God's presence, eagerness for spiritual practices, evangelistic enthusiasm

Perseverance challenge: The primary challenge in this season isn't feeling like quitting but preparing for future seasons when feelings change. Many people mistake this initial experience for what faith should always feel like, setting themselves up for disillusionment.

Perseverance strategy: Enjoy this season but recognize it's temporary. Use this high-energy period to establish sustainable practices and connections that will sustain you when emotions fade. Don't make major life decisions based solely on these initial feelings. Remember that emotional intensity isn't the measure of spiritual depth.

2. The Wilderness Season

Characteristics: Emotional dryness, questions about God's presence, spiritual practices that feel mechanical, doubts about previous experiences

Perseverance challenge: The wilderness feels like failure or abandonment when it's actually a normal, necessary developmental stage. Many quit during this season because they interpret normal maturation as something gone wrong.

Perseverance strategy: Recognize this as a growth opportunity, not punishment or abandonment. Continue spiritual practices without demanding emotional validation. Study biblical examples like Elijah, David, and even Jesus who experienced wilderness seasons. Find guides who understand this terrain rather than those offering simplistic solutions.

3. The Deconstruction Season

Characteristics: Questioning previously accepted beliefs, sorting through which elements of faith are essential versus cultural additions, intellectual wrestling, possible community tension

Perseverance challenge: Deconstruction can easily slide into total demolition without careful boundaries. Many abandon faith entirely when they only needed to discard certain unhelpful interpretations or additions.

Perseverance strategy: Distinguish between core Christian beliefs and cultural/denominational distinctives. Find conversation partners who won't shame questions but also won't celebrate abandoning faith. Seek voices who have navigated this season constructively. Remember that questioning isn't the same as unbelief—it can lead to stronger, more authentic faith.

4. The Crisis Season

Characteristics: Faith challenged by significant suffering or disappointment, intense emotions, questions about God's goodness or power, possible anger toward God

Perseverance challenge: Crisis tends to magnify whatever faith weaknesses already existed. If your faith hasn't incorporated suffering, a serious crisis can shatter it completely.

Perseverance strategy: Allow honest expression of pain while maintaining basic spiritual connection. Find communities that permit lament without demanding quick spiritual platitudes. Study biblical responses to suffering. Consider whether your theology needs to expand to include suffering rather than promise exemption from it. Remember that Jesus Himself questioned God from the cross without abandoning faith.

5. The Activist Season

Characteristics: Strong focus on living out faith through action, passion for justice or service, possible frustration with theoretical faith without practical impact

Perseverance challenge: Activism without contemplative roots often leads to burnout, bitterness, or works-based faith. Many abandon faith when their activism doesn't produce the changes they expected.

Perseverance strategy: Balance action with contemplation to maintain spiritual roots. Develop realistic expectations about what your efforts can accomplish in a broken world. Find communities that combine justice work with spiritual formation. Remember Jesus' rhythm of engagement and withdrawal, action and prayer.

6. The Ordinary Season

Characteristics: Faith integrated into daily life without dramatic highs or lows, steady spiritual practices, less emotional intensity but deeper roots

Perseverance challenge: The very normalcy of this season can feel like stagnation to those who associate faith with intense emotions or experiences. Many quit from a mistaken belief that faith should always feel exciting.

Perseverance strategy: Recognize the beauty and strength of ordinary faithfulness. Find meaning in small acts of discipline and service. Develop appreciation for steady growth that isn't always visible or dramatic. Remember that Jesus spent most of His life in ordinary faithfulness before His public ministry began.

7. The Legacy Season

Characteristics: Focus on passing faith to the next generation, deeper concern with lasting impact than immediate results, broader perspective on faith journey

Perseverance challenge: This season can bring increased awareness of time's passage and questions about whether your faith has made a meaningful difference, potentially leading to late-life doubt or regret.

Perseverance strategy: Celebrate the faithfulness that brought you this far. Find ways to share your faith story, including both successes and failures. Invest in mentoring relationships where your experience can benefit others. Remember Paul's perspective at the end of his life: "I have fought the good fight, I have finished the race, I have kept the faith" (2 Timothy 4:7).

Understanding these seasons prevents panic when your faith experience changes. The goal isn't to force yourself back into a previous season but to learn how to persevere through each season's unique challenges.

The 30-Day Perseverance Challenge

Want to strengthen your spiritual staying power? Try this 30-day challenge designed to build your perseverance muscles:

Week 1: Building Your Foundation

Day 1: Perseverance Inventory
Take stock of your current faith perseverance. Rate yourself from 1-10 in areas like:

- Maintaining spiritual practices when you don't feel like it
- Continuing faith through disappointment
- Sustaining belief during doubt
- Staying connected to community when it's difficult

Identify your strongest and weakest areas, noting patterns.

Day 2: Your Perseverance Story
Write about a time when you persevered in faith despite difficulty. What helped you continue? What almost made you quit? What was the result of your perseverance? If you can't think of a faith example, use another area of life where you've shown perseverance.

Day 3: Obstacle Identification
List the specific obstacles that most threaten your faith perseverance right now. For each obstacle, note whether it's primarily emotional, intellectual, relational, practical, or spiritual in nature. This targeted awareness helps you develop appropriate responses.

Day 4: Minimum Viable Practice
Create a "spiritual survival kit"—the absolute minimum daily practice you commit to maintaining even on your worst days. This might be as simple as a one-minute prayer or reading a single verse. The key is identifying something so doable you can maintain it through any circumstance.

Day 5: Your Why Statement
Draft a personal statement describing why your faith matters to you at the deepest level—beyond family expectations, social benefits, or cultural habit. What would be genuinely lost if you abandoned faith? This core motivation becomes an anchor during difficult seasons.

Day 6: Perseverance Partnership
Identify at least one person who can provide accountability for your spiritual perseverance. Contact them today to set up a regular check-in system. Be specific about what kind of support you need.

Day 7: Celebration Planning
Create small rewards for consistent faith practices. For example, after a week of daily prayer, treat yourself to something you enjoy. This positive reinforcement helps establish habits that will sustain you when motivation is low.

Week 2: Counter-Conditioning Your Quitting Triggers

Day 8: Expectation Examination
Identify any unrealistic expectations you hold about faith—that it should always feel good, immediately solve problems, or progress in a straight line. For each

unrealistic expectation, write a more biblical alternative that better prepares you for the real faith journey.

Day 9: Emotions Aren't Facts
Practice distinguishing between feelings and reality. Each time you think "I don't feel like God is present" or "I don't feel like praying," rephrase it to "I don't feel God's presence right now, but that doesn't mean He's not here" or "I don't feel like praying, but I can still choose to pray." Notice how this small language change creates space between feelings and actions.

Day 10: Refusal of the First Quitting Thought
When the first thought of giving up on a spiritual practice arises today, consciously refuse it. Don't argue with it or analyze it—simply say "No, I'm not quitting" and continue. This builds the mental habit of perseverance before discouragement builds momentum.

Day 11: Perseverance Role Models
Identify three people (biblical, historical, or contemporary) who demonstrate exceptional faith perseverance. Read about how they navigated their most difficult seasons. What specific strategies can you adopt from their examples?

Day 12: Comfort Audit
Examine how comfort-seeking might be undermining your perseverance. Where do you abandon spiritual

practices when they become uncomfortable? Where do you choose the easier path rather than the faithful one? Commit to embracing one specific uncomfortable-but-faithful choice today.

Day 13: Spiritual Memory Book
Create a physical or digital collection of your most significant faith moments—times when God felt especially real, prayers were dramatically answered, or you experienced breakthrough. This "evidence collection" provides reinforcement during doubting seasons.

Day 14: Community Survey
Ask three mature believers about their strategies for persevering through faith difficulties. What has helped them continue when they felt like quitting? Take notes on their responses, looking for patterns and practical ideas you can implement.

Week 3: Practicing While It's Easy

Day 15: The Five-More-Minutes Rule
When you feel like stopping a spiritual practice today (prayer, Bible reading, worship, etc.), push five minutes longer. This small stretch builds perseverance capacity without being overwhelming.

Day 16: Resistance Training

Intentionally choose a spiritual practice that feels particularly difficult for you right now. Instead of avoiding it, engage it directly for a manageable time period. Just as physical resistance builds muscle, spiritual resistance builds perseverance.

Day 17: Failure Recovery Practice
If you miss a spiritual commitment today, practice immediate recovery rather than using it as an excuse to quit entirely. Missed morning prayer? Pray mid-day instead. Skipped Bible reading? Do it before bed. This builds the crucial skill of getting back on track quickly after inevitable falters.

Day 18: No-Results Faithfulness
Engage in a spiritual practice today with zero expectation of immediate results or good feelings. Do it simply as an act of faithfulness, trusting the long-term process rather than demanding instant impact. Notice how this shifts your approach from consumption to commitment.

Day 19: Monotony Embracing
Intentionally engage in a repetitive spiritual practice, embracing rather than fighting the monotony. Pray the Lord's Prayer slowly ten times, write out the same Bible verse repeatedly, or sing the same worship chorus for fifteen minutes. This builds capacity for faithfulness when faith feels boring.

Day 20: The Second Wind Experiment

When you hit the point of wanting to quit a spiritual practice today, acknowledge the feeling but continue for at least five more minutes. Often, like runners who push through the initial fatigue, you'll find a "second wind" where engagement becomes easier again. This teaches your brain that the quitting impulse is often temporary.

Day 21: Mid-Point Motivation
Review your progress at the challenge's midpoint. What's working? What's most difficult? Recommit to completing the full 30 days, reminding yourself why perseverance matters. Share your commitment with your accountability partner.

Week 4: Preparing for Long-Haul Faith

Day 22: Crisis Contingency Plan
Create a spiritual emergency plan for major faith crises. What are the absolute minimum practices you'll maintain even in your worst moments? Who will you contact? What resources will you turn to? Having this plan in place before crisis hits dramatically increases your chance of persevering through it.

Day 23: Consolation/Desolation Awareness
Throughout today, practice naming your current spiritual state as either "consolation" (feeling connected to God, energized for spiritual things) or

"desolation" (feeling distant, dry, or resistant). This naming helps you recognize that both states are normal parts of faith, not indications that something is terribly wrong.

Day 24: Perseverance Language
Consciously change language that undermines perseverance. Replace "I'm trying to pray more" with "I'm committed to daily prayer." Substitute "I should read the Bible" with "I will read the Bible." Notice how commitment language creates different mental expectations than aspiration language.

Day 25: Progress Not Perfection
Review your spiritual practices this month. Rather than focusing on failures or inconsistencies, intentionally celebrate progress, no matter how small. Write down three specific ways you've grown in perseverance, even if they seem minor.

Day 26: Long-Term Vision
Write a letter to yourself to open in one year, describing the kind of faith person you want to become through consistent perseverance. Be specific about the practices you're committing to maintain and why they matter to you.

Day 27: Sustainable Rhythm Design
Create a sustainable weekly rhythm of spiritual practices that accommodates your real life rather than an idealized version. Include daily, weekly, and

monthly elements, with different versions for normal seasons, busy seasons, and crisis seasons.

Day 28: Accountability Structure
Formalize the accountability relationship you established earlier. Schedule regular check-ins for the next three months, be specific about what you want to be held accountable for, and establish how your accountability partner can most effectively support you.

Week 5: Integration and Moving Forward

Day 29: Challenge Review
Reflect on the entire 30-day experience. What did you learn about your perseverance strengths and weaknesses? Which practices made the biggest difference? What surprised you? What will you continue beyond the challenge?

Day 30: Perseverance Commitment
Create a personal perseverance covenant that outlines your commitments to continuing faith even through difficult seasons. Include specific practices, accountability measures, and reminders of why perseverance matters to you. Sign and date it as a formal commitment to staying the course.

This challenge won't make faith difficulties disappear, but it will strengthen your capacity to endure them rather than being derailed by them. The goal isn't perfect implementation but developing patterns that support lifelong faith.

The Kick in the Pants: Quitting Is Easy—Finishing Is Worth It

Let's get real: you're probably going to want to quit your faith journey at some point—maybe multiple points.

There will be days when prayer feels pointless, when God seems absent, when Scripture feels lifeless, when Christians disappoint you, when doubt screams louder than belief, and when continuing your spiritual practices feels like the absolute last thing you want to do.

And in those moments, you'll have a choice: to join the masses who walk away when faith gets hard, or to be one of the few who persevere even when every feeling and circumstance suggests throwing in the towel.

This isn't about white-knuckling your way to heaven out of fear. It's about recognizing that anything truly valuable in life—marriages, friendships, parenting, careers, mastering skills—involves seasons where you keep showing up even when you don't feel like it.

Why would the most important relationship of all be any different?

As Galatians 6:9 reminds us, "Let us not grow weary of doing good, for in due season we will reap, if we do not give up." The harvest comes for those who persist through the long middle season between planting and reaping—who continue to water, weed, and tend even when nothing appears to be happening.

Faith isn't built in the easy seasons—it's built in the trenches. It's forged through disappointments, questions, dry periods, and failures. The depth and authenticity that make faith actually worthwhile come precisely through persevering when everything in you wants to bail.

If you only follow Jesus when it's easy, exciting, or emotionally fulfilling, you're not actually following Jesus. You're following feelings, and feelings make terrible masters. They change with the weather, fluctuate with your hormones, and respond to what you ate for lunch. Building your faith on feelings is like building a house on quicksand—it can't withstand the first serious challenge.

The good news? You don't have to be strong enough to persevere through your own white-knuckled determination. Actually, that approach fails pretty quickly. True perseverance comes from holding onto the One who is holding onto you. It's about recognizing that God's grip on you is stronger than your grip on Him.

As Paul confidently declared, "I am sure of this, that he who began a good work in you will bring it to completion at the day of Jesus Christ" (Philippians 1:6). Your perseverance isn't ultimately about your impressive spiritual stamina but about God's faithful commitment to complete what He started in you.

This doesn't mean you're a passive player in the process. You still need to show up, engage the practices, and make the daily choice to continue rather than quit. But it does mean you're not solely responsible for the outcome. You can keep going not because you're so spiritually awesome but because God's grace is sufficient even for your weakest moments.

So when the feelings fade, when the doubts creep in, when the prayers seem to hit the ceiling, when the community lets you down, or when suffering makes you question everything—remember that these aren't signs your faith is failing. They're opportunities to develop a faith that's deeper than emotion, sturdier than circumstance, and truer than the easy-believism that collapses under the first real test.

Look at the spiritual giants throughout history. They all experienced profound struggles, doubts, and dark nights of the soul. What distinguished them wasn't the absence of difficulty but their refusal to abandon faith when difficulty came. They kept showing up, kept praying even when it felt like shouting into the void, kept serving even when they didn't see results, kept believing even when their emotions screamed otherwise.

As the writer of Hebrews reminds us, we're surrounded by "so great a cloud of witnesses" (Hebrews 12:1)—people who have run this race before us and proved it can be completed. They're cheering you on from the finish line, urging you not to give up when the middle miles get tough.

Because here's the truth: on the other side of perseverance is a depth of relationship with God that the quitters never experience. There's a richness that comes only through weathering storms together, a trust that's forged in the crucible of doubt overcome, a love that's proven genuine by enduring through disappointment.

Don't settle for the shallow faith of fair-weather disciples. Don't join the crowds who bail when Jesus' teachings get challenging or when the emotional high wears off. Don't be the rocky soil where faith springs up quickly but withers at the first sign of trouble.

Be the one who stays. Be the one who keeps showing up. Be the one who, at the end of the journey, can say with Paul, "I have fought the good fight, I have finished the race, I have kept the faith" (2 Timothy 4:7).

Because the prize isn't for those who start well but for those who finish. And finishing? That's worth everything.

Conclusion

So, Now What?

Congratulations on making it to the end of this book without throwing it across the room, unfollowing me on social media, or starting a prayer chain about the state of my eternal soul. If you've read all thirteen chapters, you've now consumed roughly 100,000 words about how to not suck at being a Christian. The question is: What the hell are you going to do about it?

Because here's an uncomfortable truth: reading a book about spiritual disciplines is about as useful as watching YouTube videos about exercise while eating Cheetos on your couch. Knowledge without action isn't wisdom—it's just trivia.

There's a reason James wrote, "Be doers of the word, and not hearers only, deceiving yourselves" (James 1:22). He understood our remarkable capacity for spiritual self-deception—nodding along to convicting truths while secretly exempting ourselves from actually applying them. We bookmark challenging passages, highlight profound insights, and share inspiring quotes on Instagram, all while continuing to live exactly as we did before.

So let's be clear about something: The goal was never for you to become an expert on prayer, Bible study, fasting, or any other discipline. The goal was for you to actually pray. To actually study Scripture. To actually practice silence. To actually worship. To actually serve. Not perfectly, not impressively, but consistently.

Because spiritual disciplines aren't spiritual achievements to be mastered; they're relational pathways to be walked. They're not about impressing God, others, or yourself with your amazing spiritual prowess. They're about positioning yourself to be shaped, filled, guided, and used by the God who loves you.

Think of these disciplines as the soil, water, and sunlight that allow the seed of faith to grow into something substantial. Without them, your faith remains theoretical—a nice idea without roots or fruit. With them, your faith becomes embodied—a living reality that transforms how you experience God, yourself, and the world around you.

What Real Growth Looks Like

Now, let's talk about what's actually going to happen when you start practicing these disciplines, because false expectations are faith-killers.

First, you're going to suck at this. Seriously. Your early attempts at contemplative prayer will feel awkward. Your first experience with fasting will make you hangry enough to snap at small children and pets. Your initial efforts at evangelism might be so cringe-worthy that even Jesus will be tempted to pretend He doesn't know you.

This is normal. No one plays Mozart the first time they sit at a piano. No one runs a marathon the first time they put on running shoes. And no one becomes a spiritual giant the first time they try lectio divina or sabbath rest.

Growth is gradual, inconsistent, and often invisible while it's happening. You won't feel dramatically different after one good quiet time. You won't experience supernatural peace the first time you practice silence. You won't suddenly stop wanting to punch that annoying guy at work because you served at a soup kitchen once.

But here's what will happen: Over time—weeks, months, years—these practices will slowly reshape your spiritual muscles. You'll start noticing subtle shifts in how you respond to stress, temptation, and difficulty. You'll find yourself naturally thinking in more biblical patterns. You'll catch glimpses of God's presence in moments where you previously saw only randomness or chaos.

The change will be less like a lightning strike and more like the gradual shifting of continental plates—imperceptible in any given moment but world-altering over time.

The Rhythms, Not the Rules

One of the quickest ways to derail your discipleship journey is to turn these practices into rigid rules that determine your spiritual worth. "I missed my Bible reading today; God must be disappointed." "I got distracted during prayer again; I'm a terrible Christian." "I haven't fasted in months; I'm spiritually lazy."

This legalistic scorekeeping transforms life-giving disciplines into soul-crushing obligations. It replaces relationship with religion, joy with judgment, and freedom with fear.

Remember: These disciplines are means, not ends. They're how you connect with God, not how you earn His approval. They're practices, not performances. They're rhythms, not rules.

Think of them as standing invitations rather than binding commandments. God isn't standing over you with a spiritual clipboard, marking tardies and absences. He's inviting you to the practices that facilitate authentic connection with Him—connection that transforms you not through guilt or shame but through love and truth.

When you miss a day (or week, or month) of any particular discipline, the invitation remains open. There's no spiritual detention hall, no divine demerit system. There's just the gentle reminder that the pathway to life-giving connection is still there whenever you're ready to walk it again.

This isn't permission for half-hearted discipleship. It's the recognition that transformation happens through grace-fueled consistency, not perfectionism-driven intensity. It's about developing sustainable rhythms that can weather the dramatic changes in seasons, circumstances, and emotions that are inevitable in any human life.

Pick Your Path, Not Your Performance

Looking at all thirteen disciplines at once is overwhelming. Trying to master them all simultaneously is a recipe for burnout and discouragement. Spiritual formation is a marathon, not a sprint, and trying to sprint a marathon only ensures you'll collapse before the first mile marker.

So here's what I want you to do: Choose one. Just one discipline that resonated most deeply with you as you read. Maybe it addressed your most obvious spiritual weakness. Maybe it connected with a hunger you've felt for a long time. Maybe it just seemed like the least terrifying option on the list.

Whatever your reasons, pick one discipline and commit to practicing it consistently for the next 30 days. Not perfectly. Not impressively. Just consistently. Set realistic parameters that match your actual life, not some idealized spiritual fantasy where you have unlimited time, energy, and focus.

If you choose prayer, maybe that means five minutes every morning before checking your phone. If you choose service, perhaps it's one intentional act each week. If you choose simplicity, it might be removing one unnecessary thing from your life each day.

The specific commitment matters less than the intentional choice to begin somewhere real rather than wishing vaguely for spiritual growth without practical action.

After 30 days, evaluate what changed—not just in your circumstances but in your awareness, attitudes, and automatic responses. Then either continue that discipline while adding a second one or switch to a different discipline that addresses your next growth edge.

The goal isn't collecting spiritual merit badges for practicing all thirteen. The goal is allowing these practices to shape you progressively into someone who increasingly reflects the character and priorities of Jesus in your everyday life.

Community, Not Just Personal Piety

One final critical point: These disciplines were never meant to be practiced in isolation. The most vibrant, sustainable spiritual growth happens in the context of authentic community, not in the vacuum of individual effort.

We've inherited a dangerously individualistic approach to faith that reduces spiritual formation to a private transaction between "me and Jesus." But that's not how the early church understood discipleship, and it's not how most Christians throughout history have approached these practices.

Prayer, study, fasting, worship, service—all were communal activities as much as personal ones. They were shared experiences that shaped not just individual souls but entire communities of faith.

So don't try to do this alone. Find at least one other person who's serious about growing spiritually and commit to practicing these disciplines together. Check in regularly. Share what's working and what isn't. Be honest about your struggles and celebrations. Hold each other accountable without judgment or comparison.

This partnership creates sustainability that solo spirituality rarely achieves. It provides encouragement when motivation wanes, perspective when discouragement sets in, and wisdom when you hit inevitable roadblocks.

Moreover, many of these disciplines—like service, hospitality, and confession—explicitly require other people. You can't practice them in your spiritual man cave, however well-appointed it might be with prayer journals and devotional books.

The way of Jesus is inherently relational, both with Him and with others. Trying to grow spiritually while avoiding authentic community is like trying to learn to swim without getting wet—theoretically interesting but practically impossible.

When You Fail (Not If)

Let's be painfully clear about something: You will fail at these disciplines. Repeatedly. Spectacularly. Sometimes hilariously.

You'll set out to pray for an hour and end up making grocery lists in your head after three minutes. You'll commit to fasting and find yourself elbow-deep in a bag of chips before lunchtime. You'll try to practice contentment and find yourself rage-shopping on Amazon after seeing your neighbor's new car.

This isn't pessimism; it's reality. We're deeply flawed humans trying to develop spiritual capacities that don't come naturally to us. Failure isn't just possible; it's guaranteed.

The question isn't whether you'll fail but how you'll respond when you do. Will you use failure as an excuse to quit entirely? Will you beat yourself up with shame and self-condemnation? Or will you recognize failure as an essential part of any growth process, get back up, and try again?

The disciples who walked with Jesus in the flesh failed constantly. They misunderstood His teachings, bickered about status, fell asleep when He asked them to pray, and ultimately abandoned Him in His moment of greatest need. Yet these same flawed followers became the foundation of a movement that changed the world.

The difference wasn't that they suddenly became spiritual superheroes who never messed up again. It's that they kept showing up, kept learning, kept trying—even after their most embarrassing failures.

That's the model we're called to follow. Not perfect performance but persistent presence. Not flawless execution but faithful engagement. Not never falling but always getting back up.

When you fail (again, not if), don't waste energy on elaborate self-flagellation or dramatic vows to try harder next time. Simply acknowledge the failure, receive the grace that's always available, and take the next small step of faithfulness.

This fail-receive-restart cycle isn't a detour on the path of spiritual growth; it is the path. It's how we learn dependence on God rather than self-sufficiency. It's how we develop genuine humility rather than religious pride. It's how we experience grace as a daily reality rather than a theoretical concept.

So fail boldly, knowing that your failures don't disqualify you from God's love or purpose. They just remind you why you needed Jesus in the first place.

The Point of It All

Let's zoom out for a moment and remember why any of this matters. Because it's easy to get so focused on the practices themselves that we forget their purpose.

These disciplines aren't about becoming super-Christians who impress God and intimidate others with our spiritual prowess. They're not religious hoops to jump through to earn celestial gold stars. They're not even primarily about self-improvement, though that happens as a byproduct.

These disciplines are about one central reality: growing in your capacity to love God and love others as Jesus did. Everything else is secondary.

If your prayer life is "impressive" but you're still a jerk to your family, you've missed the point. If your Bible knowledge is encyclopedic but you show no compassion to those in need, you've gained information without transformation. If you can fast for days but still harbor unforgiveness toward those who've hurt you, you've practiced physical discipline without spiritual growth.

As Paul wrote in 1 Corinthians, you could speak with angelic eloquence, understand all mysteries, have mountain-moving faith, and give away everything you own—but without love, it amounts to nothing.

The disciplines are meant to expand your capacity for this kind of love—love that's patient and kind, not envious or boastful, not arrogant or rude, not insistent on its own way, not irritable or resentful. Love that bears all things, believes all things, hopes all things, endures all things.

That's the measuring stick. Not how many chapters you read, minutes you prayed, or days you fasted. Not whether you did it perfectly or consistently or impressively. But whether these practices are slowly, imperfectly, but genuinely increasing your capacity to love as Jesus loved.

Because at the end of your life, God won't ask for your spiritual résumé. He won't be impressed by how many Bible verses you memorized or how many prayer journals you filled. The question will be whether you allowed these disciplines to shape you into someone who loved God with your whole being and loved your neighbor as yourself.

That's the point. That's always been the point.

Now What?

So here we are, at the end of the book, and I'll ask again: What are you going to do about it?

Will you close these pages, think "That was interesting," and continue exactly as you were before? Or will you choose at least one concrete way to begin incorporating these disciplines into your actual life—not someday when everything is perfect, but today, in all its messy imperfection?

The choice is yours, and it's one you'll make not just once but every single day. The spiritual life isn't built on dramatic moments of commitment but on the accumulated weight of thousands of small choices that no one sees and few would find remarkable.

It's choosing prayer over scrolling first thing in the morning. It's opening Scripture when Netflix seems more appealing. It's practicing gratitude when complaint comes more naturally. It's serving when you'd rather be served. It's a million tiny decisions that, taken together, determine the trajectory of your spiritual formation.

These choices will rarely feel momentous in the moment. They won't come with soundtrack swells or emotional highs. Most days, they'll feel ordinary, unremarkable, even boring. But don't be fooled by the absence of drama. The most significant spiritual growth often happens in these quiet, seemingly insignificant moments of faithfulness.

So choose. Not perfectly. Not permanently. Not impressively. Just choose the next faithful step, however small it might seem. Then choose again. And again. And again.

Because the secret to not sucking at being a Christian isn't found in dramatic spiritual experiences or revolutionary insights. It's found in the humble, ordinary, daily choice to show up and engage with the God who is always present, always working, always transforming those who place themselves in the path of His grace.

You don't have to be perfect. You just have to be in it for real.

You don't have to get it right every time. You just have to keep coming back when you get it wrong.

You don't have to feel it to do it. You just have to do it until you start to feel it again.

To paraphrase G.K. Chesterton, anything worth doing is worth doing badly. So go do these disciplines badly. Do them imperfectly, inconsistently, and inadequately. Just do them. Because showing up imperfectly is infinitely better than perfect intentions that never materialize into action.

Start small. Start where you are. Start with what you have. Just start.

And may the God who began this good work in you bring it to completion in the day of Christ Jesus.

Now what are you waiting for? The book is over. Go live the life.

A Letter to Myself in 10 Years

Dear Future Me (the one with more gray hair and hopefully more wisdom),

So... how's it going? Did we actually do any of this stuff, or did we just write the book and go back to scrolling Instagram? Be honest. I know where you live.

By now, you're either nodding along thinking, "Wow, I've grown so much in these disciplines," or you're wincing because you fell off the prayer wagon around day three and have spent the last decade mainly talking to God while looking for parking spaces.

I'm genuinely curious: Have we stopped making everything about us yet? Has that humility chapter actually sunk in, or are we still finding subtle ways to be the hero in every story we tell? I hope you've finally stopped rehearsing witty comebacks in the shower for arguments that happened three years ago. That was getting weird.

Speaking of weird, please tell me we've grown in the community department. Are we still doing that thing where we say we "value deep relationships" while systematically avoiding any conversation that might make us uncomfortable? I hope we've found people who know the real us—not just the polished, "I've got my stuff together" version we present at church.

How about the Bible? Have we moved beyond our highlight-reel approach to Scripture? You know, where we memorize the encouraging verses about God's blessings while conveniently skipping the parts about denying ourselves and loving difficult people? Just checking.

On a more serious note, I genuinely hope we've kept showing up for Jesus, even on the days when we didn't feel like it. I hope we've learned that spiritual discipline isn't about perfection but persistence. That the days when prayer feels like talking to the ceiling are often doing more in us than the spiritual high moments.

I hope we've failed—a lot—and gotten back up every time. I hope we've stopped being so surprised by our capacity for selfishness and so shocked by our need for grace.

Most of all, I hope we've relaxed a little in the best possible way. Not by caring less about following Jesus, but by trusting more in His work rather than ours. By finding freedom in the fact that our spiritual progress isn't ultimately dependent on our white-knuckled effort but on His faithful completion of what He started in us.

If you're reading this, Future Me, and you've totally forgotten all of it—congrats, time to reread the book. But something tells me that's not the case. The God who's been patient with us this far isn't likely to give up now, no matter how slowly we're learning.

So keep going, you older, hopefully slightly less clueless version of me. One day at a time.

With both eye-rolls and genuine hope,
Past You

P.S. If we've finally mastered fasting by now, I'd be seriously impressed. If not, I'm not even a little surprised.

Acknowledgments

First and foremost, I'd like to thank God, who—despite having infinite options for messengers—chose someone who once got lost in their own bathroom and regularly talks to houseplants. Your standards are refreshingly low, Lord, and I'm genuinely grateful You're still using me despite knowing all my browser history.

To my editor, who somehow read my initial draft and didn't immediately change careers: your patience deserves some kind of medal, possibly made of chocolate. Thanks for translating my 3AM caffeine-fueled ramblings into something resembling human communication.

To the baristas at seven different coffee shops who watched me stare blankly at my laptop for hours while occasionally typing furiously for 90 seconds: thanks for pretending I was a normal customer and not someone having a public breakdown in slow motion. Special thanks to the one who stopped asking if I needed a refill and just started bringing them silently, like a caffeinated guardian angel.

To my cat, Professor Pickles, who contributed several key passages by walking across my keyboard while I was in the bathroom: your literary insights are matched only by your ability to vomit precisely where I'll step first thing in the morning.

Since I lack what normal authors call "a support network" or "actual human friends," I must acknowledge the characters from The Office who kept me company during the writing process:

Jim Halpert, for teaching me that smirking at the camera is a legitimate response to spiritual nonsense.

Dwight Schrute, whose dedication to arbitrary rules reminds me daily what legalistic Christianity looks like.

Pam Beesly, who demonstrates that sometimes the most spiritual act is simply rolling your eyes and making it through the day.

Michael Scott, whose desperate need to be liked mirrors my own publishing ambitions a little too accurately.

And especially Creed Bratton, my spiritual doppelgänger. Like Creed, I've written substantial portions of this book from unusual locations (including once from inside the ball pit at a McDonald's PlayPlace where I was definitely too old to be) and frequently have no idea what's going on. I'm not saying I printed this manuscript using the toner from the church office copier, but if anyone asks, I've been in Texas. Ciao.

Lastly, I'd like to thank whoever's actually reading this acknowledgments section. Most people skip these pages entirely, which means you're either my mom (hi Mom, sorry about Chapter 7) or you're exactly the kind of thorough, slightly odd person I wrote this book for. We should probably be friends, though I should warn you—I'm already at capacity with my fictional relationships.

This book exists by the grace of God, three miracle deadline extensions, and possibly a small temporal anomaly that created extra hours in several Tuesdays. In the immortal words of Creed Bratton: "That is Northern Lights Cannabis Indica... no, wait, that's just the Holy Spirit."

Next Steps

Congratulations. You read a book. Now comes the part that actually matters: doing something about it.

I'm not going to waste your time with cheerleading or empty motivational nonsense. You've had enough words. What you need now is action. Here's what you're going to do:

1. Pick one discipline from this book. Just one. Don't overthink it. Pick the one that made you most uncomfortable—that's probably where you need to start. Write it down on a piece of paper and put it somewhere you can't avoid seeing it. Bathroom mirror works well.

2. Start tomorrow. No, scratch that. Start today. Not when you "feel ready" or after you "do more research." Today. Five minutes is better than zero

minutes. Imperfect action beats perfect intention every time.

3. Tell someone what you're doing. Not for attention. For accountability. Text a friend right now with these exact words: "I'm working on [discipline]. Ask me how it's going next week." If they don't ask, get better friends.

4. Get rid of one thing that's competing with this discipline. Delete an app. Cancel a subscription. Throw away the video game. You know exactly what's stealing your time. Don't pretend you don't.

5. When you fail (not if), don't waste time feeling bad about it. Just start again. Guilt is useless without repentance, and repentance means changing direction, not just feeling sorry.

6. Schedule these disciplines like you schedule everything else that matters. You put dentist appointments on your calendar. Your spiritual health deserves at least the same consideration as your teeth.

7. Don't wait for your church to offer a program about this. Be an adult and take responsibility for your own growth. Waiting for someone else to spoon-feed you spirituality is how you got into this mess in the first place.

8. Read your Bible. Daily. Not an app that gives you one verse with a pretty sunset background. The actual Bible, with context and difficult passages included. Even when it's boring. Especially then.

9. Pray like you're talking to someone who's actually there. Because He is. Cut the religious language and just have a conversation.

10. Find people who are better at this than you and spend time with them. Spiritual maturity is contagious. So is spiritual laziness. Choose wisely.

Look, I don't care if you liked this book. I care if it changes how you live. A year from now, no one will ask you if you read a book about spiritual disciplines. They'll simply observe whether you're becoming more like Jesus or not.

The evidence of whether this was worth your time won't be found in how many passages you highlighted but in how you treat your spouse, manage your anger, spend your money, and use your time.

Don't wait to feel spiritual enough. You won't. Start anyway. Grow anyway. Jesus is worth it.

Now put the book down and go do something.

Small Group Discussion Guide

How to Use This Guide

This is a discussion guide, not a lecture series. Ask the questions. Wait for answers. If no one speaks for 30 seconds, that's fine. Discomfort leads to growth. Don't fill the silence with your own voice.

Each meeting should take exactly one hour. Start on time. End on time. People respect what you respect, and that includes their schedule.

Refreshments are optional. Coffee is not.

Chapter 1: Prayer – Actually Talking to God

Summary: Prayer isn't complicated. You talk. God listens. Then you listen. Most people fail at the last part.

Questions:

1. When was the last time you prayed without asking for something? What happened?
2. What do you actually believe happens when you pray? Not what you're supposed to believe—what you actually believe.
3. How much of your prayer is talking versus listening? Give a percentage. Then explain why that number needs to change.

Challenge: For the next seven days, spend the first five minutes of your day in complete silence before God. No talking. No asking. Just listening. Report back next week with what you learned, even if it's just how difficult silence is for you.

Chapter 2: Bible Study – Knowing What You Claim to Believe

Summary: Most Christians own Bibles they don't read and quote verses they don't understand.

Questions:
1. Without looking at your phone, recite one Bible verse you've actually applied this month. Explain how.
2. What parts of the Bible do you skip because they make you uncomfortable? Be specific.

3. How often do you read the Bible when no one is watching? Daily, weekly, or mostly when you're in trouble?

Challenge: Read one entire book of the Bible this week. Not a verse. Not a chapter. An entire book. James takes 20 minutes. Philippians takes 14. Choose one, read it in one sitting, and come back with one thing that surprised you.

Chapter 3: Fasting – Hunger as a Spiritual Alarm Clock

Summary: Your stomach makes a surprisingly effective prayer reminder when it's empty.

Questions:
1. What's your real reason for not fasting regularly? Fear, inconvenience, or have you just never considered it?
2. What comfort or habit do you need a break from more than food? Social media? Netflix? Shopping? Your own voice?
3. What's one specific area of your life where you need clarity that might benefit from focused hunger and prayer?

Challenge: Fast from something for 24 hours before our next meeting. Could be food. Could be screens. Choose something that will actually cost you something. When you feel the hunger or craving, pray specifically about one situation where you need wisdom.

Chapter 4: Worship – Beyond the Music

Summary: Worship isn't a Sunday activity. It's directing your attention to what actually deserves it.

Questions:
1. What do you give most of your attention, affection, and money to? That's what you're actually worshiping.
2. When was the last time you worshiped God when you weren't being led by someone with a guitar? What did that look like?
3. What makes you genuinely stand in awe? Nature? Achievement? Art? How could that become a pathway to worship rather than just appreciation?

Challenge: Spend 15 minutes this week worshiping God without music, without other people, and without using any words you've heard in church. Just honest, original praise from you to God.

Come back and tell us if it felt weird, refreshing, or both.

Chapter 5: Solitude – Being Alone With God

Summary: You can't hear God when you're never quiet. Turn off your phone.

Questions:
1. What's the longest you've been completely alone in the last month? No people, no devices, no distractions.
2. What are you afraid might happen if you were truly alone with your thoughts and with God for an extended period?
3. When you're by yourself, what do you immediately reach for? Your phone? TV remote? Food? What are you avoiding?

Challenge: Spend two hours in complete solitude before our next meeting. No phone, no music, no book, no people. Just you and God. Bring one insight from that time to share with the group, even if that insight is how uncomfortable you were.

Chapter 6: Community – The People Who Keep You From Drowning

Summary: Your spiritual growth is directly tied to who you spend time with. Choose wisely.

Questions:
1. Who knows the real you—your actual struggles, not just the sanitized church version? Name them.
2. What's one area of your life where you need someone to hold you accountable, but you're afraid to ask?
3. Are you more focused on finding the perfect community or being the kind of person others want in their community? Explain.

Challenge: Have one completely honest conversation this week where you share a current struggle with someone you trust. Not a past victory—a present weakness. Ask for both prayer and practical accountability.

Chapter 7: Confession – Bringing Your Crap Into the Light

Summary: Secret sin is like mold. It grows best in dark, damp places.

Questions:
1. What's one sin you've confessed to God repeatedly but never told another human about? You don't have to share it now, just acknowledge it exists.
2. What would it actually cost you if people knew your real struggles? Job? Reputation? Relationships? Is keeping the secret worth that price?
3. Who could you trust with your darkest confession? If you can't name someone, why not?

Challenge: Confess something you've kept hidden to either someone in this group or a trusted friend before we meet again. Nothing vague. Something specific that you've been ashamed of. Experience what it feels like to be fully known and still accepted.

Chapter 8: Hospitality – Making Room for Outsiders

Summary: Jesus ate with sinners. You should too.

Questions:
1. When was the last time you had someone in your home who couldn't benefit your career, social standing, or comfort? Be specific.

2. What's stopping you from regularly opening your life to strangers and outsiders? Time? Money? Fear? Selfishness?

3. Who are the "tax collectors and sinners" in your world that religious people avoid but Jesus would eat with?

Challenge: Invite someone to your table who would be surprised by the invitation. Not family. Not a close friend. Someone on the margins of your world. Share a meal with no agenda except genuine interest in their life.

Chapter 9: Service – Getting Over Your Need to Be Important

Summary: You're never more like Jesus than when you're serving someone who can't repay you.

Questions:
1. What's the last thing you did that benefited someone else with zero benefit to yourself?
2. What kind of service do you avoid because it feels "beneath you"? Cleaning? Manual labor? Anything involving bodily fluids?
3. Do you serve to be seen or to meet needs? How can you tell the difference?

Challenge: Serve in a role this week that involves no recognition, no leadership, and no special skills. Clean toilets. Pick up trash. Serve food to the homeless. Do something purely because it needs doing, not because anyone will notice or thank you.

Chapter 10: Simplicity – Having Enough Without Having Everything

Summary: Your life is too complicated, your schedule is too full, and your closets have too much stuff.

Questions:
1. What's one thing you purchased in the last month that you didn't actually need? Why did you buy it?
2. What's cluttering your life right now that you need to say "no" to? A commitment? A relationship? A possession?
3. If your spending reflected your actual values, what would those values be?

Challenge: Get rid of 25 things you don't need before our next meeting. Not junk—things you've been keeping that someone else could use more than you. Then delete one app from your phone that sucks more time than it adds value.

Chapter 11: Stewardship – Managing Your Sh*t

Summary: Everything you have is on loan from God. Act like it.

Questions:
1. What are you doing with your money that you'd be embarrassed for Jesus to see your bank statement?
2. How much of your income did you give away last month? An actual percentage, not a feeling.
3. What's one resource (time, talent, money) you're currently wasting that could be redirected toward something meaningful?

Challenge: Track every single expenditure for one week. Every coffee, every subscription, every impulse purchase. Categorize them as either "kingdom investment" or "personal consumption." Calculate the ratio. Come prepared to discuss what needs to change.

Chapter 12: Humility – Getting Over Yourself

Summary: You think about yourself way too much. So do I. Let's stop.

Questions:
1. When was the last time you admitted you were wrong and actually changed your mind?
2. What's one area where pride is preventing you from growing? Career? Parenting? Ministry? Relationships?
3. Who intimidates you with their success? Why? What does that reveal about your own pride?

Challenge: Do something this week where you intentionally take the lower position. Let someone else get credit for your idea. Serve in a role "beneath" your abilities. Choose obscurity when you could have chosen visibility. Come back and tell us what it taught you.

Chapter 13: Perseverance – Sticking With It When It Sucks

Summary: Faith isn't a feeling. It's showing up when you don't feel like it.

Questions:
1. What spiritual discipline were you once excited about that you've since abandoned? Why did you stop?
2. When was the last time you continued a spiritual practice through a dry season with no emotional reward? What kept you going?
3. What area of your spiritual life are you currently tempted to give up on? Why?

Challenge: Choose the spiritual discipline from this book that you're most likely to abandon. Commit to practicing it daily for the next 30 days, regardless of feelings or results. Find someone in this group to check in with weekly about your progress.

Final Note to Group Leaders

Don't end with discussion. End with action. Ask each person to write down one specific commitment before they leave. Not a general intention—a specific action with a deadline.

Accountability without relationship is just legalism. Make sure you're fostering both.

And remember: The point isn't to create impressive Christians. The point is to create faithful ones. Sometimes the loudest person in the room has grown the least. Look for quiet transformation, not just enthusiastic participation.

Oh, and one more thing: Be the kind of leader who actually does these things, not just talks about them. Nothing undermines a discussion faster than a hypocritical leader.

Good luck. God is patient. You should be too.

Resources

Most people fail because they spend too much time planning and not enough time doing. They collect resources the way hoarders collect newspapers—piling them up without ever using them. That said, here are a few tools I begrudgingly admit might help you stop sucking. I've kept this list intentionally short. You don't need more options. You need to pick something and start.

Bible Reading

Bible, ESV (Crossway)
Hardback. No study notes. No inspirational sidebars. Just the text. You need fewer distractions, not more commentary. Get a pen. Write in the margins. It's a tool, not a museum piece.

Read Scripture App (The Bible Project)
For when you lack context or get stuck. Short videos explain books and themes without being condescending. Free. No annoying notifications. Clean design that doesn't look like it was made in 2003.

Robert Murray M'Cheyne Bible Reading Plan
One year. Four chapters daily. Whole Bible completed. Old Testament once, New Testament and Psalms twice. No cherry-picking the easy parts. Printable. No app required. Been working since 1842.

ESV Reader's Bible, Six-Volume Set (optional)
For serious readers only. No verse numbers. No chapter headings. No distractions. Just the text as literature. Expensive but worth it if you're tired of reading Scripture like a technical manual.

Prayer

A Simple Kitchen Timer
Set it for 10 minutes. Pray until it beeps. When your mind wanders (it will), gently return to prayer. Repeat daily. Prayer is more about showing up consistently than feeling spiritual. The timer keeps you honest.

The Valley of Vision (Bennett)
Puritan prayers. Dense. Theological. Zero fluff. Will make your "bless this food" prayers seem appropriately pathetic. Use as a model, not a script.

PrayerMate App
Digital prayer list that actually works. Organizes prayer requests into categories. Sends reminders. Free version has everything you need. No social feed. No performative nonsense.

A $1 Notebook
Write your prayers. Dating them helps you track God's faithfulness over time. When you die, someone might find it interesting. Probably not, but at least you'll stay focused while you're alive.

Accountability & Community

The Common Rule (Justin Earley)
Practical habits for limiting technology and creating space for real relationships. Not revolutionary, just sensible. Actually doable for people with jobs and families.

Meetup App
Find groups with shared interests. Join one. Show up consistently. Relationships take time and repeated exposure. This isn't complicated, just uncomfortable. Deal with it.

Marco Polo App
Video messaging that works for accountability partners. More personal than texting. Less intrusive than calls. Send updates on your progress without coordinating schedules.

A Standing Commitment
Pick a day. Pick a time. Pick a place. Show up every week without fail. Consistency beats intensity. The best accountability system is the one you'll actually use. Coffee shops work fine. So do diners, parks, or living rooms.

Spiritual Discipline Tools

The Ruthless Elimination of Hurry (John Mark Comer)

Practical guide to slowing down. Not just theory. Actual steps. Will make you uncomfortable, which means it's working. Pairs well with deleting social media apps.

Spiritual Disciplines Handbook (Adele Ahlberg Calhoun)
Over 60 practices explained simply with concrete next steps. Skip the ones that sound too mystical for your tradition. There are plenty of others. Not a book to read straight through. Use as a reference.

Day One Journal App
Digital journaling without the distraction of social media. Password protected for honest reflection. Searchable. Syncs between devices. Free version works for most people.

Freedom App
Blocks websites and apps that distract you. Schedule recurring blocks during prayer or study time. Yes, you need this. Your willpower is weaker than you think.

A Physical Alarm Clock
So your phone can stay outside your bedroom. This single change will improve your sleep, your morning devotions, and your marriage. $15 at Target. Lifechanging.

Final Note

These resources won't make you spiritual any more than owning cooking utensils makes you a chef. They're tools, not magic. The point isn't to accumulate resources but to use them consistently.

Pick one item from each category. Start there. Add others only when you've established the habit of actually using what you have. The most effective resource is the one you'll actually use, not the one with the best reviews or the most features.

And for God's sake, don't buy more books until you've read the ones you have.

www.ingramcontent.com/pod-product-compliance
Lightning Source LLC
Chambersburg PA
CBHW050058170426
43198CB00014B/2379